THE REAL INDIA

J. D. REES

GYAN

Published by

Gyan Publishing House
5, Ansari Road
Daryaganj, New Delhi-110002
Phone: 011-47034999, 9811692060
E-mail: books@gyanbooks.com

Distribution Network
gyanbooks.com
India, USA, Canada, UK, Australia

ISBN: 978-93-7097-061-8 (PB)

First Published, 1908

2nd Impression 2025

Printed at: Gyan Press, Delhi.

THE REAL INDIA
Author: J. D. REES

THE REAL INDIA

Yours very truly J D Rees

THE REAL INDIA

BY

J. D. REES, C.I.E., M.P.

LATE ADDITIONAL MEMBER OF THE GOVERNOR-GENERAL OF INDIA'S COUNCIL
AND SOMETIME TRANSLATOR TO THE GOVERNMENT OF MADRAS
IN HINDUSTANI, PERSIAN, TAMIL, AND TELUGU

WITH A FRONTISPIECE

METHUEN & CO.
36 ESSEX STREET W.C.
LONDON

PREFACE

I ACCEPTED an invitation, without which I would not have embarked upon such an undertaking, to write this book because among the many works lately published on India, most are avowedly written from the point of view of the tourist, and many, avowedly or otherwise, for party and political purposes, while others have their origin in disappointment or resentment, and some are frankly seditious and disloyal. It seemed to me a duty to accept, while so many and great slanders upon our fellow-countrymen in India are published, and while the real India and its inhabitants are overlooked amidst the din of controversy, the screams of sedition from Bengal, the cries of the party of the Hindoo Congress, and the writings and speeches of such as, even if they have visited India, were there delivered over blindfolded and tongue-tied to the interested interpreter.

The first chapter contains a sketch of the past history of India, showing the perpetual state of warfare and oppression which existed up to the time of the Mogul Empire, and how little good government was enjoyed by the people during the latter period which is now represented by agitators as the Golden Age. The consolidation of the British Empire is hardly noticed, since that is the most familiar period of Indian history, but a glimpse is given of the anarchy and misery which followed upon the break up of the Mogul Empire and the predatory predominance of the Mahrattas.

A brief account is then given of the land system of the British Government, showing how much more favourable to the landowner and cultivator it is than that of our predecessors in title, whose system nevertheless it closely follows. The constitution of the Government of India is explained, its financial system, the policy pursued towards the native states and, on the frontier, the causes and character of the present unrest, and the connection therewith of the Hindoo Congress, the character of the reforms suggested by Mr Morley and Lord Minto, and now under the consideration of the local administrations and of the general public. A chapter follows on social reform, and incidentally some account is given of the domestic life of the Indians, a fascinating subject, and a mirror, as it seems to me, in many respects, of life in the pantheistic and polytheistic times, with which we were familiar, when we read the classics in school. A final chapter deals with the economic conditions of the country, and the economic policy of the Government of India.

The vulgar spelling is advisedly adopted. The so-called scientific method would be very useful, if the object was to transliterate the words as given in English into their original vernacular forms. But no one wants to perform this feat. The vulgar spelling moreover serves its purpose. If a British soldier says interrogatively to a Bengali villager, "Dum Dum," he will be shown the way to that storied station, but if he says "Dam Dam," he will be ignored as a profane and provocative foreigner. It would be no use to tell the soldier, he should pronounce his vowels continentalwise, because he would regard such advice as absurd, well knowing that neither he, nor his adviser, ever will do anything of the kind.

My grateful acknowledgments are due to the proprietors of *The Times*, *Morning Post*, *Pall Mall Gazette*, *Nineteenth Century*, *The Fortnightly Review*, *The Empire Review*, *The National Review*, *Macmillan's Magazine*, *Journal of the Society of Arts*, *Journal of the East India Association*, and to Messrs Kegan Paul, Trench, and Messrs Macmillan for permission to make use of former books, contributions, and articles, and I have to acknowledge my indebtedness to the Imperial Gazetteer of India for 1907.

It may not be out of place here to say that this book has not been written by a man who spent six weeks in India for that purpose, but by one who served for upwards of twenty-five years in the India Civil Service, and passed through most of the grades from Assistant Magistrate to British Resident, and Additional Member of the Governor - General's Council, before retiring on qualifying for a pension, "*contentus exacto tempore vitæ . . . uti conviva satur.*" I passed the high proficiency test in Persian and in the chief languages of Northern and Southern India, and served as Government Translator in those languages and as Government Reporter on the Indian Press for many years. I have also endeavoured to improve my knowledge of the East and its problems by travel in Persia, Arabia, China, Corea, and Japan, and also in European and Asiatic Russia, in which countries I spent a year, before qualifying as a Russian interpreter.

I do not know how far the above qualifications will carry me, but hope, at any rate, that some information, and no cant, may be found between the covers.

J. D. REES

LONDON, *February* 1908

CONTENTS

CHAPTER VI

Native States

CHAPTER VII

Russia in the East

CHAPTER VIII

Unrest

CHAPTER IX

Unrest

CHAPTER X

The Congress

CHAPTER XI

Proposed Reforms

CHAPTER XII

Social Reform

CHAPTER XIII

The Economic Policy of the Indian Government

CHAPTER XIV

Conclusion

The Frontispiece is from a Photograph by Messrs Elliott & Fry.

THE REAL INDIA

CHAPTER I

EARLY HISTORY

The Brahmins—Greek Writers—Invasions—Arab Conquests—Mahmud of Ghuzni—Timour—Moguls—Akbar—Aurangzeb—Sikhs—Nadir Shah

THE poverty of language is responsible for describing as a country the vast sub-continent which stretches from the eighth to the thirty-sixth degree of latitude, from the roof of the world beyond the Himalayas to the Southern Ocean, which includes 1,766,597 of square miles, and a population of 300,000,000. The provinces under immediate British administration comprise upwards of 61, and the native states upwards of 38 per cent. of the whole, and of the population 62,461,000 inhabit the latter area. Of the British provinces Burma is somewhat smaller than Austria-Hungary; Bengal and Bombay are both bigger than Sweden, and Madras is about the same size as Prussia and Denmark taken together, while, of the native states, Hyderabad is rather larger, and Cashmere rather smaller, than Great Britain. So little do different parts of the empire resemble one another that the density of the population varies from 11 to 1920 to the square mile in different regions in the wide area extending from the Persian frontier to the Chinese march, and from the passes of eternal snow to the burning jungles of Malabar. One male in 10, and one woman in 144, is literate, and in educational eminence the order of precedence is Burma, Madras, Bombay, and Bengal. The native states of Cochin and Travancore, however, rank higher in this respect than any British province, and therein Christians are 25 per cent. of the population as against 1 per cent. throughout India. Four-fifths of the Christians of Madras are found south of that city, and of all our co-religionists in the continent two-thirds are found in the same Presidency. Agriculture in some form is the occupation of about two-thirds of the whole population, though nearly three millions are now employed in exotic occupation such as railways, telegraphs, cotton and jute mills, coal and gold mines, and tea and coffee estates.

It is believed that in the times succeeding the stone ages Upper India was inhabited by more or less dark-coloured tribes, who were gradually driven southwards by fairer peoples from the north, of Aryan stock, but whose descendants are still found in various remote and hilly tracts. The Hindoos hold that the earliest of their Vedas or historic hymns was written 3000 years before the birth of Christ, when the eleventh dynasty was reigning in Egypt, and the great Pyramid of Cheops had already stood 1000 years, but it is considered doubtful if the book and religion of the Vedas really existed more than 800 years before the foundation, in the sixth century, of the religions of Zoroaster, Buddha, and Confucius. Later Vedas describe conditions not unlike those at present existing, with the caste system well established, and the Brahmins occupying that position of pre-eminence which the spread of English education has only confirmed, albeit the recipients are now anxious to rule India without any help from Britain but that of her arms, and without any of that supervision which ensures equal justice to all castes and classes.

The Brahmins simplified the Vedic faith, and made it intelligible to the people as a religion of one God in three revelations of the Creator, Preserver, and Destroyer, and they absorbed into the Hindoo Pantheon the masses of the people who worshipped the forces of nature and their manifestation in man.

As long ago as the time when Æschylus, Sophocles, and Euripides were writing in Greece, they had worked out a system of philosophy, law, medicine, and music, much of which, through the agency of the Arab scholars at the Abbasid court at Baghdad, was introduced into Europe. Their chief epics are the Mahabharata and the Ramayana, the former of which relates to contests which took place round Delhi two or three hundred years before the date of the epics of Homer.

The Brahmins had hardly established their ascendency, when Buddha rose, about 540 B.C., to found the religion which still in point of numbers is the greatest in the world. The same century witnessed the foundation of the system of Zoroaster, which obtained in Persia till it was driven out by the Mahomedans, when a small minority fled and settled on the west coast of India, to found the commercial prosperity of Bombay, to provide representatives for the Indian Legislative Councils, and, until the present day, two members to the British Parliament.

The system of Buddha inculcated the efficacy of works, the uselessness of priests, the futility of sacrifice. It flourished as a rival to Brahminism till the eve of the Mahomedan conquests in the ninth century, when it was driven to the north and north-east of the Himalayas, and to the farther east, after absorbing the indigenous tree and serpent worship, and refining the coarser superstitions of the aboriginal Indians.

To the Greeks, to whom we owe so much in so many other directions, we also owe our earliest accounts of India. Although the father of history wrote of the Eastern Ethiopians, and Darius, son of Hystaspes, added part of the north-west of the subcontinent to the Persian empire, it was not until the expedition of Alexander (327 B.C.) that the Greeks came in actual contact with what is now called the Punjaub, and the country lying between it and Persia proper. Of the Greek writers, Ktesias (*circ.* 400 B.C.), survives in mere fragments. But even in his time the indigenous Indians were subject to foreign domination, or were secured from subjugation in inaccessible mountains, propitiating by presents the Kings of the immigrant Aryans. Megasthenes was sent as ambassador by Seleucus, the ruler of a fair fragment of Alexander's divided empire, to Chandragupta, king of Palibrotha, or Patna, about 300 B.C. His writings are of great value, and any traveller in the Punjaub to-day can confirm his statement that the inhabitants exceed the ordinary stature, and are distinguished by their proud bearing. Subsequent historians have noted, as he did, that, under ordinary circumstances, during war in India, husbandmen were regarded as a class sacred and inviolable, whereby warfare was rendered less terrible than it is in civilised countries. Manucci, however, one of the best witnesses, dissipates this comfortable theory by actual relation of what occurred in the reign of Aurangzeb.

At the present day, when socialism raises it head, all may admire, as he did, laws "which bound everyone equally, but allowed property to be unevenly distributed."

Amateur critics of the policy of the Government of India may learn from Megasthenes (confirmed by Strabo, 20 A.D.) that the Indians paid land tribute to the king, "because all India is the property of the Crown, and no private person is permitted to own land. The husbandmen tilled the land on condition of receiving one-fourth of the produce."

Those who think that the English introduced strong drink into India will learn with surprise from this ancient writer that the Indians of his day drank wine. Some light is also thrown upon a subject which even now excites controversy by the statement that women bore children at the age of seven, and became old at forty. A Greek merchant wrote the "Periplus of the Erythrean Sea" probably about 80 A.D., and he tells of trade in slaves, horses, mules, butter, ivory, pearls, silk and porphyry, besides many kinds of plants and their produce, including spice, indigo, and frankincense. Much business was done too in rice, pepper, and wine, in iron, copper, gold, precious stones, and wearing apparel. In all these substances, the author traded, making voyages from Berenice in the southern extremity of Egypt, to African, Arabian, and Indian ports.

Arrian, the pupil of Epictetus, and contemporary of Marcus Aurelius, writing about 150 A.D., recorded the fact that superintendents holding an office analogous to that of Chinese censors, reported everything that took place to the king, where the people had such an one, or to the magistrates where they were self-governed—that is to say, where there were independent towns like the Greek republics. He found the caste system in full force and vigour. If these ancient writers mixed fable and fact, the inhabitants of India at the present day hardly distinguish between mythological and historical periods, and it is remarkable that, with the exception of these old Greek writings, no histories have been composed about India until the time of the Mahomedan conquest. The Hindoos, indeed, are not chroniclers, and in the past they preferred, as to a great extent they do at present prefer, speculation and philosophy to facts and deductions of more immediate practical value. Thus peculiar importance attaches to such information as we have regarding the Græco-Bactrian kingdom. It is with some surprise we find Philostratos recording that the Pythagorean philosopher, Apollonius, in the preceding century, had been received on the banks of the Indus by a Greek-speaking king, the simplicity of whose life and personal appointments survives to this day amongst the princes of South-Western India, who have never come under the immediate influence of foreign rule. These Greek writers constantly refer to the considerable commerce carried on between Rome and the Malabar coast until the third century of our era, and 600 years previously Herodotus realised more fully than we do to-day in England "that there are many races of Indians who do not speak the same language as one another." Twenty centuries ago the Romans realised the propinquity of India better than we do to-day: "*Quantum enim est quod ab ultimis litoribus Hispanæ usque ab Indos jacet. Paucissimorum dierum spatium.*"

These old writers describe the complex and civilised

character of life in ancient Indian cities, where there were inspectors of industrial arts, and entertainments, of births, deaths; of retail and barter; of weights, measures, and manufactures, and of military and naval affairs.

While Pliny tells us that the companions of Alexander had written that India was a third part of all the world, and the multitude of its inhabitants was past reckoning, the Census Commissioner in 1901 records the fact that India is, in point of population, about a fifth part of the whole world, and that its inhabitants number nearly 300,000,000.

To this day the Indian Peninsula deserves the description given to it in the third century by Dionysius, who praises the lovely land of the Indians, "last of all lands, upon the very lips of the ocean, where ascends the sun, scattering heat and radiance over the works of gods and men." The India of classical times included, of course, Afghanistan and the surrounding regions. Seleucus was so occupied in founding the monarchy of Syria that he handed over to Chandragupta the Greek conquests in the last-named country, and in India, and his grandson, Antiochus, entered into a treaty with Asoka, the grandson of Chandragupta, in 256 B.C. For a hundred years subsequently the Greek rulers of Bactria fitfully invaded India, but, beyond an occasional discovery of coins, little trace of their domination remains. From the time the Greek invasions ceased, those of the Scythians or Tartars, and of the Turks or Turkomans, commenced. The tribes of Central Asia then began to make those descents into the more favoured country upon the south-east and south-west of their cold and barren home, which culminated in the devastation of Genghis Khan and Timour the Tartar. They drove the Greek dynasty from Bactria, destroyed the Greek settlements of the Punjaub, and founded a kingdom in Cashmere.

These inroads continued till the fifth century, during which time the indigenous inhabitants strove with varying success to withstand the invaders. The Scythians and Tartars belonged to four great races: the Mongolians from the country north of the Great Wall of China; the Tungusians, to which the present Manchu dynasty of China belongs; the Ugrians, or Fins, who settled in the west of Asia and the north of Europe, to which branch the Magyars of Hungary belong, and the Turkish, the most famous, which occupied the middle country extending from Lake Baikal to the land of the Slavs.

In 614 Chosroes had advanced the Persian boundary to the neighbourhood of Constantinople and to the Nile, and on his return from this successful campaign he was invited by an emissary of Mahomed to embrace the religion which subsequently became that of Persia, and also of the great swarm of barbarians, one branch of which founded the Mogul Empire in India.

During the wars of the Emperor Heraclius with the Persians, the latter joined forces with the Avars, who, however, besieged Constantinople, whereupon the distracted Emperor entered into alliance with the Turks, but no sooner had he thus triumphed over the Persians than the Arab followers of Mahomed commenced to conquer the provinces he had hardly rescued from the successor of Cyrus. Thus Islam marched towards India. The prophet Mahomed, born in 569, a homeless and friendless fugitive in 622, in 630 declared war upon Heraclius, Emperor of the East, and within a hundred years of his death, in 632, his successors had defeated the feeble descendant of Chosroes on the field of Cadesia, in 710. The conquest of Khorassan was followed by that of Transoxiana, when for the first time the Crescent appeared on the banks of the Indus, and the connection of the Mahomedans with India was commenced, in that full tide of glory and fanaticism which spread the faith of Islam from the Guadalquivir to the sands of Sind.

To the era of Mahomedan conquests succeeded one of letters, and the rivals who divided the inheritance of Islam—the Fatimite in Africa, the Ommeiad in Spain, and the Abbasid in Baghdad—vied with one another in the encouragement of learning.

Meanwhile India, to which expeditions had been sent in the reign of Othman in 636, and later in 662 and 664, had rest till 712. Though in the ninth century the Arabs took Crete and Sicily, and threatened Rome, the adoption of a Turkish guard by the Caliphs was only one of many signs of the seeds of decay. Africa and Spain became independent kingdoms, Syria and Egypt were usurped by Turkish slaves, and indigenous Persian dynasties reigned in Persia and Khorassan.

In like manner, the loosely consolidated Empire of the Turks lasted only from 545 to 750, though the Emperors of Rome and China paid tribute to its head; and its broken fragments existed as separate and independent kingdoms, of whose history we know very little, until Mahmud of Ghuzni (1001 to 1030) rose to power and pre-eminence, and organised no less that thirteen invasions of India.

It was in 650 that the Caliph Othman's Governor of Kufa reduced the Persian borders of the Caspian

Sea, and converted its inhabitants to the faith of Islam, while the Governor of Busra subdued the provinces of Seistan, Kohistan, Nishapur, Ghor, Herat, Merv and Balkh.

A further move in the direction of India was made in 664, the Caliph Moawiya's general, penetrating as far as Multan. In 712, the Arab General Kasim invaded Sind and settled in the Indus valley, which the Mahomedans retained till 828, though it was not till the days of Mahmud of Ghuzni that any permanent occupation was effected. Mahmud was the son of Sabuktegin, who was a Turk of the household of Alptegin, Governor of Khorassan, under the Samani dynasty, which ruled over Transoxiana, with its capital at Bokhara, and had risen to eminence during the reign of Mamun, son of Harun al Raschid.

Alptegin made himself independent, with a capital at Ghuzni, and Sabuktegin became his son-in-law, and ultimately his successor. The latter prince took Khandahar and marched to the Indus, where he defeated the Hindoo King of Lahore, upon whom he came down, as the historian Ferishta says, like the wolf on the fold.

Sabuktegin died in 997, and upon his deathbed he said that in the efforts man makes to avert disease, with the hope of recovery, he resembles the condition of the butcher and the sheep which is often bound down and shorn of its fleece, so that at last, when the moment of death arrives, it permits itself to be quietly bound, believing the occasion to be that of another shearing, and resigns its throat to the knife.

No sooner was he secure in the succession to his own kingdom than Mahmud looked towards India. In 1002, when Ethelred was massacring the Danes in England, Mahmud was returning home from a massacre of Hindoos, and his first invasion of India. During successive expeditions he acquired enormous booty, and extended his kingdom in all directions, taking Samarcand and Bokhara, then the most celebrated cities in Central Asia, capturing Kanouj, upon the Ganges, and defeating the Rajah of Lahore. But in 1030 he yielded his body to death and his soul to immortality, after an inspection of all his great possessions, of which he gave away nothing, so that the poet Sadi tells of one who saw him long after his death in a dream, his body bereft of flesh, but the eye of covetousness burning brightly in the sunken socket.

In Mahmud's kingdom, while the population was chiefly Persian, the administration was chiefly Turkish, and his authority in India was vague and ill-defined. Of his successors, one caused the fables of Pilpay, the Anwar-i-Soheili, to be translated into Persian, thereby causing their dissemination over most parts of the world. His dynasty ended in 1186 and the house of Ghor, which succeeded, produced a conqueror in Mahomed, who, imitating the example of Mahmud, made war upon the Indian rajahs. He was assassinated in 1206, whereupon one of his Turkish slaves, Kutub, of the Kutub Minar, made himself independent at Delhi, and died from a fall at polo in 1210. Other slave kings ruled over Delhi till 1288 during which period the Moguls under Genghis Khan, came to the banks of the Indus, Sind was permanently subjected to Mahomedan rule, and Behar and Bengal were added to the crown of Delhi. In the middle of the thirteenth century the court at this capital was the only Mahomedan court not overthrown by the Moguls, and it became a place of refuge for the many princes expelled from their thrones by Genghis Khan. One of these kings, Ghiyas-ud-din, was a patron of letters, and a friend of the poet Sadi. Among other wise sayings of his is this: "that it is better for a king to be obstinate than vacillating, as in the first case he might chance to be right, but in the latter he is sure to be wrong."

The Tartar house of Khilji now reigned at Delhi (1288-1320), and of its kings one Ala-ud-din, repulsed the Moguls, and conquered the Deccan and Malabar. Next came the house of Tughlak (1321-1414), founded, like many another royal family, by a successful general. Firuz Tughlak lost Bengal and the Deccan, but he constructed the still existing Karnal canal, abolished all petty and vexatious taxes, and died in 1388, leaving behind him an enviable reputation. His successors lost other provinces, and in 1398 Timour the Tartar, commonly called Tamerlane, after conquering Persia and Transoxiana and invading Georgia, Mesopotamia and Russia, was proclaimed Emperor of India. Genghiz Khan was a Mongol, but his army was chiefly comprised of Turks, and when he died, in 1227, he had overthrown all the independent kingdoms of Tartary, and taken Northern China, Khorassan and Transoxiana. Timour himself was a Turk though he revived the Tartar, Mongol or Mogul Empire. He annexed Persia and reduced Turkestan to obedience, but within one hundred years from his death, in 1405, Persia and Transoxiana were overrun by nomad Turkmans, and his descendant, Babar, flying from the Uzbegs, founded the Mogul Empire in India. Timour entered the country in which his descendant was to found the greatest of its Oriental dynasties by way of Cabul, took Delhi, from which Mahomed Tughlak had fled, and slaughtered 100,000 prisoners.

He cared little for the consolidation of his conquest, and left it a prey to disorder. From 1414 the Seyyids ruled as lieutenants of Timour's dynasty, and when the Lodis succeeded, in 1450, they held the Punjaub and Delhi, other provinces having become independent during the anarchy which followed upon the invasion of Timour. Little indeed is known of the course of events in India during the century which preceded the accession of Babar, a period remarkable in the world's history for the termination of the domination of the Moors in Spain (1491), the discovery of America by Columbus (1494); the arrival of the Portuguese in India by way of the Cape of Good Hope, the accession of Henry VIII. in England, and the conquest of Mexico by Cortez. The blight of the Mongol invasion had left India completely cut off from participation in world politics and commerce, and there was little for such chroniclers as existed to relate, beyond a tedious procession of wars and rebellions. Babar, then ruling in Cabul, invaded India during the reign of Ibrahim Lodi, claiming the country as part of the inheritance of Tamerlane. He destroyed Lahore in 1524; in 1526 defeated Ibrahim on the fateful field of Panipat, and, in the words of the historian Elphinstone, "founded a line of kings, under whom India rose to the highest pitch of prosperity, and out of the ruins of whose empire all the existing states in that country are composed."

The latter statement is accurate, but if the condition of the people, rather than the power and glory of the ruler, be regarded as the test, exception must be taken to Elphinstone's assertion that under the Moguls India rose to the highest pitch of prosperity. It would be foreign to the purpose of this little work to describe the reigns of the great Moguls, a task already performed by master hands. They governed, no doubt, as we do, through the agency of Hindoos, in our case and in theirs alike, chiefly Brahmins, and the best of them were tolerant and humane. In contemporary writings and speeches constant reference is made to the golden age of native Indian rule, and though the Moguls were foreigners, as we are, they were Asiatics, and the existence of a solidarity of sentiment, wanting in our case, may be admitted. But by common consent Akbar was the best and most tolerant of the emperors of this line, and no subsequent ruler had so able a Hindoo minister as Todar Mal. Yet it was Akbar who laid it down, as the governing principle of revenue administration, "that there shall be left for every man as much as he requires for his own support till the next crop be reaped, and for that of his family and for seed. Thus much shall be left to him, what remains is the land-tax." Aurangzeb, who collected nothing south of the Vindhya Mountains, in 1707 obtained £38,000,000 land revenue, and a total revenue of £80,000,000, while the English collect but £84,000,000 total, and under £20,000,000 land revenue from their immensely larger territories. The accomplished Orientalist, Mr Irvine, has just published a translation of the "Storia do Mogor" by Niccolai Manucci, who lived between 1653 and 1708 with Prince Dara Shekoh and Aurangzeb. No better witness exists, and Manucci tells us that every time a general won a victory the heads of villagers were sent as booty to Agra, and after twenty-four hours were deposited along the highway in pillars built for the purpose, each to accommodate a hundred heads. Aurangzeb was one of the ablest and most powerful of his line, which produced many great men, but Manucci sums up his reign by saying: "in no part of his Empire was there any justice, no one thought of anything but how to plunder, the revenue was collected by violence, and no remissions were allowed for loss of crops." In a subsequent chapter I will endeavour to describe the land revenue system now in force in India, but it is impossible to pass by Elphinstone's statement, capable as it is of such serious misconstruction, and refuted as it is by the best contemporary witness. The Great Moguls governed the greater part of India for two hundred years from 1526, and were nominal emperors till the mutiny of 1857. Manucci in no way confirms the popular belief that this was the golden age. Indeed he says: "In these days everybody's thought is to steal, and whatever happens it rarely reaches the ears of the king, the orders coming from whom his officers do not obey. Those who are the most distant from the court suffer most." He relates too an anecdote of a Portuguese he knew, who preferred death to becoming a Mahomedan, which throws an interesting light on contemporary Christianity, and adds: "It is now forty-eight years that I have been in India, yet never have I seen a Mahomedan become a Christian. I have seen on the Coromandel coast and in Bengal a few Malabaris and Bengalis, poverty-stricken Hindoos, become Christians, but it was from compulsion of hunger, or to get married to some Christian. Even then they never refrained from Hindoo practices." As to the justice of the Great Moguls, Aurangzeb, starting to wage war against the Deccani Kings of Bijapur and Golconda, gave orders that eighty men should be bound and beheaded in a kneeling position on either side of the route he would traverse; which slaughter of innocent peasants was by way of sacrifice and prayer for success in his enterprise. The founder of the Mogul dynasty, Babar fortunately bequeathed to posterity the memoirs of his adventurous life written in the Turkish language. His father was fifth in descent from Tamerlane. He was therefore a Turk, though his mother was a Mogul, a race of which he himself speaks with contempt in his memoirs, but the Indians use this generic term for a Mahomedan who enters India from beyond Afghanistan. Babar, a brave, simple and pleasure-loving monarch, compelled all the Mahomedan princes in India to acknowledge his supremacy, and was fighting for the faith against the Hindoos in the year 1534, which saw the victory of the Protestant over the Roman Catholic religion in England. He was defeated at Buxar by one of his own lieutenants, the Governor of Behar and Bengal, and was obliged in his flight to cross the Ganges on an inflated skin. When he reached Omerkote, with only seven attendants, his Queen gave birth to the illustrious Akbar, the greatest of all the great Moguls. The revolting governor, Sher Shah, built caravanserais, wells, and avenues from Bengal to the Indus, and of his second son, who succeeded him, it was said: "Empire is no man's inheritance, but belongs to him who hath the longest sword." The second son's sword was long enough to enable the wearer to supplant his eldest brother, but was not long enough to maintain his kingdom, and the son and successor of Babar, Humayun, who died just after his return to India, left his precarious inheritance, including Bengal, to Akbar, then a youth of thirteen years, whose minister, Bairam, defeated the rebellious General Hemu in 1556 at Panipat, on which field the fate of India has several times been decided. Practically the whole of India became more or less subject to Akbar, though this statement could not have been made with any approach to truth of any one of his predecessors. The population of the conquered realms was made up of the aborigines, of Scythians and Tartars, and of the races who invaded the country from the north, and are commonly called Aryans. Buddhism was the centripetal force which had to some extent welded together this loose, amorphous mass, but in the seventh century Brahminism had revived, and in the ninth it had triumphed. In its present aspect it represents the union of the Vedic faith of the original Brahmins with Buddhism, and with the rude and elementary superstitions of the aboriginal tribes. Brahmin pantheism is capable of including everything, and would before now probably have absorbed the Christian converts but for their rejection of caste. To this day, the majority of the people of India are animists—animism being that form of faith which used to be called fetichism, or the worship of tangible and inanimate objects, in the belief that they are possessed of some mysterious power. South of the Vindhya range, the boundary between Hindustan and the Deccan, were three great Hindoo kingdoms, with their capitals, Mysore, Tanjore and Madura. The Hindoo kingdom of Vizayanagar lasted from 1118 till 1565, and disputed the hegemony of the Deccan with the southern Mahomedan kingdoms. In the reign of Mahomed Tughlak, a contemporary of Richard II. of England and of Philip de Valois of France, the empire of Delhi extended from the Himalayas and the Indus on the north-west and north-east, to the sea on the east and west, though much of Rajputana was independent. Between 1489 and 1688 there were five Mahomedan states in the Deccan, formed out of the fragments of the Bahmani kingdom, with their respective capitals: Bejapur, Golconda, Ahmednugger, Elichpur and Bedi; and the ruins of the first-named city eloquently attest the greatness of the former kingdom. They include masterpieces of Saracenic architecture, and the largest dome in the world, which covers an area of 18,000 square feet uninterrupted by supports. It was here that Ferishta resided and completed his history, a valuable mine for the later Indian historian, but one in which writers of the anti-British school do not care to dig. Besides the Hindoo and Mahomedan kingdoms, to which brief reference has been made, there remained the Rajput States which had never been conquered. Insufficient as are the materials for writing Indian history, there are, thanks to the Hakluyt Society, publications which give some idea of the internal state of the country in the fifteenth and the beginning of the sixteenth centuries. The commercial intercourse, which had been carried on between India and Rome through the Red Sea, hardly survived the division of the Roman Empire into east and west, when it was supplanted by trade with Constantinople carried through Persia by caravan. The Arab conquests next interrupted intercourse between India and the Byzantine Empire, and in the tenth century intercourse was reopened with Venice through Egypt, and in the eleventh century the republics of Genoa and Venice, consequent upon the irruptions of the Turks into Syria and Palestine, developed considerable commerce with India. This trade subsequently became a Venetian monopoly, till the close of the fifteenth century, when the Portuguese in turn profited by the discovery of America and the rounding of the Cape.

Nikitin, a Russian traveller of 1470, dwelt upon the contrast between the brilliance of the Court and the poverty of the people in the Deccan. Babosa, a Portuguese, in the beginning of the sixteenth century, described the people of Gujerat as prosperous and well-found. He speaks of the roofed and tiled houses of the town, of the trade in cloth, of the silk manufactures of Bombay, and of the dealings of the West Coast in cocoa and areca nuts, spices and drugs; nor is his account of the Malabar coast, that fertile and pleasant land, any less satisfactory.

It seems that the Mahomedan kings of the time were accessible to their subjects, and personal in their rule, though practically absolute authority was delegated to governors of provinces. The army was composed of levies, supplied fully equipped by local chiefs, and by individual soldiers who served for hire. The Hindoos had to pay the poll-tax, but they were generally employed in the administration, and sometimes as generals. The Emperor Babar in his memoirs says that the revenue officials, merchants, and work-people were all Hindoos, and much the same might be said at the present day, for the actual government is generally in the hands of Brahmins, who are supervised by a handful of Civil Servants who form a *corps d'élite*. There can be no doubt that the Mahomedan conquerors of India soon lost their fierce proselytising zeal and intolerance, and treated the Hindoos with leniency and toleration. They coined silver and gold, and Akbar fixed the rupee at very much its present weight. Before his day the Indian Mahomedans had adopted the muslin robe and slippers which they now wear, and their character, as well as their costume has changed, since they left the uplands of Central Asia for the river plains of Hindustan, whence some as a ruling class migrated to the "wide stony wolds of the Deccan." Akbar was cut off from the Afghan base which his predecessors had possessed, and partly on this account, and partly, no doubt, from statesmanship, he determined to pursue a policy of toleration and conciliation. The contemporary chronicle known as the Akbarnama of Abul Fazl, the eminent minister, throws an interesting light upon the Emperor's methods of administration. One day he came upon two bodies of Hindoos, who were quarrelling about the possession of a sacred bathing place. He first of all endeavoured to effect a friendly settlement, and finding this impossible told them to fight it out, and saw fair play. Had this solution been adopted during the recent disturbances in Eastern Bengal, little would have been heard of the Hindoo case, for the Mahomedans would have easily settled all disputes in their own favour. Akbar tried alternately violence and conciliation in order to the subjugation of the Rajput States, which was never completely effected. He took Gujerat, recovered Bengal and Behar, annexed Cashmere, and tried, with indifferent success, to subdue Afghanistan. This was the first war made by a ruler of Hindustan against that country. Sind was next subdued and Kandahar recovered, so that the Mogul Empire now extended from Afghanistan across the whole of India north of the Vindhya mountains, while the Deccan proved an insoluble problem. Those breezy uplands bred heroines, and Chand Bibi of Ahmednugger fired copper, silver, and gold coins at the Moguls, when iron was exhausted, and was firing away the Crown jewels when her valorous soul was quenched, a worthy prototype of the Ranee of Jhansi. Akbar returned to Agra from this campaign in 1601—the year in which the first East India Company was founded, and in which the first English ships reached India—and in 1605 he died. He dreamt of an eclectic religion, embracing all that was best in all the chief faiths of his own generation. Probably he was for the most part sincere, possibly, like his contemporary, Henry IV. of France, who thought Paris worth a Mass, his religion was subservient to his policy of conciliation. He discouraged suttee and child marriage, and allowed Hindoo widows to marry again, thus anticipating some of the reforms effected by the English. His religious system died with him. His revenue system was borrowed from that of Sher Shah, the Afghan king of Delhi, who died in 1545, a great monarch, who said that his life was not long enough to allow of his doing sufficient good to his people. All the cultivable lands in the Empire were measured and divided into three classes according to their fertility, the demand of the State being fixed at one-third of the gross produce, as against a rough general average of one-fourteenth which we get. Settlements were thus effected which lasted for ten years as against thirty of our present system, and measurements and classifications were recorded in the village accounts, just as they now are. Akbar's Dewan was the famous Todar Mal, and his finance minister the hardly less celebrated Abul Fazl. Sir William Hunter concluded that the revenue collected from a part of India, by the Great Mogul exceeded that received by the British from their more extended and far greater Empire, and it is probable that the land-tax of the present day is, on an average, less than a quarter of what was exacted by Akbar. There were then no police except the hereditary village watchmen, and the chief landowners were held responsible for the protection of life and property. The rural watchmen usually belonged to the robber class, but that was the case until late in the nineteenth century in the extreme south of India, where the system, now abandoned, worked fairly well. The army consisted chiefly of cavalry, and the troopers were men of the yeoman class, who supplied their own horses and weapons. This arrangement practically survives in the native cavalry regiments to the present day. The infantry of the line were paid six rupees a month, and, in theory at any rate, all males capable of bearing arms were liable to service. Akbar's successor, Jahangir, regarded his wife as a colleague upon the throne, and they reigned in a fashion not unlike that of Justinian and Theodora, her name being engraved on the coins with that of the Emperor It was in this reign, in the year 1616, that Sir Thomas Roe arrived as ambassador of James I., who sent him in the hope of obtaining more favourable terms for British trade at Surat, and on the West Coast of India, where silk, spice, pepper, precious stones, and cotton were bartered in exchange for knives and broadcloth. When Jahangir died, in 1627, his dominions were practically coterminous with those of Akbar, for his endeavours to conquer the Deccan were fruitless.

His successor, Shah Jehan, a contemporary during his long reign of Charles I. and Cromwell, and of Louis XIII. and Louis XIV., conducted the usual wars, with less than the usual unsuccess in the Deccan, into which he introduced the revenue system of Todar Mal. During the reign of Shah Jehan, the Mogul Empire reached its zenith, but Elphinstone, than whom no man was more competent to form an opinion, considers that the condition of the people must have been worse than in the most badly governed state in modern Europe. It was this emperor who rebuilt and adorned Delhi, constructing the Great Mosque, the palace, the little Musjid, and the Taj Mahal. No sooner was Aurangzeb formally installed upon his throne, in the year of the restoration of the Stuarts in England, than war broke out between Bejapur and the Mahrattas, who were a race of cultivators living in the hills of Goa and Surat, and the western extremity of the Deccan plateau. Sivaji, the national hero, began life as a brigand, and little was heard of the Mahrattas till his day, though Ferishta records that as early as 1485 the Mahomedan kings of the Deccan had already enlisted these hardy hillmen in their service. In 1648, Sivaji had acquired possession of several fortresses belonging to Bejapur, as a result of his wars with the ruler of which kingdom, he was placed in possession of considerable territory; and of Indian chiefs he first realised that infantry was of greater importance than cavalry. Aurangzeb had made the fatal mistake of reducing the Mahomedan kingdoms of the Deccan instead of invoking their aid against the rising strength of the Mahrattas. The latter continued to grow in power, and soon the states of Bejapur and Golconda commenced to pay tribute to Sivaji, who presently arrogated to himself the right to levy the famous *chauth*, or quarter of the revenue, as the price of security against attacks by his followers.

Another false step taken by Aurangzeb was the revival of the obnoxious poll-tax levied on Hindoos, and, departing from all the wise precedents of his line, he forbade the entertainment of Hindoos in the Government service. The reimposition of the tax on infidels and the revocation of the Edict of Nantes were two events of equal import to the Mogul and French monarchies. The interests of the Rajputs now became identical with those of the Mahrattas, and the latter bandits became champions of the Hindoo religion and nationality. All Rajputana was in a blaze, and the star of Sivaji was ever in the ascendant in the south, where the Mahomedan kings of the Deccan called him in to aid them to maintain their independence against Aurangzeb. In 1683 the Emperor left Delhi, never to return before his death in 1707, the intervening period being spent in vain efforts to reduce the Deccan to submission. His last years were clouded by the intrigues of his sons, as well as by the failure of his arms, and when he died, in the eighty-ninth year of his life, and the fiftieth of his reign, he said: "Everywhere I see nothing but God. I have committed many crimes, and know not how I shall be punished. The death agony presses on one, I am going. Come what may I have launched my vessel on the waves. Farewell, farewell." Elphinstone says of him that "he would indeed have been a good and great king had he not had a heart cold, calculating, and a stranger to all generous and ennobling impulses." His land revenue reached 38½ million sterling, and his total income was 77½ millions. The usual fratricidal strife followed upon his death, and resulted in the ultimate victory of Shah Alam, the eldest son, whose Viceroy in the Deccan now openly paid chauth to the Mahrattas. The new Emperor first offered the Rajputs practical independence in return for peace, and turned his own attention to the Sikhs. This religious sect, afterwards so famous in Indian history, was founded at the end of the fifteenth century by Nanak, who recognised no distinction of caste, but preached universal toleration, and the unity of the Godhead. Since the death of the tolerant Akbar they had been persecuted, and in 1675, their Guru or leader created a religious and military commonwealth, every member of which was a soldier. None were allowed to shave, and each and every one was bound to carry cold steel about his person—of which rule of conduct, the quoit in the turban is now the outward and visible sign. The Sikhs respect the Brahmins, and forbid the slaughter of cattle, but their resemblance to the orthodox Hindoo in other respects is small, and they have acquired a very distinctive character. Farokhsir was a prince of no great merit, but he fought and defeated the Sikhs, whose sectaries he treated with the utmost barbarity. The Deccan in his reign had now become almost independent under its Viceroys or Nizams, who acknowledged the Mahratta sovereignty, and duly paid their chauth or tribute. The real governors of the Empire were the Seyyids, two brothers who were king-makers, but when their creature, the king, tired of them, the Nizam of the Deccan became chief minister, while the power of the Mahrattas passed into the hands of a family of Brahmin village accountants in the Konkan. Balaji Visvanath became their Peshwa or minister, and he endeavoured to realise, as a regular tribute and revenue, one quarter of the revenue, as settled by Todar Mal, of the Mogul

Empire. During its decline and fall, however, nothing like this amount was collected, and Mogul revenue and Mahratta chauth alike were levied by force and not according to law. The different heads of account in one and the same area were collected by different agencies, in order to prevent any one authority from becoming independent of the central power at Delhi, an object which, none the less, the arrangement failed to secure. One result however, of this system was of a permanent character, for the intricacy of the accounts led to the universal use of Brahmin accountants, thereby increasing the ascendency of the caste, always so powerful in India, to which the family of the Peshwa belonged. To Balaji succeeded Baji Rao, who first invaded the northern provinces of the tottering empire, saying "let us strike the withered trunk, and the branches will fall of their own accord."

At this period rose to eminence the families of the Gaekwar of Baroda, Holkar of Indore, and the Sindhias of Gwalior, who were lieutenants of the Peshwa Baji-Rao. It was now evident that any effort to oppose the Mahrattas would be fruitless, and the Nizam therefore joined them in self-aggrandisement at the expense of the empire, the breaking up of which was precipitated by the invasion of Nadir Shah. The eastern portion of the tableland of Herat formed a kind of neutral territory between the Persian and the Mogul empires, and the Safavi Shah Hosain was involved in warfare with the Ghiljis, who occupied the western portion of that tableland. The tribesmen, however, invaded and took Ispahan, whereupon Tahmasp, the son of Hosain, invoked the aid of Nadir Kuli, a renowned freebooter of that day, who, instead of placing Tahmasp upon the throne of Persia, himself, in 1736, assumed the title of Shah-in-Shah, to which, by the conquest of Balkh and Bokhara, he gave an actuality that lofty designation had long lacked. The distracted empire of the Moguls was an irresistible temptation to such a warrior, and, a pretext for attack being soon found, he took Cabul, and as the Emperor had omitted to pay to the Afghans the subsidies they claimed, he passed unobstructed through the mountains, crossed the Indus, defeated the Imperial troops at Kurnal in February, 1739, and gave Delhi over to fire and sword. Almost immediately, however, he departed home with all the booty he could obtain, and with a treaty in his pocket whereby the Emperor relinquished all claim to everything west of the Indus. Nine years later he was assassinated, in consequence of his mad endeavours to suppress the Shiyya doctrines, which the Persians since the Mahomedan conquest ever have, and still do, profess. When Nadir Shah had left, the Mahrattas again began to harry the prostrate empire. Balaji Baji succeeded Baji as third Peshwa, but the curse of domestic dissension now fell in turn upon the Mahrattas, and the French appeared for the first time to aid the Nizam's son, Salabat Jung, to oppose them. Ahmed Khan, afterwards Ahmed Shah, of the Durani tribe, succeeded to the authority of Nadir Shah in Khorassan, and the country between the Indus and the Persian frontier in 1748, and in the same year a prince of the same name succeeded to the Mogul throne, only to make way almost immediately for Alamgir, from whose feeble grasp Ahmed Shah Durani wrested Delhi, leaving behind him a Rohilla chieftain in command, who was presently expelled, with the aid of the Peshwa's brother, Ragoba, who seized Lahore and threatened

Oudh. At this juncture, Ahmed Shah Durani for the fourth time invaded the Punjaub, and defeated the Mahrattas under Sindhia and Holkar. It was not against the Mogul emperor that the Afghan king made war, but against the Mahrattas, whose power was now, in 1760, at its height. The whole of the empire, and more of the south of India than ever acknowledged its authority, was either part of, or paid tribute to, their power. Their forces, estimated at about 300,000, and the Durani forces of 100,000, faced one another, in January 1761, upon the classic battle-ground of Panipat, with the usual result that the invaders were victorious. The Mahrattas retired to their conquests in Hindustan, and the dynasties of the Peshwa and the Mogul alike were overwhelmed in a common catastrophe.

The Mahrattas recovered a great deal of their once great power, but that of the Moguls was finally broken, and upon its fragments rose independent states, with which, and with the relations of the Europeans with which, the history of India from this date is chiefly concerned.

CHAPTER II

LATER HISTORY

Clive—Afghanistan—Mutiny—Burma—Lord Curzon—Frontier—Assam—Military Affairs—Army—Mutiny—Education—Lord Minto

GEORGE III. had sat upon the throne a year when the third battle of Panipat was fought, and already, in the reign of Charles II., the East India Company, which dated from the reign of Queen Elizabeth, had become sufficiently powerful to obtain a new charter, and the cession of Bombay. Fort St George had been founded in 1639, but it was not till 1698 that Aurangzeb granted a site upon the Hoogly for the occupation of our traders in Bengal. As the Mahomedan invaders all came by land, so did the Europeans all arrive by sea. The trade between India and Europe which passed by the Red Sea through Egypt, and paid heavy transit duty to the Sultan, fired the ambition of the Portuguese to try and discover some direct sea route whereby they could avoid the transit duties, and Vasco da Gama doubled the Cape and anchored off Calicut, in 1498, and returned to Portugal with a letter for his king from the Zamorin. Cabral, in the following year, quarrelled with the latter potentate and withdrew to Cochin, the Rajah of which state, true to the traditional policy of his house, received them with kindly hospitality. Two years later Vasco da Gama again arrived at Calicut to avenge the treatment Cabral had experienced. But Alfonso Albuquerque, "in whose presence the sea trembled," was the real founder of the Portuguese power in the East. He captured Goa, held Ormuz, and the spice island of Malacca, and with his dismissal began that decline which everywhere proceeded during the period in which the crown of Portugal was united with that of Spain, from 1580 to 1666. The Mahrattas took Bassein, the Dutch seized Malacca and Ceylon, and the Persians captured Ormuz; but it was the Dutch who struck down the Portuguese monopoly, their objective being the spice trade of the Eastern Archipelago. In 1602 the Dutch East India Company was founded; in 1605 they expelled the Portuguese from Amboyna, and in 1619 founded Batavia. With the exception of the English, the only other European country which owned land settlements in India was Denmark, which bought Tranquebar from the Rajah of Tanjore, and had another settlement at Serampore on the Hoogly. These possessions, which became famous centres of missionary activity, were sold to the English in 1845. Thus it happened that the French were the only serious competitors of our fellow-countrymen, their chief possessions being Chandarnagore on the Hoogly, and Pondicherry on the Coromandel coast. In 1746 they took from us Madras, which was restored at the peace of Aix-la-Chapelle, 1748, but the real fight for India began between Dupleix and Clive, when the former statesman endeavoured to found a French Empire by intervening in the disputed succession to the thrones of Hyderabad and Arcot, fragments of the Mogul Empire which had become practically independent. Ten years before the battle of Panipat, Clive, by his defence of Arcot, had made the English name feared and respected in

Southern India, and two years before that battle, Coote had defeated the Comte de Lally at Wandewash, after which the English remained the masters of the south. In Bengal the tyranny of Suraj-ud-Daula, and the fact that France and England were at war in Europe, led up to the important victory, but not great battle, of Plassey in 1757, and to the first extensive grant of territory to the English, which grant was largely increased in 1760 upon the deposition of the Nawab Mir Jaffar of Bengal. Subsequently their own creature, Mir Cassim, endeavoured to assert his independence with such aid as the Emperor Shah Alam, could give, whereupon the English defeated him at Buxar in 1764. Clive, however, restored Oudh to the Nawab Vizier, and obtained from Shah Alam in return for a fragment of his empire which was given back to him, the fiscal administration of Bengal, Behar, and Orissa, for which provinces there thus obtained a dual management till Warren Hastings abolished the system, and sold to the Nabob of Oudh the territory which Clive had restored to the Emperor, because, when the Mahrattas seized that potentate in 1773, Hastings considered that the British could neither pay territory nor tribute, either directly or indirectly, to the Mahrattas. The power of the latter after the battle of Panipat, was divided between the Peshwa, the Bhonsla Rajahs at Nagpur, the Sindhias at Gwalior the Holkars at Indore, and the Gaekwars at Baroda. Sindhia and Holkar restored Shah Alam to his throne in order to use such authority as remained to this shadow of a great name, and they held him prisoner till the second Mahratta War, in 1803, whereby the power of Sindhia and the Bhonslas was broken, and the Protectorate of the empire was restored to the

British. The third Mahratta War brought about the defeat of Holkar, and the fourth was waged in 1817-1818 with the Peshwa, when Poona was captured, and Baji Rao was deposed and pensioned at Bithoor, where he died, in 1853, leaving no family, but an adopted son, who subsequently became infamous under the name of Nana Sahib. In 1780 and 1790, when the British were engaged in war with Hyder Ali of Mysore, and his son Tippoo, the Nizam and the Mahrattas co-operated with the English in the first war and compelled Tippoo to cede half his dominions, which the allies divided. In 1799 he was crushed by Lord Wellesley, who also brought under British authority those fragments of Mogul and Mahratta rule, the nawabship of Arcot, and the principality of Tanjore. Not only Mysore and the Mahrattas engaged the English at this time, but the Pindaris were a sore trouble in the land. They were camp-followers of the Mahrattas, the flotsam and jetsam of distracted India, the debris of the Mogul empire, "who asked no leave of king or chief, as they swept through Hindustan." It cost Lord Hastings a regular campaign before he broke them, in 1817, in which year also the fall of the Peshwa led to the constitution of the Bombay Presidency, in somewhat its present form. The British Government, however, while it then became paramount over the greater part of India, had yet to fight against the Mahomedan rulers of Afghanistan.

Upon the death, in 1773, of Ahmed Shah Durani the usual wars and rebellions ensued, but in 1809 his descendant, Shuja Shah, was seated upon the Afghan throne, and to him the British sent a mission in order to establish a defensive alliance, with the ultimate result that he was ejected from Cabul and fled to India for protection, while Dost Mahomed, of the Barakzai family made himself king in his stead. The creation of the strong kingdom of Runjeet Singh in the Punjaub relieved India from all fear of Afghan invasions, but Dost Mahomed none the less yearned to recover Peshawar from the Sikhs, and since the Viceroy, Lord Auckland, had no power to gratify this wish, and still more because of the pressure of Russia through Persia upon Herat, the Viceroy decided to replace Dost Mahomed by his own creature — the fugitive Shah Shuja, who might fairly be expected to carry out his wishes. The thing was done accordingly, but the British reckoned without the Afghans, who, after a sullen acquiescence of two years, killed Sir Alexander Burnes and Sir William Macnaghten, and annihilated the army of occupation—a disaster which in 1842 Generals Pollok and Sale avenged. The administration of Lord Amherst (1823-1838), but for the first Burmese War, whereby Assam, Arakan, and Tenasserim were ceded to the company, had been comparatively peaceful, and Lord William Bentinck, from 1828 to 1835, had enjoyed peace broken only by ten days' war, which ended in the annexation of the little province of Coorg. Lord Auckland, however, besides being involved in the first Afghan War, was engaged in the first, or, as it is commonly called, the opium, war with China (1840-1842), at the conclusion of which Hong-Kong was ceded to Britain, and Shanghai and other ports opened to European trade. Lord Ellenborough (1842-1844) conquered Sind, the Amirs of which had been unfriendly during the Afghan War. Lord Hardinge (1844-1847) fought the hard fight of the first Sikh War as the result of which the country between the

Sutlej and the Ravi was annexed and Henry Lawrence was appointed President at the court of the youthful son of Runjeet Singh. It remained for Lord Dalhousie (1848 to 1856) to annex the rest of the Punjaub, Oudh, Satara, Jhansi and Nagpur, and a large part of the present province of Burma. In thus changing the map of India he conducted the second Sikh and the second Burmese Wars, but he also opened the first Indian railway, introduced cheap postage, organised the public works, constructed roads and canals, and inaugurated the educational system on new and permanent lines. Lord Canning declared war on Persia, which had seized Herat, and forced the Shah to renounce all claims on this fortress, or on any part of Afghanistan, and fought the second Chinese War, as a result of which all customary commercial privileges were conceded to England and other European powers, and to America. The great event, however, of this viceroyalty—the greatest event in our occupation of India—was the Sepoy mutiny, of which the immediate result was the transfer of India from the East India Company to the Crown. There is no occasion here to relate the incidents of this chapter in our history, but the conclusions of the latest historian, Field-Marshal Sir Evelyn Wood, may with advantage be recorded. He says that revolt was "the outcome of annexations, and of centralisation coupled with well-meant but mistaken attempts to govern in accordance with systems prevailing in the United Kingdom millions of Asiatics, as numerous as the peoples of Europe, and of as many different religions." The Congress is at the present day, with the aid of the Bengali Babus, and the newspapers they control, urging us to persevere in the very attempts, to which Sir Evelyn Wood, with so much reason, attributes in no small measure the greatest disaster which has occurred during our domination in India.

The tangled web of our relations with Afghanistan received another twist when Lord Lawrence (1864-1868) acknowledged Sher Ali, the son of Dost Mahomed, as Amir, and this prince was formally received as such by Lord Mayo (1868-1872) at Umballa. During the viceroyalty of Lord Lytton (1872-1876) it became known that Sher Ali had made overtures to, and received an envoy from, Russia, and, as he refused to entertain a mission sent from India, war was declared in 1878; he was defeated by General (now Field-Marshal Earl) Roberts, his son, Yakub Khan, was seated on the throne, and a British Resident, Sir Louis Cavagnari, was appointed to the Afghan court. Within a few months Cavagnari was assassinated, Yakub Khan abdicated, and the late Amir Abdul Rahman, the representative of the line of Dost Mahomed, was recognised by Lord Ripon (1880-1884) as Amir.

The chief event of the viceroyalty of Lord Dufferin (1884-1888) was the third Burmese War, due far more to justifiable fear of French intervention than to the misgovernment of King Thebaw, whose personal vices certainly, and whose political misdeeds probably, have been somewhat exaggerated. As a result of the war, Upper Burma was annexed, and subsequent Viceroyalties up to the present date resulted in no important additions to the Empire, though Lord Elgin was driven by the force of circumstances to take and retain Chitral, two years after which event occurred the most serious and widespread tribal frontier war we have had in India.

The Viceroyalty of Lord Curzon, still so recent as to be the subject of heated controversy, is chiefly remarkable perhaps for the policy pursued upon the western and north-western land frontier of India. In 1897, on the termination of the Tirah campaign, the Secretary of State telegraphed to Lord Elgin urging that, with the cessation of hostilities, our permanent position and policy should be defined, and agreeing with the Viceroy that our interference with independent tribes — so far as they can be called independent since the Durand line was drawn—should be strictly limited in order to avoid serious eventual responsibilities involved in the extension of administrative control over tribal territory. The Secretary of State also urged that the then existing arrangements should be modified in view to concentration of force. While he formally concurred with the Government of India in ascribing the concerted, simultaneous, and, till then unprecedentedly, serious, risings of the tribes to fanaticism, Lord George Hamilton could not conceal the fact that the delimitation of the spheres of British and Afghan influence, in accordance with the Durand Convention, had naturally led the tribesmen to suspect designs upon their independence. There are not a few interested in frontier politics, and among them Sir Thomas Holdich, who consider that not only was this result to be expected, but that a mistake was made in determining upon this delimitation, which necessarily largely increased our responsibilities for, and intervention in, tribal affairs. No doubt there is a difficulty in preserving a state of civilised administration up to, and ignoring violence and rapine immediately beyond, a certain point, especially when the inhabitants of either side are not a constant but a changing and interchanging quantity: but it is possible that our susceptibilites in this respect are too acute, and have led us on many occasions into interference in matters we might well have ignored, and into vain and expensive expeditions. To some, at any rate, it would appear, even from the narratives of those responsible for the action in question, that the dynastic and domestic squabbles of the petty chief of Chitral were such as we might have disregarded. Yet they led to our occupation of what a great authority describes as "a useless, expensive, and burdensome post," since invasion from the north is impossible. One serious objection to such interference is that it can have no finality. If an obligation to impose law and order on the turbulent frontier tribes lies upon us in consequence of a higher standard than that of other nations which we impose upon ourselves, why not upon similar tribes in Afghanistan?—and, if there, why not in Eastern Persia, in Persia generally, in Mesopotamia and Asia Minor? Where, indeed, in such a policy can the line be drawn? The money spent in mounting guns in solitary valleys, the treasure lavished upon fortifying natural forts, would have sufficed many times over to supply the loans solicited on very good security by Persia, our refusal to grant which threw the spendthrift Shah into the arms of the all-willing Czar. Of course, the Indian and Home Budgets are separate and independent of one another, but now at any rate it is idle to deny the fact that Persia is as much a frontier of India as is Afghanistan, but far weaker, far more vulnerable, far more the object of a rival Power's solicitude, so that Indian money might be spent on the shores of the Persian Gulf with as much propriety as upon cantonments, roads and railways in and for the benefit of Chitral, and other robber-haunted border hills. It might be argued that the charges in both cases more properly fall on the

Imperial Exchequer, which would, as regards expenditure in the Gulf, to some extent be recouped in consequence of the revival which would result therefrom, in our fast-falling trade with Persia, though neglect of the Indo-Persian question might have led to a conflagration beside which the war with the Transvaal would seem a feeble flame. Not, indeed, that Gulf questions have been neglected, even before the conclusion of the Convention with Russia. The action of the Home Government and the Viceroy, Lord Curzon, in regard to the efforts of the French to obtain a coaling station at Muscat, and of the Turks, whether or not of their own motion, to seize Koweit, was prompt, firm, and effectual.

As has been remarked above, the events of Lord Curzon's viceroyalty are of such recent date as to be still the subject of considerable controversy. There are many, however, which all must approve. He wrote off land revenue amounting to £1,320,000, and insisted upon a more lenient method of assessment and greater elasticity in collection. He reduced the salt-tax, and raised the limit of exemption from income-tax. He, or rather his Government, passed an Act in order to preserve to the hereditary cultivator in the Punjaub the land he held by restricting freedom of alienation. Whether this Act will in the end justify expectations remains to be seen, but it was a courageous effort, which also deserves praise. The same administration passed a law regulating labour in mines. Whether this was altogether needed, and whether it was desirable to deal with metalliferous and coal mines in one Act is a question of some doubt, but it was at least a measure in entire harmony with the prevailing spirit of interference with, and protection of, labour, which finds favour in so many quarters. As a fact, restrictions enforced in Britain for good and sufficient reasons, are seldom desirable, and often injurious and unpopular, in India. Witness the prohibition against taking women and children underground. Nothing is so desirable as to wean pauper agriculturists from the land to the coal mines. Nothing, for reasons into which it is unnecessary here to enter, is more likely to prevent this result than to make it impossible for his wife to bring his food, which she cannot do unless she can take the children with her.

Another Act of somewhat similar tendency dealt with labour in Assam. The Government of India regarded with suspicion contracts entered into between the agents of planters, on behalf of their employers, and the natives of Bengal, and the United Provinces, who go forth to work on tea estates in Assam, though there is overwhelming evidence that these men are well paid and well treated, and they themselves give the best proof possible that they know it, by settling in large numbers in Assam at the expiration of their indentures. It is recorded in the Census of 1901 that ex-tea-garden coolies hold 90,000 acres of land under Government and thus materially help to colonise a fertile but backward province. This last Act is not working well, and it is devoutly to be hoped that, in no long time, planters, who are most desirable settlers in India, and who are hard hit by the excessive and repeated increases of the taxation on tea, may be able to get labour immigrants, not under contract, but free, as the Ceylon planters get their coolies from Southern India. A new department of commerce and industry was created by Lord Curzon's Government, but it proved easier to create the department than to find the man. In fact, the Government came to the conclusion that it could not do better than appoint the most suitable Indian civilian they could find. It was very likely a wise decision, but it makes the creation of the department a rather nominal proceeding. In dealing with famine, Lord Curzon found everything ready to hand, and succeeded to the experience of his predecessors. Nevertheless, he dealt strenuously and effectively with the most widespread failure of crops of which there is any record, and the conspicuous success of the Government, for which, of course, the Viceroy's colleagues and subordinates in India are entitled to equal credit, did not avail to silence the bray of virulent and malevolent criticism, of the same character as that which now impugns the humanity and efficacy of the administration of Lord Minto in dealing with the epidemic of plague. It was Lord Curzon's constant endeavour to make known some at least, of the salient facts connected with Indian administration, and it was distinctly advantageous to point out the limitations within which the Government worked in respect of the extension of irrigation, of which a certain school of critics writes, as if it would be a simple matter to attach a hose to a tap at the foot of Cherrapunji and to irrigate India, as a householder in Hampstead might irrigate his back garden.

Sir Colin Scott Moncrieff's Commission found that the government might look forward to an extension of 3,500,000 acres at an outlay of 8,000,000 or 9,000,000 sterling, but there was no unlimited and illimitable field. Irrigation works can only be constructed out of taxes, and should only be constructed when a reasonable return is assured.

The opening of the Quetti-Nushki trade route, the delimitation of the boundary of Seistan and of the Aden Hinterland, must be put to the credit of the

Government of Lord Curzon, who broke new ground by touring around the Persian Gulf, and visiting ports, wherever the interests of British trade needed attention. With his action in respect of the partition of Bengal, the north-west frontier, and Tibet, it will be necessary to deal in other chapters, and it remains here to refer to what was accomplished during his viceroyalty in regard to military administration and education. He assumed office in 1898, and in the following year severe criticisms were passed upon the efficiency of the Indian army, notwithstanding the fact that it had done excellent work in China, and in South Africa had saved the situation at the outset, before it was realised that the campaign would be other than exceedingly brief and uniformly successful. It was, however, admittedly necessary to re-arm the native regiments, strengthen the artillery, and add to the number of the British officers. There were also other improvements and developments, which needed early attention. Lord Kitchener since 1902 had been Commander-in-Chief, and it was evident that military administration would occupy a leading place in the annals of the Viceroyalty. The military department had up till this time been managed by the Member of Council in charge, invariably a soldier of distinction, like Generals Sir Henry Brackenbury, and Sir Edwin Collen, to name two recent occupants of the post. He was the constitutional adviser of the Viceroy on military questions, and the Commander-in-Chief, who is also appointed as a matter of course (extraordinary) Member of Council is responsible for discipline, promotion, mobilisation and other functions properly appertaining to the Head of the Army. But any proposals the Commander-in-Chief made had necessarily to come before the Governor-General in Council, upon the representation of the Military Member, and through the Military Department. To this Lord Kitchener objected, and in so doing he was not singular among Commanders-in-Chief, for several of his predecessors had, on public grounds, demurred to the position in which they were placed, but either had not the power or the will to alter it. Lord Kitchener, however, was determined to create an Army Department dealing with the whole military administration, of which he should be the head. Lord Curzon, with the support it must be remembered of the Ordinary Members of his Council, held that under such an arrangement all military authority would be concentrated in the Commander-in-Chief to the practical annihilation of the necessary supremacy of the civil power, which would thus be deprived of independent military advice. The Secretary of State so far amended the proposal as to retain the Military Member of Council, while assigning to him a position in which the Viceroy and his civil councillors thought he would not be able to give them independent or authoritative advice upon the financial and administrative aspects of proposals relating to military matters. In that case they thought the Governor-General in Council would be left without expert aid and information to face the newly constituted, and largely increased, power of the Commander-in-Chief. It followed from this view that the new Membership of Military Supply in their opinion should be filled by an officer they considered competent to act as their general adviser in military matters. Lord Curzon, who had reluctantly accepted the changes, approved, after consideration by a committee, of which Lord Roberts and Sir George White, ex-Commanders-in-Chief of India, had been members, nominated as new Member for Military Supply, who was to deal in future with supply, contracts, military works, Remounts, and other departmental services, General Barrow, a very able officer, then commanding at Peshawar. The Secretary of State and the Cabinet at home, however, did not think that an officer occupying a high, and likely to occupy a higher, combatant command was likely to inaugurate the new system with an open mind, especially one who, from the appointment he had previously held in the Military Department, would naturally have a leaning towards one view of the controversial position which had been created. Lord Curzon insisted that he must have a colleague capable of giving advice to the Governor-General in Council on questions of general military policy, and it was evident he meant fully to avail himself of such advice. In short, he desired the new Member of Military Supply to be as much as possible like the old Military Member. The Government at home had another object in view and wanted to make the new policy as effectual as possible, and the situation in India resolved itself into a struggle between the Viceroy and Commander-in-Chief—Lord Curzon having explicitly said in his telegram of 10th August 1905 that, "if the view of the Commander-in-Chief is to prevail it is useless for me to remain in India since I could not frame a scheme in accordance with it." In another telegram he truly said "that the question was not one of choice of an individual, but of principles underlying future change in the administration." There was only one issue. The Viceroy resigned, and at his request the telegraphic correspondence was published, to the surprise and regret of those who realised the effect it would inevitably have upon the public mind in India. Into the technical questions at issue it is difficult for others than experts to probe. Lord Roberts had found the existing system cumbrous, dilatory, and complicated. Sir George White and Sir William Lockhart found the difficulties very great. Yet the Military Member had tended every year to become more of an expert adviser than a civil administrator, more and more a rival of the Commander-in-Chief, to whom he gave authoritatively independent opinions on purely military questions, and conveyed adverse decisions even without reference to the Governor-General in Council. Lord Kitchener's attitude met with the approval of professional opinion, and it remains to see how the new system works. It certainly was not rashly or lightly undertaken, and the Committee which reported to the India Office was one of unusual strength and ability, including the then Secretary of State, now Lord Middleton, Lords Roberts and Salisbury, Field-Marshal Sir George White, Sir James Mackay, Sir Edward Law, and General Sir John Gordon. At the same time it must be owned that opinion in India inclined to support Lord Curzon and the dissenting Members of Council. The one thing certain is that in the eyes of all India the Viceroy, hitherto regarded as the outward and visible expression of supreme power, engaged in an administrative battle with the Commander-in-Chief, and was beaten. It is not likely that the disaffected and agitator elements in the community failed to draw the obvious moral, and to regard the head of the Indian adminstration as a mere mortal after all. Mr Morley, who took office soon after Lord Minto became Viceroy, had to deal with the draft rules of business proposed by the Government of

India, in connection with which many of the largest questions of military organisation were, or could have been, raised, anew, or again. In a published despatch, the tactful and skilful character of which met with general approval, he amended the draft rules so as to provide that all matters before they reached the Commander-in-Chief, or member in charge of the Army Department, should pass through the Secretary to the Government of India in the Army Department. He went far to neutralise the serious effect upon India of this struggle and of its result, by safeguarding the fundamental principle that the Government of India in all its branches, aspects, and divisions, subject to the statutory powers of the Secretary of State, has been solemnly and deliberately confided by Parliament to the Governor-General in Council. That is to say that the army was no exception in this behalf.

Space will not allow of any detailed history of the army of India under the East India Company, of the armies of Bengal, Madras, and Bombay, and of the present unified Indian army. The first began with the enrolment of sepoys in 1748 in Madras by Major Stringer Lawrence, in order to enable us to fight the French, who in 1748 had captured the southern capital. Each Presidency army was originally separate and distinct, and it was the military genius of Robert Clive which made the native troops into good soldiers, and enlisted all the likely material which came to hand. The extension of the Company's rule after Plassey was accompanied by corresponding development in the military forces. In 1764 the Bengal sepoys mutinied for higher pay, and in 1768 the European officers conspired because camp allowances in cantonment were stopped. The armies of native princes at this period were of huge dimensions, of little cohesion, and of less training. The Mahratta forces, which enjoyed great mobility and powers of endurance, were, however, organised by Sivaji into formidable foes, but even they were hardly professional soldiers, like the Sikhs, who, after the dissolution of their army, returned to the plough but have ever since supplied us with soldiers, than whom there are no better, serving any Power. The Presidency armies, after frequent trials of strength with loosely organised native levies, were themselves reorganised in 1796, after which, and in 1805, further vast territories were annexed, so that after the third Mahratta War the three Presidencial armies consisted of 24,500 British, and 130,000 native troops. Then in 1806 occurred the mutiny at Vellore, and afterwards Madras European officers in turn conspired for higher pay.

In 1824 there was another reorganisation, and in 1846 local corps, such as the Corps of Guides, and the Punjaub Irregular Forces, were enrolled for duty on the frontier. On the eve of the Mutiny, the army consisted of 39,500 British and 311,000 native troops, the latter out-numbering the former by nearly eight to one. During the great crisis the Punjaub frontier force, the Hyderabad contingent, and the Madras and Bombay armies remained loyal, and it is believed that dislike of the mutinous Bengal army, which finds an echo in the distrust with which the natives of other provinces regard Bengali pretensions at the present day, was at least one of the factors making for loyalty elsewhere. It is the opinion of an able writer in the Imperial Gazetteer of India, General Sir Edwin Collen, that among the causes of the Mutiny were measures political, domestic, and military, which were carried out to satisfy the craving for improvement according to Western ideals, and if this were so in 1857, it is certainly not less so half-a-century later, when the outcry of a few denationalised extremists is accepted far too readily in many quarters as the voice of India. Not a fluent Bengali, who has broken with all the ideals and habits of his own country, and is regarded by the Hindoo masses with dislike and suspicion, but will prate about representative government, improvement and progress to willing, and easily deluded, ears in this country. Of course the annexation of Oudh was a great predisposing cause, and then again the Government of India proceeded upon the assumption that an administration which violated the received ideals of Western government must necessarily have been odious to the native population. There is very little proof, however, that this was the case, and it is quite certain that some of the very features of our rule of which we are most proud are those which are particularly unpopular with the natives. Brahmins thought they saw signs of the destruction of their influence in the suppression of suttee, and the legal remarriage granted to Hindoo widows, and of course the substance used for lubricating the cartridges was made of animal fat. It is a singular circumstance that, in spite of this, cotton goods for India continue to be sized with some such substance, though it is believed that a vegetable substitute might easily be devised. Last year a Bengali agitator addressed a meeting at Assansole saying that sugar was refined with pigs' and cows' blood. It is also notorious that British officers in India are less in touch with the natives than they were formerly. Many indeed are wholly dependent upon interpreters who fasten like leeches upon men in authority and carefully keep all information from their ears, and this is true not merely of such travellers as are only too willing to believe evil of their fellow-countrymen, but even of well-disposed and moderate men who are like clay in the hands of the potter, when they fall into the clutches of astute and intriguing Babus, with axes to grind. Meanwhile, so little does the native of the country agree with the said Babu, that he would exclaim with the old Pindari :

> "I had rather be robbed by a tall man who showed me a yard of steel,
> Than fleeced by a sneaking babu with a belted knave at his heel."

One predisposing course towards the Mutiny in the opinion of good soldiers was the diminution in authority of the commanding officers, another was the all-pervading and all-powerful influence of the Brahmins in the Bengal army. Yet at the present moment an agitation is proceeding in India which is entirely caused by, and restricted to, Brahmins, and other high castes in sympathy with them, who even now have an immense and preponderating influence in the government of the country but would fain be rid of the impartial supervision of British officers, who refuse to let them plant their heels upon the necks of the lower castes and classes. Again, disaster in Afghanistan had broken the charm of invincibility, which had previously attached to our arms, just as at the present moment the pricking by Japan of the Russian bubble, which we had always shown an obvious reluctance to try to prick, has undoubtedly impaired the belief of the East in the natural and inevitable superiority of Western over Eastern arms, and just before the

Mutiny stories were in circulation in India about our difficulties in the Crimea, which had their counterpart quite recently in the alarmist rumours regarding our position in South Africa, nor was the existence of secret agents conspiring against the Government and endeavouring to debauch the Sepoys, wanting then, nor is it lacking at the present day. Nothing indeed was necessary to cause the unrest, which is now happily subsiding, to break out into overt acts of hostility but weakness and vacillation in high places, of which fortunately there has been none. Mr Morley has said that patience and firmness are the watchwords of the present situation, and he has shown himself not only able to formulate the right policy, but to carry it into effect. Fortunately, there is no doubt at all about the loyalty of the Sepoys at the present moment. Indeed, they treated the overtures of the agitators with the utmost contempt. None the less has the situation recently been one which cannot but inspire with grave misgivings those who are familiar with Indian conditions, and all must unite in thanking heaven that the crisis found a statesman at the helm. After the Mutiny, the European army of the East India Company was transferred to the Crown, and a Royal Commission advised that the European forces should be 80,000 strong and that the Indian troops should not exceed them by more than two to one in Bengal, and three to one in Madras and Bombay, recommendations which were adopted, and remain in force to the present day. The British troops serving in India are lent to, and paid for by, the Indian Government, from which a capitation grant of £7, 10s. has been levied since 1890. This represents the cost of enlisting and training the recruit, and certain other charges, but Sir Henry

Brackenbury and four other members of the Indian Expenditure Commission thought that no charge should be made on this account. Differences of opinion between the Home and Indian Governments regarding allocation of the charges have frequently been, and still are, under consideration. In 1893, Parliament passed an Act abolishing the offices of Commander-in-Chief in the Madras and Bombay armies, and withdrawing the power of military control from the governments of these Presidencies. Before this measure was carried out the Bengal army had become unwieldy, which was bad, and tended to become homogeneous, which was worse, and it was decided to divide India into the four territorial commands of the Punjaub, Bengal, Madras and Bombay, each under a lieutenant-general. It was subsequent to this date, in 1899-1900, that India despatched the force which saved Natal, the British infantry having been armed with the Lee-Metford rifle in the previous year. Since 1903, the army, consisting of five commands since the separation of Burma from Madras, is made up of 74,170 British and 157,941, native troops, and this brings the narrative down to the time of Lord Kitchener, who, besides initiating the important administrative changes, of which a full account has been given above, has also commenced to introduce a new scheme of military organisation, the leading features of which are recognition of the fact that the chief function of the army is the defence of the north-west frontier, and that the forces in time of peace should be organised and trained in units of command similar to those in which they will take the field in time of war. In pursuance of this policy, many small military stations are being abandoned and troops concentrated in large cantonments in three Army Corps of ten Divisional Commands, each of which will supply a full division to take the field. Regiments are organised on the "class," or on the "class squadron," or "class company" system. The Gurkha regiments, for instance, are all Gurkhas, and in some cases four companies of a regiment may be Sikhs and four Mahomedans, and so on. Enlistment is for general service within or without British territory, and, if necessary, beyond the sea. The volunteers in India are now 34,000 strong, including reservists, and they may yet do, as they have done in the past, good work at critical times. Some of the native states maintain armies in addition to Imperial service troops, but though these levies number 93,000 men in all, they are not a very formidable force. Nepaul has an army of 45,000 men, and could raise many more if needed, while the standing army of Afghanistan numbers from 65,000 to 70,000 regular troops, organised more or less like those of the British Government, and 20,000 irregulars. All these troops are well armed, and every Afghan is a first-rate fighting man.

The above brief excursus upon the army arose out of the differences which occurred during Lord Curzon's Viceroyalty, and in like manner it would be difficult to appreciate the action taken by the Government of the same Viceroy, during his term of office, which extended to nearly twice that of the average holder, without briefly reviewing a few of the more salient events in the history of education. Under the old Hindoo system, advanced instruction was strictly confined to the upper castes, and under the Mahomedans education was inseparably connected with mosques and shrines. Early in the last century a knowledge of English became a marketable acquirement, and missionaries and philanthropists at home and in India brought pressure to bear on the Government in favour of popular education. Two parties arose—the Anglicists and the Orientalists; the former contending that the knowledge and science of the Western world should be conveyed to the natives by the medium of English, and the Orientalists desiring that vernacular education should be supplemented by the study of the classical languages of the East. The Anglicists carried the day, led by Lord Macaulay, whose famous minute, which has been so frequently eulogised, in which seas of treacle and butter and kings thirty feet high are held up to ridicule, is really a very shallow piece of writing and reasoning. It would be equally easy to ridicule the beautiful mythology of the Greeks, whose influence upon the development of civilisation has been unequalled, and it is very unlikely that Macaulay had read the literature he professed to despise. The consequences of the decision at which the Government arrived have been, and will be still more, momentous, for it may be regarded as certain that Orientalism will never again have strength enough to raise its head. In 1854 Sir Charles Wood (Lord Halifax) directed the constitution in each province of Departments of Public Instruction, the creation of universities at Presidency towns, the establishment of training colleges, the multiplication of vernacular schools for elementary education, and the introduction of a system of grants in aid to schools maintained by private bodies or persons, English being prescribed as the medium of instruction in the higher branches. From this date up to 1882 great progress was made, to review which, and to criticise the whole system, a commission was then appointed, with the result that the general principles of the Act of 1854 were reaffirmed, amended, and supplemented.

At the end of 1902, 4,000,000 students were under instruction, in twenty years the number of pupils in primary had increased by 49, and in secondary schools by 180, per cent. and more than 23,000 undergraduates and students of various professions were receiving instruction in 200 colleges, in spite of which, in 1901, only 98 per 1000 in the case of males, and 7 per 1000 in the case of females, were able to read and write.

Burma, the native states of Travancore and Baroda, Madras, Bombay, and Bengal is the order of merit for literacy, though claims, wholly unsustainable as the Census shows, are frequently made for Bengal that it is the most educated part of India. As a matter of fact, of the greater provinces, only two—the Punjaub and the United Provinces—occupy a lower position in the list, and it is not surprising that the more degraded, bloody, and immoral forms of Hindooism find their home in this province, to which fact, were proof needed, the writings of recent travellers and observers amply testify. It is not, however, only in Bengal that education somewhat lags behind the ideals set before the Government, for only one-sixth of the boys of school-going age were following the course of primary instruction in 1901-1902. Secondary, is more developed than primary, education, and a very valuable Resolution of the Government of India not long since was issued deprecating the undoubted sacrifice of the vernacular languages to English in the secondary schools. Higher education, such as it is, has spread far and wide, and in 1901-1902 nearly 15,000 students became Bachelors of Arts, but it was admitted by the Indian Universities Commission that the acquirements of Indian graduates were in many cases inadequate and superficial. These youths live during their university course with their friends or in lodgings, with results which are admittedly unsatisfactory, and to remedy which the Indian Government is encouraging the hostel system.

Education has made less way amongst the Mahomedans, and in the case of females presents, of course, peculiar difficulties. The proportion of girls under instruction is highest in Madras, and the difference of the attitude towards this question in different provinces is illustrated by the fact that in Burma 74 and in Madras 52 per cent. of the girls at school are found in boys' schools, while in the Punjaub the like figure falls to 1 per cent.

Space does not allow of any consideration of the Chief's Colleges, the technical and industrial, the arts, engineering, medical, agricultural, veterinary and normal colleges and schools, but all are represented in the complete and complex educational system of India. Everywhere the State maintains a position of strict religious neutrality. No religious instruction is given in Government schools, and private institutions, provided their secular education is satisfactory, may give instruction in any religion whatsoever. The all-important question of moral training was considered in 1887-88, and suitable text-books, physical training, and athletic sports were recommended as an antidote to the want of reverence, respect, and religious obedience, which merely secular education are said, and probably rightly said, to promote. Great care is taken in the selection of the text-books; a difficult matter where so many languages are spoken, but, in fact, the measures taken have not availed to scotch, much less kill, evils, the existence of which cannot be denied.

The educational situation called for the Viceroy's attention. Lord Curzon was not the man to pass by any nettle which needed to be grasped, and he himself presided over a conference of educational officers which he called together to consider the situation. He was under no illusion as to the delicate ground on which he was treading, nor indeed was he mistaken as to the necessity for reform. He appointed a Director-General of Education, and a University Commission, he further legislated upon the University question, and he had the courage to say that the vernacular languages were being neglected and degraded in the pursuit of English, and very often bad English, for the sake of the mercantile value of the latter language. He made primary education a charge upon provincial revenues, and supplemented these charges by permanent annual grants. He laid down tests for the official recognition of secondary education, and he realised that our higher instruction trained the memory at the expense of the mind. He also introduced important reforms into training colleges, and primary and industrial schools. The University legislation of his Government was the cause of his being overwhelmed with obloquy by the babus of Bengal. Here it should be observed in passing that "babu" is an honorific title which an educated Bengali gentleman gives to himself, and if it now connotes any other significance, such can only be due to the chief characteristics of those who bear it. Five universities, founded on the model of London University, as it was in the beginning, control the instruction given in nearly 200 colleges, which, however, were practically under no inspection, and in respect of which no uniformity of standard or ideals were required. It was to the interest of the weaker colleges to lower the standard, nor were they checked in this aspiration by the governing bodies of the universities. The object, on the contrary, of the senate was to turn out the largest number of graduates, and Lord Curzon's Commission of 1902 having clearly brought to light the chief defects of the system, the Indian Government determined to provide all universities with new senates, mainly composed of teachers, and to leave each university to frame its own regulations and inspect its own colleges. The action taken was exceedingly unpopular, particularly with the Bengali babus, and with the Bengali press which represents them in such a full-blooded and uncompromising fashion.

The charge was that Lord Curzon desired to officialise the universities, and to insist upon a standard of efficiency so high that it would crush the weaker colleges which had been found so useful to the babu class in the manufacture of graduates. There is no reason for supposing that the reconstructed senates have dealt severely with the less satisfactory colleges, but there is no doubt that Lord Curzon has been overwhelmed with obloquy for action in itself praiseworthy. This feeling was intensified by the delivery of his Convocation Address in 1905, in which he stated that the highest ideal of truth is to a great extent a Western conception, and that truth took a high place in the moral codes of the West before it had been similarly honoured in the East. This comprehensive and unnecessary generalisation naturally gave very great offence. Every Oriental scholar will remember the well-known lines of Sadi :

دروغ مصلحت آمیز
به از راست فتنه انگیز

"Better to lie with good intent,
Than tell the truth, if harm is meant";

and in the Mahabharata falsehood is said to be permissible in five cases—marriage, love, danger to life, loss of property, or the benefit of a Brahmin. But it is a fact that those who are accustomed to associate with the natives of India in other than an official capacity by no means accuse them of being generally untruthful. Indeed, the Hindoos and Mahomedans, apart from the atmosphere of courts of all sorts, may fairly be described as truthful and straight-dealing people. The contrary impression would no doubt be created upon those who had had all association with them through interpreters, in whose case, the Italian proverb *Traduttori traditori* is peculiarly appropriate.

Since his arrival in India Lord Minto has issued a very important resolution on the subject of primary education, and the very serious problems to be solved are at present believed to be occupying the earnest attention of his Government.

CHAPTER III

THE LAND SYSTEM

Its Critics—Their Case—Permanent Settlement with Individual Holders desirable—Famines Past and Recent—Remedies

THE land revenue system of India, upon which, in recent years, many and great assaults have been delivered, was not invented by the British, but was inherited by them, like so many other systems which form an integral part of their administration, from their predecessors in title. In a former chapter passing reference has been made to the fact that, in the reign of the most moderate of all the great Moguls, the land-tax was so regulated that nothing was left to the cultivator beyond what sufficed for the subsistence of himself and his family, together with enough seed for sowing next season's crop. Passing reference was also made to what the earliest writers on India have recorded on this all-important subject. That it is all important, no one can doubt, seeing that two-thirds of the people of India are engaged directly or indirectly in agricultural pursuits, so that if our land policy is bad it would be difficult, indeed, to claim that our administration in general was good, The argument that the British grind the people down, and that the severity of the land system has led to the frequency of famines, is noticed in its proper place, though it is in itself not worthy to be answered.

Among the critics are Mr R. C. Dutt, C.I.E., and

others with more or less qualifications for expressing opinions upon this very technical subject. From time immemorial the Government has been entitled to a certain proportion of the produce of all land, the rights to which have not been limited, and the procedure by which that proportion is determined is called the settlement of the land revenue. Such settlements are of two kinds: permanent, by which the demand of the State is for ever fixed, and temporary, by which the State demand is revised at recurring periods. The permanent districts cover the greater part of Bengal, parts of the United Provinces and of Madras, and certain other isolated tracts. At one time, the extension of the permanent settlement throughout India was advocated, and critics of the school of which Mr Dutt may be regarded as an example urged that had this policy been carried into effect forty years ago, India would have been spared the worst famine of recent years. It is held by the same school, and this is a most important plank in the Congress platform, that in consequence of the permanent settlement the cultivators of Bengal are more prosperous than those of any other part of India. If it were a fact that the cultivators of Bengal enjoyed exceptional prosperity, there would, indeed, be some reason for the inference that the permanent settlement was the cause. But there is, in fact, no ground whatever for any such assertion. Bengal, as a whole, and particularly the new province of Eastern Bengal, possesses exceptional fertility and means of communication, a monopoly of the production of jute, and the possession of the greatest city in India as one of its capitals. Yet not all these advantages avail to save Bengal from serious drought whenever the monsoon failure reaches that region. Noticing earlier famines in this province that of Behar in 1873-1874 cost the State 6,000,000 sterling, while in the famine of 1897 more than three-quarters of a million of the population were on relief. A careful consideration of the history of famines during British administration, and of such information as is available on the subject in ante-British days, lends no support whatever to the contention that Bengal has been saved from famine by the permanent settlement, or that its cultivators enjoyed any exceptional prosperity, over and above such as is due to the climate and geographical causes. Still less is there any ground for thinking that the cultivators and tenants of the State-created landlords in Bengal enjoy, owing to the permanent settlement, any exceptional prosperity. On the contrary, it was because they were especially impoverished and oppressed that the Government of India was compelled, by a series of legislative measures, to place them in the position of greater security which they now enjoy. This legislation has not only no connection with the permanent settlement, but has been designed to confer those benefits which that settlement has altogether failed to secure. Absentee landlordism, unsympathetic management, bad relations between landlord and tenant, the multiplication of middlemen and unhappy relations between owners and cultivators obtained in Bengal to a greater extent than elsewhere in India, and it is not in the land settlement, but in the new laws which have been passed to check these abuses, that the Bengal cultivator has found salvation.

That criticism has been more generally levelled against the temporarily settled districts is due to the fact that the agitation has been directed from Bengal, whence also the sinews of war have been provided. It is in no way due to the fact that conditions in such districts are at all inferior. Of the two sub-divisions of this category, the Zemindari, Malguzari, or Talukdari tenure—in which the landlord pays the revenue to the State, whether he cultivates himself or through some rent-paying tenant — obtains in the Central Provinces, the United Provinces, and the Punjaub. The Government of India has always held, and has led the way in holding, that in such cases a limit should be placed to the rent the landlord may demand from his tenant, and it would indeed be little less than absurd to dwell upon the necessity for Government taking a moderate share when it deals directly with the tenant, and to ignore the necessity for equal moderation in the demands of the landlord. It is equally necessary to protect the cultivator whether he pays rent to the Indian landlord or revenue to the British Indian Government. In accordance with these principles, legislation has proceeded in Bengal, the Central, and the United Provinces, with little or no co-operation in this behalf on the part of those who are in a position to assist in carrying out this policy. It has further been argued that where the land revenue is paid to the State by the landlord the demand should be limited, as a fixed and invariable rule, to one-half of his rent or assets. It has been shown that the ruling power has always been entitled to a share in the produce of the soil. Indeed, this doctrine has been laid down in far stronger terms by the earlier writers upon India, who speak of the land as belonging to the State. In the regulation of 1793, the Government share was fixed by estimating the rent paid by the tenants, deducting therefrom the cost of collection, allowing the landlords one-eleventh as their share, and appropriating the balance, or ten-elevenths, as the share of the State. The word landlord in this connection means the intermediary between the cultivators and the State, and the landlords in the sense in which we use the term in this country are the holders under the permanent settlement to which reference is made above, such as the landlords of Bengal, who, though not the natural leaders of the people, have been placed in a position of power and pre-eminence by the action of Lord Cornwallis's Government. The British Government, however, while necessarily adopting the principle that it was entitled to its share of the landlord's assets, began at once to moderate its severity, and in the middle of the last century the demand had been limited to two-thirds, while before the Mutiny it was laid down that about one-half and not two-thirds of the well-ascertained net assets should be the Government share. No Government, however, has any right to forego revenue the collection of which is conceded by immemorial custom, and by the universal consent of those who pay it, unless it can tap other sources with greater convenience to the tax-payer, and it need hardly be stated that of all countries in the world subject to a civilised and scientific administration of which we have knowledge India is that one in which new sources of revenue are most difficult to find, and in which the inhabitants, while it never enters their heads to question any customary payment, are most rapidly aroused by the imposition of any new tax. The Government, therefore, never bound itself to demand more than 50 per cent. of the actual rental of the landowner, and the settlement officers, in the interests of the people, were under an obligation to take into consideration any prospective increases of income in determining what the net assets were. Nevertheless, the movement has steadily progressed in a downward direction and prospective assets have been included; allowances have been made for improvements, for vicissitudes of seasons, and for local circumstances. In the Central Provinces, the Government inherited assessments of 75 per cent. from the Mahrattas, but while the amounts landlords are allowed to demand from their tenants have been strictly limited, the amounts the Indian Government takes from the landlord have been progressively reduced.

The general tendency throughout temporarily settled Zemindari districts has been to reduce the Government share below 50 per cent. of the net assets, and it is not a little extraordinary that the Congress agitation, which is so intimately connected with the landlord interest, has persuaded the representatives of British democracy in Parliament that it is desirable that the Government should abandon the taxes to which it is entitled, which are levied from landlords, and spent in a great measure on the cultivator, the inevitable result of which would be that the amount remitted would have to be made up in some other way from the masses who are less able to pay.

Turning to the temporarily settled districts in which the peasant proprietor prevails, the cultivator paying directly to the State, the provinces which best illustrate this tenure are Madras, Bombay, Burma, and Assam. It has been urged by the critics of British rule that the Government share should be limited to 50 per cent. of the value of the net produce after liberal deductions for cultivation expenses, and should not exceed one-fifth of the gross produce; even in those parts of the country where, in theory, one-half of the net, is assumed to approximate to one-third of the gross, produce.

Others contend that a definite and fixed share of the gross produce should be adopted as the State demand. Few, indeed, of those who have any personal acquaintance with this problem would approve the latter recommendation, for it is exceedingly difficult to estimate what the average produce is, depending as it does upon the industry and resources of the cultivator, the nature of the crop, the fertility of the holding, and the vicissitudes of seasons. In the Madras Presidency, it was found that the gross produce standard favoured the more, and prejudiced the less, fertile districts. In that Presidency and elsewhere, the net produce has been valued at rates far below the current prices, the out-turn per acre has been underestimated, and liberal deductions have been made for unprofitable cultivation, distance from markets, and vicissitudes of seasons, so that the actual rates used for assessment are far below the nominal share, in some cases falling 20 per cent. short of one quarter, not of one half, of the net produce. The one certain thing is that the introduction of the cast-iron system suggested by the critics would largely increase the burdens of the people, who themselves are naturally and notoriously unfavourable to any rigid rule of revenue administration. The adoption of the gross-produce standard put forward as an alleviation of the cultivator's burdens would lead to an all-round increase of assessments—indeed in Madras and the Central Provinces the exaction of one-fifth of the real gross produce would double the liabilities of the ryots. Turning to

Bengal, the figures, which have not been contested, show that rents are much below one-fifth of the gross produce, and this proves, were proof necessary, that the cultivators in Government temporarily settled estates are much better off than those under proprietors with permanent settlements. In regard to the Punjaub, grossly inaccurate statements have been circulated by those who have endeavoured to associate the people of this province with the agitation current in Bengal. In the peasant proprietary districts of the former province the Government demand nowhere exceeds one-fifth, and is often far lower, going down below an eighth of the gross produce. The last Famine Commission, presided over by Sir Antony MacDonnell, naturally paid special attention to this subject, and reported that the incidence of land revenue on the average value of the produce was less than 4 per cent. in the Central Provinces, 7 per cent. in Berar and most of the Punjaub, and in the Deccan from 7 to 8 per cent. Only in Gujerat, which suffered severely during the famine, but where the profits on cultivation are very high, did the incidence amount to the 20-per-cent. standard which was recommended in a certain memorial, which led to general inquiries in this behalf being made. A further recommendation has been pressed on the Government, to the effect that temporarily settled districts should never be settled for less that thirty years, the term which generally obtains, though in the Punjaub a shorter period of twenty years is the recognised rule, while in very backward districts, such as Burma, Assam, and Sind, even shorter periods are allowed. The criterion is, the more or less prosperous condition of agriculture in the particular province. Where there is much waste land and fluctuating cultivation, where communications are being improved, population increasing and prices rising, postponement of resettlement may be unjust to the general tax-payer, but the interests of the masses invariably escape notice at the hands of critics who belong to the Brahmin and upper classes, who now administer India under our supervision, but who would have no objection whatever to governing altogether on their own account. It cannot be denied that the resettlement of provinces is a serious operation, disturbing and unsettling the minds of the cultivators concerned, and at the present moment the ryots of Orissa are dreading a resettlement of their province, which may be accompanied by an enhancement of revenue. The Government of India is of opinion that many of the objections urged to revision of settlement have become, or are fast becoming, obsolete. The process is now more rapidly completed, and the necessary records are more elaborate, though it may be contended that the people are not so appreciative as is the Government of the changes which operate in this direction. The mere possibility of enhancement is not pleasant to them, and it would be good policy not only to extend the term in all cases to thirty years, but also seriously to consider once more whether it would not be advisable to make a permanent settlement with each individual holder. Not only might this prove good revenue policy in the end, but it would infallibly attach every single peasant proprietor to the fortunes of the British Government, by the strongest possible tie. Nor is it possible to deny that the multiplication of cesses is regarded by the Indian cultivators as an injustice. They and their ancestors for thousands of years have paid rent or revenue, but land-cesses for furthering the services of Western civilisation, such as sanitation and education, are altogether new imposts, the necessity for which they do not allow, and the imposition of which they bitterly resent. An increase in the land revenue may be borne—

> "The sirkar cannot send the rains,
> Although it hath to levy toll,
> And barren fields and empty wains
> Are bitter to the sirkar's soul—"

but cesses are a new and foreign thing, and hated accordingly. As a matter of fact the local rates are lower in the peasant proprietor provinces of Bombay and Madras than in the landlord province of Bengal, where they reach 6¼ per cent. on the rental. It may safely be affirmed that the average cultivator does not regard primary education as a proper subject for taxation, and he does hold with all his might that such taxation should be limited to objects directly connected with the land. These objections do not apply to cesses levied for the remuneration of village officers, such having been a charge on the community from time immemorial. In thus criticising the local cesses and rates imposed by the British Government, it must always be remembered that in the landlord districts numerous other unauthorised village cesses are habitually levied, notwithstanding the endeavours of the Government to put an end to the practice—efforts in which it is in no way supported by its critics, the most active of whom are closely connected with the landlord classes.

The principle of exempting from assessment the occupier's improvements has been adopted by the British Government, first of all the rulers of India;

and the profit arising from such improvements has been secured to the cultivators in perpetuity in Bombay and Madras, and for lengthy periods in Bengal, the Punjaub, the United, and the Central, Provinces. In spite, however, of the many and great advances made by the British Government, all in the direction of leniency of assessment, it is well not to forget that, in the eyes of those chiefly concerned, the object of a new settlement is to increase the payments previously made, and there is probably no measure that would be more popular with the masses than a permanent settlement, not such a settlement as was made in Bengal, with which indeed no serious statesman would now propose to interfere, but which none the less was conducted upon principles which benefit the classes at the expense of the masses, principles the exact opposite of which would be adopted in any such permanent settlement as is contemplated in these pages. It is, of course, the case that the principle that the State has a right to a share in the produce of the land carries with it a claim to a share in any increment of the produce or value, and it might fairly be argued that the State cannot be called upon to surrender increased values produced by the development of the country, the introduction of new staples, increase of population, or any rise in the productivity of the soil, due to expenditure upon irrigation and communications, incurred by the exchequer. It is, however, an important factor in the consideration of this matter that two-thirds of the people of India are engaged in agriculture, and that active efforts are being made by agitators to persuade the agricultural classes to adopt an attitude of hostility towards the British Government. Whether it is justifiable to forego a prospective increase of revenue, which would benefit the general tax-payer, is ordinarily a question to be answered in the negative, but in India, by such surrender, not less than two-thirds of the population would be immediately and immensely benefited. It is indeed true that there is no precedent in native rule for any step of this nature, but it is also true that we have since 1835 been busily occupied in preaching a new dispensation from the West, in which Oriental customs, Oriental faiths, and Oriental principles of administration are treated with scant reverence, if not openly held up to the ridicule of the rising generation. The strongest objection would be taken by the Bengali critics of the Government to the introduction of a permanent settlement with individual peasant proprietors, without a similar concession being granted in temporarily settled Zemindari districts, wherein it is difficult to make prices the basis of assessment. It might, however, be urged with much weight that in ryot-wari, or peasant proprietary areas, the only ground for enhancement should be a rise in prices, and though the extension of this principle would involve the surrender of increment resulting from the construction of public works at the cost of the general tax-payer, it is by no means certain that such surrender would not be amply compensated by the general content on the part of individual proprietors, and by their greater attachment to our rule.

Not only have the Bengali critics asserted that the land revenue assessments are excessive, but they have not hesitated to allege that such assessments have been responsible for the frequency of famine. Throughout the last century there has, however, been a progressive reduction in assessment, which in the second half thereof has been increasingly manifest, so that, if there be anything in this allegation, the famines of the earlier, should have been more serious than those of the later, part of the nineteenth century. But the contention of the critics is that the contrary has been the case.

Nor is there any support whatever for the assertion that the most highly assessed parts of India have suffered most severely, a contention disproved by the Famine Commission. Indeed, in the famine of 1899-1900, the districts most severely affected had been exempted from paying their increased assessments, and the districts that suffered most in 1896-1897 were such as for years had known no enhancement. A low land-tax, like the few pence an acre paid on unirrigated land in the Deccan, is the outward and visible sign of a poor peasantry, near the margin of subsistence. So fallacious is the inference that a low assessment means a prosperous peasantry. But where the land is rich, and the assessment light, are the people there famine-proof? Gujerat answers this description as well as any part of India, and there was the pressure most severe in 1899-1900, when the Deccan cultivator stood up erect under the loss of his crops, and the comparatively rich Gujerati succumbed, when the crop failure affected 400,000 square miles, 25,000,000 of people in British India and 75,000,000 in native states, the loss in crops being equivalent to £50,000,000 sterling. The Government spent upwards of £10,000,000 on relief, and not much more than 2 per cent. of the population affected succumbed, more from privation and disease than starvation. Then it is asserted that the increase, only 2·42 per cent. of the population between 1891 and 1901, is a proof of far greater mortality, since between 1881 and 1891 there was an increase of 11·2 per cent. But who is in a position to say that 11·2 per cent. is the normal rate of increase of the Indian population, as to which we know nothing, and have only two or three counts to place to our credit. The Central Provinces, twice desolated by the severest visitations, showed a fall of 8 per cent., while in ante-British days it would have been nothing exceptional had half the population, under similar circumstances, disappeared. In Madras, the province to which, in complete ignorance of the facts, the Congress school of critics has imputed an assessment exceptionally severe, the increase in the population at last Census was the highest—namely, 7·4 per cent. To determine the normal rate of increase in India, excluding the results of monsoon failures, would be to eliminate what is a regular feature recurring at irregular intervals, but never known to have been absent from one part or another of the congeries of countries we call India for more than a short term of years. It is unfortunate that crop failure is invariably described as famine. Tracts in which there are scarcity and distress of varying degrees of intensity are alike called famine-stricken. The State, in its efforts to prevent famine laying hold of the people, long before acute distress prevails brings into operation its relief code, or rules for the prevention of famine, commonly called the Famine Code, and in any province in which these preventive measures are brought into force, famine is said to prevail. The case of the Government in this respect is parallel with that of a pious man called Barebones, the abbreviation of whose lengthy Christian name gave a very erroneous impression of his true character. Those who think the Indian administration enslaves and starves the Indians are also under the impression that when 6,000,000, or 2 per cent. of the population of India, were, in 1899-1900, in receipt of relief, 6,000,000 were starving, instead of being saved from starvation, and it would be useless to point out that a slightly larger percentage—2·2—of the population of England and Wales is annually in receipt of aid from the State.

It is devoutly to be hoped that this so-called Famine Code will never degenerate into a Poor Law, from the necessity for which India is saved by the abounding charity of the people. Their humane and civilised character enables their rulers to dispense with a Poor Law in normal seasons, and the latter in turn have declared, and take no credit for declaring, that the whole resources of the State, are available for saving the lives of the distressed. So successful is this policy that in 1899-1900, in the locality affected above all others by one of the most widespread scarcities ever experienced, in the Central Provinces, the death rate actually remained round about the normal figure. Among many deductions to be drawn from these visitations is the fact that the peasant proprietors of Madras are better able to pay their nominally higher assessment than are their brethren in Bombay to pay their nominally lower rate. It is pretty clear that it is private debts, often 50 per cent. of the value of the produce, which press, and not the Government assessment of 7 per cent. which presses, so hardly upon the cultivator. It is, moreover, a fact, to which many unprejudiced observers have testified from personal experience, that the administration of famine relief, has now reached such a pitch of perfection that, as a general rule, the workers on the famine relief works, do not show signs of emaciation and cannot be distinguished from ordinary labourers. The object of the Government is to provide them with work and food before they deteriorate in condition.

Famine photographs, which, with sinister objects, are circulated, are generally those of the occupants of the poor houses, in which are gathered together in times of scarcity the waifs and strays, the halt, the lame, the blind, the feeble and infirm, the flotsam and jetsam of a teeming Oriental population. It is interesting to know that the periods of scarcity, which are held by ignorant or malevolent critics to prove the failure of British rule, have conclusively demonstrated what otherwise might be well regarded as open to argument—namely, the superiority of direct British administration to that of the protected native states, which, during the last great visitation, were tried and found wanting. Indeed, before that, in 1897-1898, the chiefs of Rajputana and Central India had not proved very successful in caring for their own distressed people. No one could be naturally more prone to prefer Indian administration under general British supervision to direct British administration than one who has, himself, had the good fortune to be British Resident in two conspicuously well-governed native states, and who has made a study of native languages, and association with the natives of India, the chief object of his long service in India. But it must be admitted that the evidence of private and official witnesses, the reports of newspaper correspondents, and the Census figures, all alike testify to the immense superiority of our own system of relief, if, indeed, any system can be said to exist outside British limits. In the first place, we can redress the balance, by calling on a rich, to feed a poor, province, which a single financial unit cannot do. In the second place, the British Government has a positive genius for forethought and *bandobast*, or tie and twist—an Indian word meaning arrangement, but the inward expressiveness of which no translation can convey. The grim realities of actual starvation were almost confined in our districts to the hill tribes, and to the occupants of poor houses and relief works, which were flooded with refugees, already past aid, from native states. Not that the British Government accepts no responsibility for such states. It does, and laid it down as a principle that it could not allow the lives of thousands to be jeopardised by the caprice of their ruler. It is characteristic of a certain school of critics that Mr Hyndman should have written at this period: "We see by looking at the great native states that our system is the real cause of the ruin we deplore. Scarcity in their case seldom deepens into famine!" What shall be said of the equal ignorance of those who glibly assert that famines were less frequent and less disastrous before the days of British rule. Indeed it is true that fights with famine have been more frequent in our time, for our predecessors accepted these visitations as fatalities. Hindoos do not write history, and Mahomedan historians, who omitted nothing to the credit of the kings, who paid them for their chronicles, have not recorded that they made any effort to counteract the effects of failure of seasons. A certain amount of information on this subject can be gathered, however, from Ferishta, Babar, Tavernier, Bernier, Dow, Elphinstone, and Elliott, and after a careful perusal of these works, and after inquiring into the subject, not only in India, but in other Oriental countries—such as Persia, China, Turkey, Japan, and Corea—I have gathered the impression that, generally speaking, the tax-collectors of Eastern, are not more but less strict than those of European, Governments, and that the enormously high assessments of former times in India, and elsewhere, were only possible because they were spasmodically and irregularly collected. However that may be, in 1596, under Akbar, such famine prevailed that cannibalism became general, burial was abandoned, and pestilence raged unchecked. In 1615 and 1616 there was another great visitation, when wild beasts dragged the starving villagers from their huts, and devoured them in the streets. In Kattywar and Gujerat there were famines in 1559, 1631, 1647, 1681, 1686, 1718, 1723, 1747, 1751, 1759, 1760, 1774, 1780, and 1785. Of such severity were these visitations that, compared with them, the fourteen so-called famines which occurred between 1880 and 1897 were merely local scarcities, In the Central Provinces there are records of famines in 1771, 1803, 1818, 1819, 1825, 1826, 1832, 1833, 1834, 1868 and 1869. Upon these occasions, wheat sometimes sold at 3 or 4 seers of two pounds, for a rupee, and rice at 2 or 3 seers a rupee, whereas in 1899-1900 the average prices in the Central Provinces, the most afflicted part of India, were 15 and 14 seers respectively, and after the famine of 1877-1878, in that province, the cultivation only decreased by 5 per cent. In the Mahabharata the great epic poem of the palmy days of India, written before its sacred soil had been invaded by Mahomedans or Europeans, a famine of twelve years duration is recorded, in which Brahmins were driven to devour dogs. Should Burma ever again suffer, it will, no doubt, be argued that, as in the case of India proper, so in regard to its newest province, British maladministration has reduced the previously prosperous people to such straits. But Pimenta, writing of Pegu in the sixteenth century says: "The wayes and fields were full of skulls and bones of wretched Pagans, who were brought to such miserie and want, that they did eat man's flesh and kept publike shambles thereof. Parents abstained not from their children, and children devoured their parents. The stronger by force preyed on the weaker, and if any were but skinne and bone, yet did they open their intrailes to fill their owne, and picked out their braines. The women went about the streets with knives to the like butcherly purposes." To this day the skull famine, so called because the countryside was littered with skulls, is remembered in India.

No doubt our Government has not always been successful in treating these calamities. In the earlier part of last century we hardly attempted the colossal task now so successfully achieved. In Madras in 1833-1834, in Madras and Mysore in 1877-1878, and in Orissa in 1866, the mortality was very high, but the science of famine prevention was then in its infancy, and it is that science, and not famine, which is the invention of the British Government. The vernacular press often refers to India as the only country in the world ruled by a wealthy and civilised Government subject to periodical famines, but there was a time when these visitations were frequent in Europe, and the poor ate roots and acorns. These conditions have passed away with improved agriculture, the development of commercial credit, removal of restrictions upon the natural course of trade, and the opening of increased facilities of transport. Yet the critics of

Government, amongst whom in this behalf is an ex-Chief Commissioner, actually accuse improved communications of contributing to cause famine, and to the ruin of the indigenous native transport trade, and so, it is presumed, to the greater sufferings of the victims of crop failure! Nor, in fact, have these visitations by any means ceased to afflict Europe. In 1891 Russia suffered from an extremely widespread famine, and the Czar's Government, while it did infinitely less than ours does, obtained greater credit owing to the feeling abstention on the part of the Emperor, court, and capital from all amusements while the people were distressed. During the last scarcity in the Central Provinces, in some districts 40 per cent. of the population were on relief works, but it was difficult to tell that those upon relief were other than ordinary cultivators. Meanwhile, sufferers flocked in their thousands from native states to British works, and those states lost in the last ten years about the same proportion of their population as the British districts gained. So complete and comprehensive is the famine relief of these days that the question arises to what extent the poorest should be fed out of taxes paid by the poor, for the rich, and notably the landlords, who support the Congress movement, do not contribute their fair share, and there is no Indian middle class to be remorselessly bled by the tax-gatherer. I have myself shown, in the pages of *The Nineteenth Century*, that it was possible for families to earn on relief works 25 per cent. more than the average agriculturist's income. The Commissioner of the northern division of Bombay, Sir F. Lely, now a member of the Indian Decentralisation Commission, attributes the intensity of the distress in Gujerat to the fact that in a long period of prosperity the people had acquired expensive habits and had become unfit to endure poverty, so little were they brought down to poverty by previous taxation. Some friendly critics maintain that a measure restricting land alienation should be enacted for all India, but it will be necessary first to study the results of the Land Act already passed for the Punjaub, for such legislation reduces the cultivator's credit, and could probably be evaded by the moneylender. Circumstances, moreover, differ in different provinces, and agrarian legislation has been by no means successful in the Deccan. If, again, the revenue were made to depend entirely on the rain, whence would come money in rainless years to feed the victims of rainlessness? Some would say by supplementing the finances of India by a grant from England, regardless of the dictum of the late Chancellor of the Exchequer, now Lord St Aldwyn, that the finances of India are in an infinitely better condition than our own. The fact is that the collection of money in England for the Mansion House Fund apparently makes it impossible for the British public to realise that want of funds has never compelled the Indian Government to refuse relief to a single individual applying therefor, or to relax its efforts to force help upon the retiring and unwilling. There is no reason whatever why India should lose her most precious possession, her financial independence. Indeed, Lord Elgin wisely insisted that the province of private charity, as distinguished from State relief, should be unequivocally laid down before he undertook to receive the Mansion House money, which was used for such comforts and, comparatively speaking, luxuries as the Government did not think could properly be given from public funds.

The introduction of usury laws is also urged, but these indeed were practically adopted when the Indian Contract Act was so amended as to describe the agriculturist as a person entitled to special protection in his dealings with moneylenders. Irrigation of course has been suggested as the best of remedies, and various English newspapers have eloquently described the tens of millions of acres which could be rendered independent of the seasons. Little notice is taken of the fact that the Government of India has spent 32 millions sterling upon irrigation works, for which capital accounts are kept, whereby 17½ millions of acres give crops worth 34½ millions of pounds, and has in hand projects which will irrigate further millions of acres. It is an absurd contention that while the Government has done so much it is responsible for famine because it does not further do what financial and geographical reasons forbid.

So far as the mere prevention of famine goes, it must not be forgotten that successful irrigation schemes lead to a proportionate increase in the population, and it is impossible to suppose that the Government, regardless of levels and water supply, can extend irrigation at a remunerative cost, to such a degree as to make the country independent of failure of the rainfall. Lord Curzon made special inquiries to discover what additional practicable projects could be devised, and it was proved that the field was of a very limited extent. The real remedy is to be found in the introduction of foreign capital, which the present agitation must necessarily scare away; in the development of the material resources of the country, and the removal of the surplus population from the overcrowded occupation of agriculture. Tea and coffee planting, gold and coal mining, and cotton spinning should be encouraged; the rules and regulations which restrict enterprise should be still further relaxed; obstacles to the movement of labour, of which too many remain, should be abolished, the cheap supply of labour alongside the raw material being a great attraction for the capitalist of India, which, in spite of its admitted, but exaggerated, poverty, absorbs gold and silver to the value of upwards of £10,000,000 sterling per annum. Caste in no way handicaps industrial operations. On the contrary, it enormously facilitates the organisation of labour. Agricultural distress must still exist in a country dependent upon the monsoon, but in modern India there is always sufficient grain to eat, and the object is the creation of economic conditions, in which the people will have the money with which to buy food. Nevertheless, so utterly is this question—like most others relating to India—misunderstood in England, that the old-world expedient of storing grain is seriously recommended, while what the people want is the money they can only get by selling what, in former times, was stored, because there were no communications, and no markets. As to the so-called drain, most of it is incurred as interest—absurdly low from the Indian point of view—upon capital expended for the benefit of that country. It is of course desirable that the amount should be kept as low as possible, and the heavy charges for pensions and non-effective services are certainly open to criticism. The European civil agency could, in some provinces at any rate, be reduced. Few English judges are really wanted, and the Egyptian system would serve as a useful model, but the one man who cannot be spared is the British soldier, who makes it possible for so few civilians to manage so many millions. The secretariat could probably be reduced, for it can hardly be seriously contended that it is absolutely necessary that the reports of an officer getting 2000 rupees a month should be handed on to others upon 3000 or 4000 rupees a month, with assistants at 1000 or 2000 rupees a month, before they are referred to a greater mandarin at 5000 or 6000 rupees a month, who can refer the matter to a colleague upon the same stipend, when, if the latter differs with him, or if a secretary chooses, the file, *plena jam margine, scriptus et in tergo nec dum finitus*, will finally come before the head of the administration. There is, at any rate in the old presidencies of Madras and Bombay, too much secretariat rule, and any superfluous hands would be better occupied in district administration. But such savings would not seriously affect the situation. The Government of India has pointed out how imperfectly its critics realise the smallness of the land revenue compared with enormous losses resulting from the failure of crops. In the Central Provinces during seven years the loss in this behalf has been equivalent to the total land revenue for fifty years. It is clear that any reductions that could be effected in establishments, and even under the greater head of land revenue demand, would never enable the community to withstand losses of such dimensions, nor indeed is it true that abatement of taxation results in provident saving on the part of the people. It is notorious, on the contrary, that the exact reverse is the case. Excessive leniency encourages the transfer of the soil to moneylenders, landlords, and middlemen, who at once swallow up the profits intended for the cultivator. It is also established that the chief sufferers at famine time are not those who pay assessment to Government or rent to landlords, but labourers on the land, who are not immediately affected by the revenue assessment. The last Famine Commission, presided over by Sir Antony MacDonnell—than whom no Indian administrator has been a more active friend to the tenant farmers and peasant proprietors—recorded that "the pressure of land revenue is not severe, the incidence on the gross produce of the soil being light, and not such as to interfere with agricultural efficiency in ordinary years, though there is a distinct need for leniency in adverse seasons." Whilst crop failure is the primary cause, there are other factors which cause poverty and indebtedness in India, such as the ever-increasing sub-divisions of holdings, due to land hunger, and attachment to his own locality on the part of the cultivator; the decline of village industries, rack-renting on the part of certain landlords; expensive litigation, and extravagance on the occasion of marriage and other festivities.

The Government of India has long had under consideration the desirability of a gradual and progressive enforcement of such increases in assessment as it is thought desirable to effect on resettlement. Wherever a large enhancement is necessary, endeavours are made to spread it over a period of years, and this has already been arranged in several provinces, but in no case can an enhancement be welcome, and landholders in India, perhaps more than elsewhere, rapidly raise their standards of living to suit their resources for the time being. In theory, Government assessment represents the sum that may fairly be demanded on an average of seasons, but it is assessed upon the assumption that the cultivator will save from the surplus in a good, to meet the deficit in a bad, year. This assumption, however, rests upon a false basis, and the rigid demand of the land revenue must add materially to the hardships of the poor. In tracts where great variations from the average produce are not frequent, this hardship may not be felt, but where, as so often happens, fluctuations are common and large, the rigid demand of a fixed assessment cannot be other than disastrous. In Madras no revenue is charged upon irrigable land, the produce of which has not ripened owing to failure of the water supply, and in the Punjaub partial failure to ripen, from the same cause, entitles the cultivator to a proportionate abatement. In Burma and Assam unirrigated lands are exempt from payment of assessment if left unsown, but elsewhere, lands dependent upon the rainfall for water pay a fixed and very low assessment, irrespective of their produce. The desirability of making collection more elastic in respect of these lands has frequently engaged the attention of the administration, and it must be admitted that an assessment varying with the out-turn, for such a vast area, would be difficult to work, would throw great power into the hands of subordinates, and would deprive the people of the object they now have in saving for a rainless day. On the other hand, it is hopeless to expect an Indian cultivator to be thrifty and saving, and it is a highly satisfactory circumstance that the Government of India has declared that it is not satisfied that, in well-known tracts, in which the crops are liable to violent fluctuations, a fluctuating assessment should not be introduced; though any alteration in the assessment is in conflict with the terms of the existing contract, by which the landholder undertakes the liability for loss in return for an expectation of profit. It may, upon the whole, be regarded as sufficiently proved that the permanent settlement is no protection whatever against famine, that 50 per cent. of the assets is the most ever demanded from landlords, that the State frequently intervenes to protect tenants from such landlords, and to limit the rent they demand, and that in areas where the State is paid directly by the cultivator the proposal to fix the assessment at one-fifth of the gross produce, would always largely increase, and in several provinces would double, the existing Government demand. It may further be held to be proved that the policy of long-term settlements is being extended, that the principle of making allowance for improvements is generally in force, that the disturbance connected with a new settlement is diminished, and that over assessment is not a general or widespread source of poverty and indebtedness in India, and cannot be regarded as a cause of famine.

The Government of India is further prepared to concede more elasticity in collection, and to resort in a still greater degree to reduction of assessment, in cases of local deterioration, even where such reduction cannot be claimed under the terms of settlement. Notwithstanding, the complete answer which this affords to the baseless charge that the Indian administration grinds down the faces of the poor, the proposal to settle with each holder is worthy of the consideration of the Government, whose present system, however, was inherited from its predecessors in title, from whose practice it only differs in that it is infinitely more moderate and favourable to the cultivators concerned.

CHAPTER IV

THE GOVERNMENT OF INDIA

Provincial Government — Departments — Magisterial and Revenue Functions—Local and Municipal Institutions—The Police

IN accordance with the lines laid down for this little work, after briefly surveying the past history of the country, showing the circumstances under which the present dispensation arose, and the respects in which it chiefly differs from its predecessors, it is necessary to give a brief and popular account of the manner in which the British administration of India works. The Hindoo system described in the Code of Manu is an absolute monarchy, and the manner in which the king passed his day, as laid down in the Code, is practically that adopted to this day by the ruling chiefs in Travancore and Cochin, two old-world states, which have never been invaded by strangers from the north, and which are therefore, a mirror of ancient India, and of great and exceptional interest to the student and historian. The villagers enjoyed a large measure of autonomy by immemorial custom, and of the various criticisms which have been passed upon our system of government none are more weighty than those which condemn the partial destruction of the village system, inevitable though that is in view of the extension of scientific, probably far too scientific, administration. Armies, the size of which is probably exaggerated, but which no doubt were large, were maintained to defend each kingdom, which was separated into military divisions, each division supporting a body of troops. The revenue consisted of a share in the produce of the land, taxes on commerce and on shopkeepers, and a forced service of a day a month by all accustomed to manual labour, and it has already been shown that the people were, according to accounts given by early travellers, in all probability fairly contented. Under the Mogul administration, the revenue collector was magistrate and police officer as well as revenue official, and this system, against which an outcry is now being made by critics of the Congress School, has survived in the main to the present day. Sir Courtenay Ilbert, the latest writer, has divided the history of British India into three periods—from the beginning of the seventeenth to the middle of the eighteenth century, when the East India Company as a trading corporation alternately coerced and cajoled the Indian powers, and fought with its rivals, the French and Dutch; from the middle of the eighteenth to the middle of the nineteenth century, in which period the Company acquired and consolidated its territory, sharing its power with the Crown in progressively increasing proportions and, *pari passu*, being deprived of its mercantile functions and privileges, and the third period after the Mutiny of 1857, when the remaining powers of the Company were transferred to the Crown. Passing reference has been made to the conquests of Lord Clive, and during the troublous period in which Britain was at war with France, Holland, Spain, and America, India was preserved by one of the greatest men England has ever produced—Warren Hastings. The conquests and annexations of Lords Cornwallis,

Wellesley, Hastings, and Dalhousie have already been briefly reviewed, and subsequent to the Mutiny the history of India is a record of development, the only important territorial addition made being Upper Burma, acquired in 1886. It is now time, therefore, to explain how the present system of government arose, and what that system is.

By Lord North's regulating Act of 1773 a Governor-General and four Councillors were appointed to administer Bengal, and Madras and Bombay were placed in subordination to the former presidency. By Pitt's Act of 1784 the administration of the three Presidencies was placed under a Governor and three Councillors, of whom the Commander-in-Chief was one, the control of the Governor-General in Council being maintained and extended. The Charter Act of 1813 withdrew the Company's monopoly except in regard to tea and the China trade, and the Charter Act of 1833 put an end to its commercial business, and vested the entire civil, military, and legislative power in the Governor-General in Council. In 1836 the Lieutenant-Governorship of the North-West, now United, Provinces, and in 1854 that of Bengal, was created, the latter province till then having been directly administered by the Governor-General. The original intention was to make Bengal a presidency, with a Governor in Council, which forms the justification for a claim by the Congress party that this constitution should now be conceded Those who support this request can hardly have been at the pains to learn that the Governor-in-Council constitution is now anomalous, and unworthy of imitation, since it has lost all signs of independence other than outward pomp, and the power of corresponding directly upon unimportant subjects with the Secretary of State. More than this, since the abolition of the office of provincial Commander-in-Chief, the Governor possesses no power beyond that of over-riding his Council in cases of grave importance, which never can arise in a subordinate administration in telegraphic communication with Calcutta, and, even with his casting vote, he can only equal two votes of his colleagues, so that he might practically be, throughout his term of office, as powerless as Warren Hastings for a time was. It is far more likely that, in order to save the additional expense entailed, the old Presidencies will be reduced to Lieutenant-Governorships than that the latter administration will be levelled up, if indeed it be an ascent for a Lieutenant-Governor, all powerful in respect of acts within the administrative competence of his Government, to become a Governor, who might be readily reduced to a cipher in his own Council. That the men are so much better than the system is the only reason why the now three-legged constitutions of Madras and Bombay continue to work in an admittedly satisfactory manner.

The transfer to the Crown in 1858 made no difference except that the Governor-General became known also as Viceroy, though the title has no statutory basis, the Governor-General in Council being the authority responsible for the entire administration of British India, and for the control of the native states. Immediately under the central or supreme Government, known as the Government of India, are foreign relations, defence, taxation, currency, debt, tariffs, post, telegraphs, and railways, and, subject to its control, provincial governments are responsible for internal administration, the assessment and collection of the revenue, irrigation, and communications. So complete is this control that no new appointment can be created, except of a very minor character, by provincial governments ruling over perhaps 50,000,000 of people; but the latter have their own budgets, and the expenditure of shares of certain items of revenue raised within their own limits. The shares were formerly assigned for periods of five years, and formed the subject of continual controversy, but arrangements are now being made of a more permanent character. The larger provinces have their own legislative councils, which, however, can only deal with local matters, and then only with the ultimate approval of the Governor-General in Council. The latter authority deals directly with the important native states, though some of these—such as Patiala and Travancore—are under the political control of the adjacent provincial administrations, an arrangement which, in regard to the latter state at any rate, leads insensibly, perhaps inevitably, to its precious individuality being impaired, and its own admirable and indigenous systems being forced into correspondence with those obtaining in neighbouring British districts.

The Council of the Governor-General consists of six ordinary members and the Commander-in-Chief, the Governor-General having since 1786 the power to over-ride the majority of his Council in matters of grave importance, a power which has hardly ever been exercised. By the Councils Act of 1861 the distribution of the work of the various departments among the members was legalised, any act done under orders so passed being deemed to be the act of the Governor-General in Council, the members of which under this system fulfil the function of Ministers with departmental portfolios—viz. Foreign, Home, Revenue and Agriculture, Legislative, Finance, Public Works, Commerce and Industry, Army and Military Supply. The Governor-General takes the first, Revenue and Public Works are under another, and the remaining departments have each their own members. At the head of each department is a Secretary, whose position is somewhat similar to that of a Permanent Under-Secretary of State in England. The disposal of work by members is subject to reference to the Governor-General in cases of difference of opinion, or where the subjects are of exceptional importance, and the vote of the majority prevails when matters come before the collective Council at its weekly meetings. The Foreign Department deals with external politics and frontier tribes, controls the administration of Ajmere, the new North-West Frontier Province, and British Beluchistan, and transacts all business connected with native states, which cover 770,000 square miles, with a population of 64,000,000, but few of which, outside Rajputana, date from any earlier period than the eighteenth century and the chaos in which the Mogul Empire expired. Some of the chiefs, as, for instance, the Nizam of Hyderabad and the Maharaja of Travancore, coin money, tax their subjects, and inflict capital punishment without appeal; none have power to deal with external relations, or, without restrictions, with Europeans. The Home Office deals with general administration, law and justice, jails, police, education, health, and local government, with which the provincial governments are immediately concerned. It also supervises the ecclesiastical department, which consists of bishops and chaplains, but the policy of Government is one of the strictest religious neutrality. Missionary schools are eligible for educational grants, but these are solely available for secular instruction, and may be obtained on similar terms by schools of any religious denomination. The department of Revenue and Agriculture administers the land revenue and the forests, deals with famine relief, and organises agricultural inquiries and experiments. Under the care of the Finance Department are Imperial and Provincial finance, currency, banking, opium, salt, excise, stamps, assessed taxes, and the general supervision of the accounts of the whole empire. The department of Commerce and Industry was formed in 1905 to facilitate the disposal of questions concerning trade and manufactures, and a Railway Board was created at the same time to deal, in subordination to it, with matters relating to the administration of the railways of the empire. Post office, telegraphs, customs, statistics, shipping, emigration, mines, and other matters have also been transferred to the new Commercial member.

The chief executive officer of the army is the Commander-in-Chief, under the supreme authority of the Governor-General in Council. The separate armies of Bengal, Madras, and Bombay were abolished in 1895, and there are now five territorial divisions, the northern, eastern and western commands, and the Burma and South India divisions. Up till 1906 all business connected with the army was transacted by the Military Department, which was in fact the War Office, but in that year it was replaced by the two departments of Army and Military Supply, the former of which, in charge of the Commander-in-Chief, deals with cantonments, volunteers, and all matters concerning the army, except stores, ordnance, remounts, medical service, and India marine, which are managed by the department of Military Supply. These changes were effected after considerable controversy, and though the Viceroy of the day, Lord Curzon, reluctantly agreed to them he subsequently resigned office over the question of the officer actually to be appointed to the charge of Military Supply.

British India is no longer divided into three Presidencies, but into thirteen local governments, two of which, Madras and Bombay are Presidencies; five of which, Bengal, the United Provinces of Agra and Oudh, the Punjaub, Burma, and Eastern Bengal and Assam are Lieutenant-Governorships; four of which, the Central Provinces, the Andamans, Coorg, and Ajmere are Chief-Commissionerships, and the new North-West Frontier Province, and British Beluchistan. Of these local governments two, the North-West Frontier Province, and the Lieutenant-Governorship of Eastern Bengal and Assam, were created during the viceroyalty of Lord Curzon, in 1901 and 1905 respectively. In respect of the former territorial unit so much controversy has arisen that it will be necessary to refer to the matter elsewhere, and in regard to the latter, though considerable differences of opinion existed, there is, upon the whole, a most unusual consensus of opinion to the effect that the step taken was necessary. Sir Mackworth Young, the Lieutenant-Governor of the Punjaub, from which certain districts were detached, disapproved of the formation of this territory, and of adjoining border tracts over which we exercised direct influence since

1892, into a separate administration, but he pointed out, and so did Sir Dennis Fitzpatrick, an ex-Lieutenant-Governor, that when the Punjaub Government differed with the Government of India, it was only in the weight the former attached to the difficulties and risks inherent in some forward movement with which it was more impressed on account of their closer proximity. The Secretary of State had found the existing administrative conditions unsatisfactory, and the Lieutenant-Governor agreed that, if the elimination of the Punjaub Government from trans-frontier control was desired, the creation of a separate administrative unit was the best solution. Indeed, a series of eminent authorities had expressed their approval of some such scheme, and among them were Sir B. Frere, Sir H. Durand, Sir J. Browne, Sir R. Sandeman, Sir W. Lockhart, Sir C. Aitchison, Sir G. Chesney, Lord Lytton, Lord Lansdowne, and Lord Roberts, who indeed was actually designated head of a new Frontier Province by Lord Lytton, when the outbreak of the Afghan War led to the retirement of the latter from India. The weighty opinion to the contrary of Lord Elgin must here be recorded, and further notice of this important question must be deferred to a chapter on frontier relations.

By whatever designation known, the head of every Local Government is under the control of the Governor-General in Council, Lieutenant-Governors differing from heads of provinces, other than the two Presidencies, in that their charges are constituted under Act of Parliament. By the Indian Councils Acts of 1861 a legislative council may be created for any provinces not already possessing such, and a lieutenant-governor may be appointed to such province, and under an Act of 1854 the Governor-General in Council may, with the sanction of the Secretary of State, take any territory in British India under his management, and provide for its administration. Burma and Eastern Bengal were made Lieutenant-Governorships under the former, and Assam in 1874, and the North-West Frontier Province in 1901, were separated from Bengal and the Punjaub respectively, under the latter Act.

It is now necessary to refer to the manner in which the Home Government of India has grown up, and is at present constituted. The regulating Act of 1773 did not materially alter the system under which the Court of Directors and General Court of Proprietors managed the business and other affairs of the East India Company, but in 1784 Pitt established the Board of Control, with power to direct all operations and concerns relating to the civil and military government of India, the President of this board being the political ancestor of the Secretaries of State for India, and the real effectual control being transferred to that officer, though patronage and other powers were still left with the Company. This system obtained till 1858, when the government, territories, and revenues of India were transferred to the Crown. Under the Act of that year the Secretary of State is made the constitutional adviser of the Crown, and he has the power of issuing orders to every officer in India including the Governor-General, and of directing all the business relating to India, which is transacted in the United Kingdom. He may act without consulting his Council in all matters in respect of which he is not required by statute to act as Secretary of State *in Council*, and he may withhold from his Council "secret" communications regarding making war or peace, negotiation with foreign Powers, and relations with native states, or such other matters as he may regard as urgent, but no matter for which the concurrence of the Council is required can be treated as secret or urgent, and among these are the making of any grant or appropriation of the Indian revenues. The members of the Council of India are appointed by the Secretary of State, and it meets once a week. Five members are a quorum, and a subdivision into committees facilitates the disposal of the business of which it disposes. At least nine members must have served or resided in India for ten years, and in practice the most distinguished of the retired civil servants are appointed, men whose presence at the India Office gives additional weight and authority to the decisions of the statesman who occupies for the time being the great office of Secretary of State. The establishment at the India Office is paid out of the revenues of India, but cannot be increased without an order in Council, which has to be laid before Parliament, which has supreme authority over India, as over all other dominions of the Crown. In practice, however, it only legislates for India, as it did in the session of 1907, when the political constitution requires amendment, or the Secretary of State needs to issue a loan. The revenues of India are under the control of the Government of India, except that they may not be applied to defraying the expenses of military operations beyond the frontier without the consent of both Houses, except for preventing or repelling actual invasions, or upon other sudden and urgent necessity. As the Home charges, including the Secretary of State's salary, are defrayed from Indian revenues, they are not included in the annual estimates laid before Parliament, though detailed accounts of receipts and disbursements, and a report on the moral and material progress of the country, have to be so laid.

As the President of the Board of Control is the political ancestor of the Secretary of State for India, so are the writers, factors, and merchants, the official forebears of the present Indian civil servants, who were organised upon their present footing by Lord Cornwallis, after Clive and Hastings had increased their pay in order to put an end to the practice of supplementing it by private trade and other means. Nominations to this service were made by the directors, and in 1805 the college at Haileybury was established for the training of writers before they went to India. In 1853 this service, for which the principal civil offices in India were reserved, was thrown open to competitors, and in 1858 the college at Haileybury was closed. The age limits are from 22 to 24, and on arrival in India every civil servant becomes a magistrate of the lowest class, and has to qualify in law and languages before he becomes eligible for promotion. Among many matters concerning India misunderstood in England is the extent to which the natives of the country are employed in its administration. About 1200 Englishmen are engaged in the civil government, and in the more or less direct control of 300,000,000 of people, and excluding 864 civil charges which are held by members of the Indian Civil Service, and excluding all posts of minor importance held by natives, there are 3700 persons holding office in the superior branches of the executive and judicial services, of whom only 100 are Europeans. The natives manage most of the business connected with the land, dispose of most of the magisterial business, and perform nearly all the civil judicial work thoughout the empire. Sir John Strachey pointed out that, except in England, there is no country in Europe in which judicial and executive officers receive such large salaries as are given in the higher ranks of the native civil service. Appointments made in India carrying a salary of £13 a month and upwards are reserved for Indians, and under an Act of Parliament of 1870 selected natives are eligible for any of the offices formerly reserved for the Indian Civil Service. At present the public service is divided into the Indian Civil Service, recruited in England, and the provincial and subordinate services, recruited in India from amongst natives of India, and the members of the provincial services enjoy all important executive judicial and administrative appointments which are not held by the smaller Indian Civil Service recruited at home. They are also eligible for offices hitherto reserved for the Indian Civil Service, and in the discharge of their functions, and more particularly their judicial functions, they have shown conspicuous ability. Of the eight great provinces of India, Bengal, with upward of 50,000,000, is the most populous, though the United Provinces, with 48,000,000, run it close. Burma, with 170,000 square miles, is the most extensive province, followed by Bengal with 151,000 and Madras with 142,000. Burma is as big as Sweden; the United Provinces contain more inhabitants than Austria-Hungary, and the population of Madras and the area of Bombay are about the same as the population and area of the United Kingdom. British India is divided into 250 districts, the average size being three-quarters of that of Yorkshire, and the average number of inhabitants more than half the population of that county. The head of the district, the Collector and Magistrate, is the representative of Government, and the principal revenue and magisterial officer. He performs all duties connected with the land and land revenue, and has general control over, or co-operates with special officers in the management of, the police, public works, forests, jails, sanitation, and education, besides being responsible for the guidance of municipal and district boards, for the peace of his district, and for the administration of the Famine Code in times of scarcity. He is assisted by subordinate civil officers, by a superintendent of police, and a civil surgeon. There are also similar sub-district units, in charge of native officers, who administer, very satisfactorily, charges varying from 400 to 600 square miles. Below them again are the village officers, headman, accountant, watchman, and so on. The judicial administration consists of the High Court, the District and Session Courts, the Court of the District Magistrate and his assistants, and the Courts of the Subordinate Magistrates, while there are also Courts of District Munsifs and Subordinate Judges courts, both of which only try civil cases. The law administered is Hindoo, founded upon the Institutes of Manu, Mahomedan, based on the Koran, and customary, which is greater than the other two, but the growth and development of which has been somewhat checked by the more or less rigid adherence of our courts to written Hindoo and Mahomedan law.

The idea of territorial as opposed to personal law

is of modern and European origin. It has always been assumed that the English brought their own legal system with them, so that in 1726 their common law was introduced into the three presidency towns. In 1780 the Declaratory Act laid it down that Hindoo and Mahomedan laws were to be applied to Hindoos and Mahomedans, a principle which was incorporated into subsequent Acts, though the influence of Western jurisdiction has necessarily largely leavened the *corpus juris* administered in India. It is, however, clearly established that no Act of Parliament passed subsequently to 1726 applies to any part of British India unless expressly extended thereto. Brief reference has already been made to the creation and constitution of the Legislative Councils, and in 1892, by the Indian Council Act, the supreme and local councils were enlarged, the elective element was tentatively introduced, and provision was made for discussion of the Budget.

The Indian Statute Book contains several enactments enabling the executive, in times of trouble, to suspend the regular law, and supersede the ordinary course of justice. By the Act of 1892, to which reference is made above, the Governor-General must summon additional members for the purpose of legislation, not less than ten and not more than sixteen in number, one half of whom must be, and more than one half of whom usually are, non-officials. The nominations to five seats are made on the recommendation of members of the legislative councils at Madras, Bombay, Calcutta, and Allahabad, and of the Calcutta Chamber of Commerce. At present it generally happens that, of twenty-four members of the Council sitting to make laws and regulations, one-third are natives of India, but by reason of the permanent official element provided by the ordinary members, the Government majority is assured. Ample opportunity is given for the expression of the views of the public, and opinions are invited broadcast before any legislation is effected. Members have the privilege of asking questions and discussing the Budget, but cannot propose resolutions, or on the latter occasion divide the Council. Every measure passed requires the Governor-General's consent, and may be disallowed by the Sovereign. Nor has the Council authority to repeal or alter the Army Act, or any enactment enabling the Secretary of State to raise money in the United Kingdom. It possesses, however, power to make laws binding native Indian subjects anywhere, for European British subjects, and for servants of the Government in India in the native states, and for native officers and soldiers, wherever they are serving. In like manner the Legislative Council of local governments consists, besides the members of the Executive Council, of not less than eight, and not more than twenty, other members, of whom at least half are non-official. In the four great provinces of Madras, Bombay, Bengal, and the United Provinces some of these members are appointed on the recommendations of groups of district boards, universities, chambers of commerce, and the like bodies. Codification of law in India has been carried a long way on the road to perfection, since Lord Macaulay, the first law member of the Governor-General's Council, and the moving spirit on the Indian Law Commission, drafted the Penal Code. Other commissions followed, but the work is now done by Government, under the guidance of the law members, and codification, always useful, is particularly valuable in a country in which the judges and magistrates are not generally professional lawyers. European officers and soldiers remain subject to military law, but native troops are governed by the Indian enactments in that behalf. In native states, as a rule, laws are passed by the ruling chief, with the advice and approval of the political officers representing the British Government, to which, however, various rights are reserved arising out of the fact that, for international purposes, native states are regarded as part of the British Empire. Under the Indian High Courts Act of 1861, the Crown was empowered to establish High Courts for Bengal, Madras, Bombay, and (later) the United Provinces; the judges were to be appointed by the Crown, and at least a third of their number were to be barristers. Every province is divided into Sessions divisions, presided over by the Sessions judge, for whose sentence of death confirmation is required from the highest Court of Criminal Appeal. After the Sessions Courts come those of the magistrates of different classes, and elaborate arrangements are made for the right of appeal and for revision. Civil suits are never tried by jury in India, but by the District Judge, Subordinate Judge, or Munsifs and Courts of Small Causes. The civil courts of the grades below that of district judge are almost entirely presided over by natives of India, while eight Indians occupy seats on the benches of the High Court, and two are judges of the Chief Court of the Punjaub. An appeal from the High Court in civil and certain criminal cases, lies to the Judicial Committee of the Privy Council. Civil courts are generally excluded from adjudication of matters relating to the assessment and collection of the land revenue, which are for the most part disposed of by the collectors, sitting as revenue courts. Considerable criticism is at present levelled at the combination in the person of one officer of the functions of collector and magistrate. It may be safely stated, however, that this system, which was inherited, as has been observed above, from our predecessors in title, is by no means unpopular with the masses, and that they do not desire that separation of these functions, which is in fact the rule only in the most advanced western countries. In the dearth of more serious causes for complaint this separation is one of the planks of the Congress platform, and since it is quite evident that in the hands of a corrupt or tyrannical officer such powers might be abused, it is hardly necessary here to repeat the arguments which are annually brought forward in favour of separation, a reform which is indeed now under the consideration of the Government of India. It may, however, be remarked that district magistrates try very few cases; that appeals from the decisions of their subordinate magistrates do not lie to them; that the creation of stipendiary magistrates for the disposal of criminal cases only throughout the country, would cost a great deal of money; that the English educated classes who expect to be, and would be, appointed to these offices, would naturally and necessarily be gainers by the change, and that there is every reason to believe that the masses of the people would prefer that the present system, which provides for disposal or revision by European magistrates, should be continued.

It is notorious that the people cry out for adjudication by British magistrates wherever possible, and consider them more trustworthy and impartial than their own fellow-countrymen. The exclusive jurisdiction over Europeans on the part of the Crown Courts and the independence of all other tribunals, formerly claimed for them, have now disappeared. European British subjects may only, however, be arraigned before a judge or magistrate who is a Justice of the Peace, and when tried before a district magistrate, sessional court, or high court, can claim a jury of which not less than half the members must be Europeans or Americans. Otherwise Europeans and Indians are subject to the same criminal and civil jurisdiction. Among the punishments authorised is whipping, in the case of males, for theft and certain other offences, and, in spite of objections raised by humanitarian societies, this short and sudden remedy is by no means unpopular amongst a people whose ancestors before the advent of British rule were subject to mutilation as well as to death, imprisonment, and fine. In describing the general features of the administration of India, nothing was said regarding local and municipal government, a subject of too great importance to be disregarded. Villages may be divided into the joint or landlord village, the type prevailing in the United Provinces, Frontier Province, and the Punjaub, and the individual or ryot wari village, which prevails outside Northern India, where the revenue is assessed on the individual cultivator, and wherein there is no joint responsibility. In both cases the usual staff of village officers exists, and the artisans and traders necessary for a self-sufficing unit. The Indian village is still an important factor in the administration, and the headman, accountant, and watchman have special functions to perform in connection with the collection of the revenue and the maintenance of law and order. But under Hindoo and Mahomedan government no system grew up in the villages, corresponding with that which is usual in Europe. Representation has always been altogether foreign to the Hindoo genius, and the management of villages and of towns resided, not in representatives of the people, but in tax-collectors, police officers, and other officials. In the days of Akbar, the Kotwal, who was the chief authority in magisterial, police, and fiscal matters, was directed "not to suffer women to be burnt against their will, nor a criminal deserving of death to be impaled, to allot separate quarters to butchers, hunters of animals, sweepers, and washers of the dead, and to restrain men from associating with such stony-hearted, and gloomy dispositioned creatures. He was to amputate the hand of any man who was the pot companion of the executioner, and the finger of such as held communication with his family." Such directions as these, however, from the Ain-i-akbari, can hardly be regarded as relating to municipal administration, and that system is in fact a British exotic. True it was introduced in 1687 into Madras city after a pattern which then obtained, and still obtains, in London, but the people, then as now, abhorred the taxes levied for sanitary services. Nevertheless, the municipalities have continued to exist in the Presidency towns, and the elective system was introduced into them between 1872 and 1878. District municipalities were first attempted in 1842, based upon the voluntary principle, which naturally failed amongst a people who have ever been, and are now, hostile to the whole principle of local self-government.

The law in this behalf was from time to time altered

and strengthened, and the election of municipal commissioners was made permissive. Lord Mayo went further, but it was reserved to Lord Ripon to make a great and general advance. He regarded the elective system as a means of political and popular education, and widely extended its bounds, and he gave towns power to elect non-official chairmen in place of the executive officers. At the same time, municipal revenues were relieved of the maintenance of the police, on condition that they incurred equivalent expenditure on education, medical relief, and local public works. Lord Ripon's system practically remains in force, and in 1901 there were 742 district municipalities in the empire, in the great majority of which some of the members are elected, and some nominated by the Local Government.

The elected members vary in number, from one half in Bombay, to three quarters in the United Provinces and Madras, and not more than a quarter of the members of the committee may be salaried officers of Government in Madras, Bombay, and Bengal, while considerable powers of control are in all cases reserved to Government and its officers. About two-thirds of the aggregate municipal income is derived from taxation, and the remainder from other sources, including Government contributions. It may safely be stated that the only tax levied by municipalities which is not exceedingly unpopular is one to which, in the eyes of European economists, particular objection attaches—the *octroi*, to which the people have no particular objection, because they regard it as identical with the town or transit duties which were levied under Indian rule. The administration of Calcutta, by its municipality, has been a constant source of anxiety to the Government, though it would be unjust to regard it as a failure in view of the great difficulties with which it had to contend. In 1899 the number of commissioners was reduced from 75 to 50, of whom 25 are elected, 15 are appointed by the local government, 4 by the Bengal Chamber of Commerce, and other native associations, and 2 by the Commissioners of the Port, and the action of Government, though called for by the imminence of plague, was resented by the advanced politicians of Bengal as interference with popular government. The development of local institutions in rural areas has been accomplished through the agency of local boards, which in the beginning, like municipalities, partook of a voluntary character.

In 1871 Acts were passed in every province dividing the country into local fund circles, and creating consultation boards nominated by the Government, with the Collector as president. Local taxation was now introduced, and in 1882 Lord Ripon replaced the local committee by a network of boards, on which the non-official element preponderated, and the elective principle was recognised in the same way as in municipalities, but the degree to which this system has been introduced is not constant, but varies in different provinces. Provincial rates yield 60 per cent. of the income of local boards, and of these the land-cess is the most important.

Although the extension of local self-government has always been regarded in some quarters as a stepping stone of the progress towards an ill-defined and indefinite goal, before reaching which the inhabitants of India must have entirely changed their character and outlook, yet it must be admitted that it is almost the most unpopular of all branches of our administrative activities.

The writer, whose duty it has been to administer local boards and municipalities, and to review the reports of these bodies in the secretariat, would confess that, for his part, he found on all sides nothing but discontent with the taxation imposed for this purpose, and dissatisfaction with the result. These feelings do not extend by any means to the lawyer class, who almost invariably acquire power and influence upon such boards, but the aristocracy, and the masses of the people, whose feelings such aristocracy pretty faithfully represents, have no hesitation in expressing to any European, with whom they are on terms of friendship, their dislike and distrust of the whole business, and particularly of that very representative principle which is regarded as its glory by its founders and admirers. Officers of the Government rarely place themselves in communication at first hand with the people, other than with those who have been denationalised by Western education, and who take care in every district to form a camarilla, through which alone information reaches the English officer, who cannot, without a knowledge of the native languages, and considerable originality and determination of character, break loose from his bonds. It is only by incurring the absolute enmity of the class which is known in Bengal as the Babus, and exists to some extent in every province, that the English official can associate at all with those who represent ninty-nine in one hundred of the population of his charge. So difficult is it to perform this feat, so absolutely necessary is it to the success of the intrigues of the Babu class to prevent communication between the people and their rulers, that slanders are widely circulated concerning the official who would seek the truth, and efforts, by no means always unsuccessful, are freely made to damage him with his superiors, by means of anonymous charges, in the concoction of which the writers and agitators of India are extremely adept. There is no feature of local self-government which is so thoroughly unpopular as the representative principle. No man of any position amongst his countrymen will submit himself, at any rate in rural districts, to the ordeal of election, or the chance of having to accept as his colleagues persons of low caste and slight consideration. There is, too, an indisposition to accept the vexatious and exacting requirements of public life, and little doubt exists that the inhabitants of the districts, if they could be polled, would, by enormous majorities, vote for leaving all administrative business in the hands of the impartial and professional administrator who represents the British Government, and is their local providence. Another branch of the administration which is subject to perpetual criticism, on the part of the Babu class, is the police—not the village police, but the regular established force, working under Government. In 1902, Lord Curzon's Government appointed a commission to inquire into the police administration, a measure which is held by very competent authorities to have conduced in no small degree to that want of respect for authority, that disposition to disaffection, and that spirit of unrest which has of late been only too conspicuous in Eastern Bengal, and which spread, not without active assistance from the agitators of Calcutta, to other parts of India, and particularly to certain districts in the Punjaub.

CHAPTER V

REVENUES AND TAXATION

Salt—Opium—Expenditure of the Government—Exchange Compensation—Railways—Home Charges—Pensions—Currency and Banking

IT is doubtful if any country in the world can show such an advance in prosperity as can British India during the sixty years ending with the year 1900, in which the total value of imports and exports has risen from 28 to 246 *crores of rupees, and the gross revenue from 21 to 113 crores. The expenditure has increased *pari passu*, as salaries have been raised in amount, and increased in number, public instruction and medical relief have been organised, and vast sums have been spent in irrigation, railways, post office, telegraphs, and sanitation. It is claimed on behalf of the Government that the growth in the revenue is due to increasing prosperity and better management, and not to increasing burdens on the tax-payer, and, as shown in the chapter on land revenue, this contention may be considered to be fairly sustained. In regard, however, to local cesses and rates, it is doubtful if the people who pay would complacently accept the position taken up by their rulers, and whether they would not prefer to be without some of the services of Western civilisation, and to retain some of the money collected from them on this account, either to keep it in their own pockets, bury it underground, or

* A crore of rupees is £666,666.

to spend it according to their own inclinations upon festivals and ceremonies. The comparison made with the year 1860 in the latest official publication on this subject is not altogether conclusive, because sources of taxation had been tapped before that date which were new to the people of India, Income-tax, for instance, is at a lower rate than that imposed in 1860, but there was a time before 1860 when there was no income-tax at all, and it was subsequent to 1860 that the unpopular municipal and rural rates came into being. Of the total income of £85,000,000 sterling in 1904-1905, more than £6,000,000 were derived from sources other than taxation and land revenue, and the latter receipt, the largest of all the individual items, in Europe would fall to the private landlord. The direct taxation of the Moguls, raised from a much smaller population and cultivated area, and at a time when the purchasing power of the rupee was much higher, was heavier than that now levied by the Indian Government. One of the most important reforms introduced into the existing financial system was Lord Mayo's innovation of making a fixed grant to each local Government for provincial services, and thus giving them an interest in effecting economies which had previously been wanting, but hardly had the benefit of this change made itself felt, when that decline commenced in the value of silver which so severely tried the stability of Indian revenues.

Next Lord Lytton endeavoured to obtain an annual surplus of 1½ crores, to be applied to the reduction or avoidance of debt, and thus to provide for expenditure on famine, and in 1882 the general import duties were abolished, though they subsequently had to be reimposed. Meanwhile exchange continued to fall, and a drop of a penny meant an addition of over a crore to the expenditure. The action of Russia on the Russo-Afghan frontier in 1885, and the conquest of Upper Burma, led to further charges, which resulted in the necessity for a general tax on non-agricultural incomes in excess of 500 rupees per annum, and the increase of the salt-duty to 2 rupees 8 annas per maund of 82 pounds. Between 1892 and 1895 exchange fell from 1s. 3d. to 1s. 1d., in 1893 the mints were closed to the free coinage of silver, and the Government definitely adopted the policy which has led to the stable rate of exchange at 1s. 4d. and to the practical attainment of a gold standard. In 1894 the general import-duty of 5 per cent. was reimposed, a countervailing excise-duty being levied on cotton goods produced by Indian mills. In 1900 the value of the rupee reached the 1s. 4d. rate, and from 1895, when the effect of the new policy began to be fully felt, up to the present day financial prosperity has increased, though two exceptionally severe crop failures have occurred, and plague has fastened upon the country. These two famines cost sixteen, and the military operations on the frontier of 1897-1898 accounted for five, crores. During this period, the duty on cotton cloth was largely reduced, cotton twist and yarn were exempted, and a counter-vailing duty was imposed to protect Indian sugar against the competition of bounty fed beet sugar from Europe. In 1902-1903, the Government remitted 2 crores of arrears of land revenue which had accrued in the famine, and in 1903-4, the salt-tax was reduced from 2½ to 2 rupees per maund, and all incomes of less than 1000 rupees per annum were exempted from income-tax. In 1905-1906, the salt-tax was further reduced to 1½ rupees, and the grants to local governments were largely increased. The Budget for the current year provided for increased expenditure on police and education, and the local cesses levied for the payment of village officials were abolished—a welcome remission, though this is the particular service remunerated by local cesses, to which the payers have the least objection. Of the gross revenue of British India about 26 per cent. is raised from taxes proper, as against about 83 per cent. in the United Kingdom, and the land revenue forms about 39 per cent. of the total net receipts, as against 44 per cent. thirty years ago.

The revenue derived from opium is obtained chiefly from the export of this product to China, where the local product has become a formidable competitor in spite of decrees by the Emperor forbidding the use of the drug. At present, however, the Indian Government is under an engagement to gradually reduce the export, year by year, till it altogether ceases, provided that the Chinese Government furnishes proof that the production of native opium has been correspondingly diminished. This engagement as a firm agreement is limited to three years, at the expiry of which the British Government will be free to reconsider the position—as free, that is, as that Government ever can be, when pressed by bodies possessing considerable interest with the electorate, and desiring to abolish the opium trade, without regard to the results to the Indian revenue, and whether or not the abolition results in any diminution of the consumption in China. The latest authority, Major Bruce, thinks the English Government could as easily abolish beer drinking as the Chinese Government, even if in earnest, could appreciably reduce the use of opium in China.

There was a time when opium yielded 16, but it

now furnishes only 7 per cent. of the total net revenue. The receipts from salt, the consumption of which has largely increased in recent years, amounted to 8 crores in the last year of the 2½ rupees duty, when the average incidence, which now has fallen to about 3d., was 5d. per head of the population. Under the term excise is included not only the revenue from intoxicating liquors, but also the duty on opium consumed in the country, where the drug is used chiefly as a medicine and preventive of fever. In malarial tracts the people are absolutely dependent upon it, and prisoners in jail from such regions if deprived of their dose run the risk of losing their lives. The use of opium has also proved highly beneficial to Indians in malarial parts of Africa, as appears from reports submitted to the Colonial Office. The wholesale condemnation of the use of this drug because of its misuse in China and elsewhere obscures the fact that it plays a very valuable part in the *pharmacopœia*, and is a specific in regard to malarial diseases, from which 19 per mille of the people of India die, as against 2 per mille per annum victims of the plague, of which we hear so much more, because even the ingenuity of the virulent critics of British rule in India can hardly assert that malarial fevers, which have been the scourge of the country throughout its history, were, like plague, invented by the British Government, or brought about by the oppression and excessive taxation of its unhappy subjects. But *post hoc propter hoc* is good enough argument where the English in India are concerned.

The customs duties are levied for revenue purposes only. They have no protective power, and they tend to decline in consequence of the rapid growth in the local production of petroleum, and the development of the Indian cotton trade. Of the stamp revenue, which amounted to 5 crores in 1902-1903 more than one-third is collected in Bengal owing to the exceptionally litigious character of the inhabitants of that region. Of the ordinary heads of expenditure, the charges for civil administration naturally show a disposition to increase, one reason for which has been the grant of compensation allowances to officers of Government for the loss caused to them by the fall in the value of the rupee upon their remittances to England. Little or no exception could have been taken to this measure provided its operation had been confined to Government servants, who had entered the service under an express or implied understanding that they would be paid in rupees at the rate of ten, or about ten, to the pound. But there is much reason for holding that to extend the concession to officers who joined the service when exchange had fallen, and was falling rapidly, was hardly fair to the tax-payer, who was in no way responsible for such fall. The question is one of little interest now, but it gave rise at the time to some acrimonious criticism, for which there was, it would appear, no little justification. The expenditure under general administration police and education, shows a progressive increase, that for education being 83 lakhs more than in 1876-1877, though there will perhaps in the future be still further increases, in consequence of the changes contemplated by Lord Minto's Government.

Under the item, political pensions, 40 lakhs annually are spent, and when the administration is accused, as it frequently is, of niggardly dealing with these pensioners, it should be remembered that the latter have been confirmed in the receipt of handsome stipends, whereas before, they were as a rule merely new and precarious occupants of the thrones, and more or less royal cushions, from which they or their ancestors have been deposed. Many of the families who have been subjects of much superfluous sympathy, were of mere mushroom growth, and would certainly have been swept away, but that they found salvation in the consolidation of British rule.

No outline of the finances of India, however brief, would be in any sense complete without a reference to the railway system, which is destined to become a very large contributor towards the revenues of the country. In 1850, and succeeding years, English companies constructed eight railways, upon a guarantee of 5 per cent. on their total outlay with half the surplus profits. Without such a guarantee British capital would not have been attracted to India, where it has performed such valuable work for the people of the country, and where, moreover, capital from no other quarter was at all likely to have been attracted. All the old guaranteed railways have now been purchased by the Government under a provision in their contracts in that behalf. When the system above described had been in force for twenty years the Government began to borrow money for construction. With these funds, only such lines were constructed as were expected to yield sufficient to cover the interest on the capital outlay within a reasonable time, and other railways required for protection against famine were built out of revenue. In order, however, to expedite the completion of the necessary programme, the aid was invoked of private companies, whose contracts were far more favourable to the State, and far less generous to the proprietors, than those given on a 5 per cent. sterling guarantee. At the end of 1904-1905 India was provided with 27,728 miles of railway of which some 20,000 belonged to the State, and the capital outlay was 202 crores, of which 59 crores were spent on the purchase of the companies' lines. The result the railway account shows is that between 1876 and 1881 there was an average net loss of 120 lakhs, and between 1899 and 1905 an average net gain of 111 lakhs. There is no doubt whatever that in the future railways will prove a valuable source of revenue to the State, and they have already saved the lives of millions during seasons of widespread failure of crops.

For forty years past officers, designated consulting engineers, had exercised supervision over companies' lines, and they were, in the case of Madras, Bombay, and Burma, attached to those Governments, and in other cases directly under the Government of India, which of course directly exercised control over guaranteed lines. After various modifications in the secretarial arrangements and in the agency maintained at headquarters for the conduct of railway business a Railway Board was created. After a report had been received from an officer, Mr Robertson, specially deputed to examine the problem, it was considered that the management of the railway system should be entrusted to practical railway men, less tied up in red tape than the Government officials previously engaged in this responsible duty. Accordingly, the railway branch of the Government of India Secretariat was abolished in 1905, and a Railway Board, consisting of a chairman, Sir F. Upcott, and two members, one with English, and one with Indian, railway experience, was created to take its place. This board works under the department of Commerce and Industry created by Lord Curzon's Government, and the care of irrigation and civil works, which alone now fell to the Public Works department, was transferred with that department to the charge of the department of Revenue and Agriculture. Certain defects in this arrangement have, however, already become apparent, and Mr Morley has appointed a commission, with Sir James Mackay, the negotiatior of the last trade treaty with China, at its head, to inquire into the whole subject. This commission has not yet reported and meanwhile important changes are taking place in Southern India owing to the purchase by Government of the Madras railway, an old 5 per cent. guaranteed line, the mileage of which is being distributed between the South Indian and Southern Mahratta narrow-gauge systems.

The national debt of India in 1904-1905 was £133,000,000 sterling, and 122 crores of rupees, and the total debt, taking both classes together, rose from £103,000,000 sterling in 1876 to £214,000,000 sterling in 1905, but whereas in 1876 there was a charge against revenue for railways and irrigation works of over a crore of rupees, in 1905 these works, after paying all interest charges yielded a profit of nearly 5 crores. In 1903-1904, Sir Edward Law, then Finance Minister, showed that the excess of debt of assets in 1902 was only 33 crores, the whole Government debt being shown on one, and the capitalised value of railways, canals, and other commercial assets on the other, side. The subject of military expenditure looms largely in considering the financial system of the British Indian Empire, upon which it has produced, and continues to produce, so great an effect. The advance of Russia, and the conquest of Upper Burma in 1885, the introduction of improvements in armament, equipment, and organisation in 1890, 1891, and similar improvements which have been continually effected subsequent to that date; the raising of the pay of the native soldiers in 1895, and of the British soldiers in 1898 and 1902; the establishment of cordite, gun casting, and small arms factories, redistribution and reorganisation; the supply of new guns and rifles, and the expenditure on military works, have brought the average figures for the quinquennial period 1896-1897 to 1900-1901 to 23 crores against the quinquennial average of 17 crores in the period 1876-1877 to 1880-1881, and the figure for 1904-1905 rose to 27 crores. In spite of criticisms levelled against the military adminstration, which is further noticed elsewhere, it can hardly be seriously contended that an army of 230,000 is excessive for a vast empire, with many thousands of miles of land frontier, and a population approaching 300,000,000.

Of the extraordinary expenditure of the Government of India, the largest item has been famine relief, or, as it should be called, prevention of famine, upon which, between 1876 and 1903, 26 crores were spent while the cost of military operations during the same period was 22 crores. Within this time occurred the Afghan War of 1878, the Upper Burma expedition of 1885-1886, the Chitral campaign of 1895-1896, and the Tirah and other frontier campaigns of 1897-1899, and also three great crop failures, that of 1876-1878, in South India, and of 1896-1897 and 1899-1900 in Upper India, the Central Provinces, Bombay, and other regions.

Indian accounts are kept in three sets—those of the Home Government, of the Government of India, and of the Local Governments. The decentralisation policy was initiated by Lord Mayo in 1870, and subsequently further developed with the intention of giving Local Governments an inducement to develop their resources, and economise in their expenditure, to obviate the need for interference in the details of provincial administration on the part of the Central Government, and at the same time to maintain the unity of the finances, so that all parts of the administration should receive a proper share of the increase of revenue.

Under the existing arrangement, the Government of India delegates to local governments the control of the expenditure on the ordinary provincial services, together with certain heads of revenue, or a proportion of certain heads of revenue, sufficient to meet these charges. Thus salt, customs, opium and tribute are wholly Imperial heads ; stamps, excise, land revenue, assessed taxes, forests aad registration are divided between the Imperial and Provincial Governments, and local taxes are wholly provincial. The Government of India entirely controls charges connected with foreign affairs, with the public debt, the army, Indian marine, and the home charges of the central administration. It also keeps in its own hands post and telegraphs, mint and railways, and its expenditure amounts to three times as much as that of all the provincial governments put together. The local governments have no borrowing powers, but fall back on the Government of India when their own resources are exhausted—as was the case in Bombay, for instance, during the last famine. It was very clearly laid down by Sir James Westland, with the approval of Lord Elgin and his colleagues, that the whole resources of

India were at the disposal of the Government of India, and that local governments were merely delegates, and exercised such functions as they were permitted to perform under the control of the central administration. Arrangements with the local governments, which formerly lasted five years only, have now been made of a more permanent character. Permanent they can never be made, for the financial fortunes of the provinces must always stand or fall with those of the Central Government. The changes made, however, are in the right direction, and in future Budget day at Calcutta will cease to resolve itself into a wrangle as to which of the provincial governments is the milch cow of the Government of India. The net expenditure in England chargeable to Indian revenue is about £17,700,000 sterling, of which £6,500,000 are railway revenue account, £2,800,000, interest and management of debt, £1,800,000, stores, £1,300,000, army effective charges, £400,000, civil administration, £200,000, marine, £4,700,000, furlough and pension allowances of civil and military officers. These are the payments which are commonly described by hostile critics of British administration as the drain, or as the tribute paid to England. But, of the £17,000,000, upwards of £11,000,000 are payment on account of capital and materials supplied by England, and cannot properly be regarded as an administrative transaction. The charge of £4,700,000 for furlough and pension allowances stands, it must be confessed, on a different footing. It is of no avail to say that such a payment is unprecedented, because the Indian Empire is unprecedented, and no precedents can be expected, but, inasmuch as the salaries paid by the Indian Government to its servants are by no means ungenerous, it may very fairly be argued that this is an exceptionally large amount for the Indian tax-payer to find for the benefit of officers who have left the country. To the furlough allowances no reasonable exception can be taken. They must necessarily be pitched upon a scale analogous to that of the salary in each individual case. But when a public servant enjoys good pay during the whole of his service, retires, and returns to his own country, perhaps in the prime of life, to live for many years as a pensioner, it is hardly reasonable that he should claim to be altogether relieved of the necessity for making provision for himself after his retirement, and that a generous scale of pensions operates in encouragement of extravagance, can hardly be denied.

The class of pension often selected for adverse criticism is that of the Indian civil servant who receives £1000 a year, but it should be understood that, of this sum, he has subscribed an amount equal, as a minimum, to one half of the whole, by compulsory payments to the pension fund, and, in the case of an officer of long service it frequently happens that his payments to the provident fund would entitle him to a pension of this amount. There are indeed many public servants who draw higher pensions than £500 a year, which is the maximum received by the Indian civil servant from the Indian tax-payer. It would probably be generally admitted that British officers serving in India are able to make some provision for their old age, though the cost of living has largely increased, family expenses are exceedingly heavy, and no Indian civil servant who has not considerable private resources can possibly hope, on his return to

England, to take any part in public life, or to end his days in other than modest obscurity. This is a regrettable fact, because the sound common-sense views and experience of this class of the unemployed, are not by any means represented by those of their cloth, whom want of success and disappointment, or a naturally anti-English turn of mind, inspires with sufficient energy to push their way through to platforms, from which to criticise their own kith and kin and the administration, willing and concurring agents of which they have apparently been for the greater part of their lives. However this may be, it is eminently desirable that home charges, other than those represented by interest upon capital and materials, should be kept within the lowest possible limits. Mr Morley has given practical proof that he entertains this view by effecting a reduction in the salaries of the members of his own Council, a measure which has met with some adverse criticism in India. It is true that retired officers of the Indian Government who have secured employment in the city, or elsewhere, might find it difficult to accept a seat on the Indian Council, with the consequent loss of emolument. But on the other hand it must be remembered that a very small proportion of retired civil servants, of the class and age from which Members of Council are recruited, can, or at any rate do, obtain, after their retirement, employment so remunerated that they would incur loss of income by accepting a membership of Council. In the vast majority of cases the officers the Secretary of State would desire to appoint would be as ready to take the appointment at £1000 as at £1200 a year. Officers who serve in administrative appointments in India occupy a position of power and importance, which can hardly be realised by those who spend their lives in England, and it is only fair that proper provision should be made for the evening of their days. It is, however, out of the question to attempt to provide them from public funds with pensions at all proportionate to the dignity of the appointments they held in India, and it is probable that, in regard to officers appointed in the future, terms might be imposed providing that in no case should any pension from Indian revenues exceed £500 a year, exclusive of such amounts as any officer may subscribe towards the cost of his own pension. Judges of the High Court appointed from England receive a pension of £1200 a year for less than twelve years' service in India—that is, £100 a year for life for every year spent in the country, an amount only exceeded, it is believed, by that paid to an ambassador who passes twelve years in that grade after a long life spent in the public service. This exceptionally large pension was attached to the office of High Court judge to induce barristers of eminence, in large practice, to leave this country and take up judgeships in India. It would be idle to ignore the fact that men of the class these terms were intended to attract do not avail themselves of the offer, and that judges of equal capacity, to a great extent, perhaps for the most part, natives of India, could be obtained on more favourable terms. Here, perhaps, is an opportunity of effecting a reduction in the home charges, and there may be other concrete cases. Every such reduction will be unpopular, and will be resisted by the officers affected, but the critics of the home charges have their eyes fixed upon cases like these, and being, as they are, for the most part, lawyers they fasten upon every appointment made to the High Court benches in India, which affords any justification for the views they entertain. These appointments are not in some cases such as an impartial judge can consider altogether satisfactory, but that is only an additional reason for giving the fullest consideration to every complaint for which there appears to be any justification. The dispenser of patronage can only appoint men who are willing to go. The men the terms were intended to secure will not go. But that would be a good reason for reducing the pay, not for overpaying the men who will accept.

For the rest, the great advance in revenue and prosperity is so obviously due to the use in the country of British capital that it is idle to entertain the theory that the empire is exploited for the benefit of the British capitalist, who indeed manifests a preference for almost any other field of investment. Without a Government guarantee it is at present difficult to attract capital at all, and the action of the Bengali agitators, who have succeeded by intrigue in awakening a slight echo in the Punjaub, will not tend to diminish the previously existing shyness of the investor.

The expenditure in England is defrayed by the sale of telegraphic transfers, and from the sale of Council bills, and, as the imports of India are exceeded by her exports, purchasers in Europe have to remit the difference. In order to this end, they buy bills on India from the Secretary of State, who pays the home charges with the proceeds, and the buyers send the bills to India to be cashed by the Government. This simple and effective system was subject to considerable disturbance when the exchange value of the rupee fell to 1s. 1d. in 1894-1895. In that year the sterling value of the bills paid was £15,770,000, to discharge which the Government of India had to pay 28 crores of rupees, while at the rate prevailing in 1872 it would have had to pay only 16 crores, the difference of 12 crores being more than half the amount of the net land revenue, the greatest asset of the Indian Government. The satisfactory condition of Indian finances, and the progressive improvement which has marked the last thirty years, are obscured by the use of the word famine for those periodical crop failures which must, and do at longer or shorter intervals, affect some part or another of the vast subcontinent of Asia dependent upon a precarious monsoon. If the use of this word were abandoned, and famine relief were called by its proper, and now thoroughly justified, name of prevention of famine, less heed would be paid to the foolish charges brought against the Government of oppression and starvation of their subjects. In fact, there is an increasing land revenue accompanied by a diminishing incidence on the cultivated area, and a steady rise in the receipts from salt, excise, customs, and income tax, all satisfactory proofs of developing resources. The latest published figures show that the value of exports and imports, including bullion, have risen from 61 and 37 crores respectively, in 1876-1877, to 129 and 86 crores. The number of cotton and jute mills has increased since 1878 from 78 to 237. In the same period, the coal produced has been multiplied sevenfold, and the supply of petroleum has leapt in a year or two from 6,000,000 to 56,000,000 of gallons. The number of joint-stock companies has more than, and their capital has nearly, doubled. The black cloud of falling exchange has disappeared, but a little cloud has appeared in the possible extinction of the opium revenue. It can only be hoped that the opinion of those who believe that when India ceases to supply China with opium, the supply in China will cease, will be justified, but the loss of revenue will in any case be a serious matter, though not such as the Government cannot surmount without the help of the mother country, to the receipt of aid from which would attach, whether express or implied, conditions which must impair the financial independence of India. The great expansion hitherto experienced in the land revenue cannot be maintained; indeed, if the view expressed in Chapter III. of this little volume be adopted, no further development can be expected. The Government always welcomes any increase in the production in India of articles at present imported from Europe, albeit such increase must necessarily be attended with a decline in the customs revenues. Indeed, it has itself worked two collieries through the agency of the North-Western Railway, and either directly or through the agency of a subsidised company has produced iron and steel in Bengal. *Svadeshi* was really invented by the Government, which, as Lord Minto has said, welcomes its development, provided it be of an economic, and not of a spurious political, character.

In connection with the finances of India it is necessary to refer briefly to the introduction of the gold standard. Under the Currency Acts of 1835 and 1870, silver was received without limit for coinage at the mints of Calcutta and Bombay, and the gold value of the rupee of 180 grains weight, and of 165 grains of pure silver, depended upon the gold price of silver bullion. The fall in the value of silver, which began in 1873, not only caused great loss to the Government of India in discharging its sterling obligations in England, but also, owing to frequent and violent oscillations in the rate of exchange, checked the flow of British capital into India, and disturbed the commercial and economic relations between the two countries. It was decided, therefore, to introduce a gold standard, and in 1893 the mints were closed to unrestricted coinage, and bullion and gold coin were received in exchange for rupees at the rate of 1s. 4d. to the rupee. In consequence of these measures the average rate of exchange for 1898-1899 had been pretty well established at a figure very closely approximating to 1s. 4d. In 1899, therefore, sovereigns and half-sovereigns were made legal tender at 1s. 4d. to the rupee, which, while remaining legal tender up to to any amount, yet became a token coin representing $\frac{1}{15}$ of a sovereign, though no sovereigns have actually been coined in India. Gold does not circulate freely, except in large centres, but between 1900 and 1904 about £17,000,000 sterling were issued in this form, most of which has probably been withdrawn from circulation, and *more Indico* hoarded by the possessors. Lest the Indian Government should at any time be unable to satisfy a demand for gold, by which failure the rate of exchange would probably be adversely affected, a special Gold Reserve Fund has been formed on which Government could draw if the stock in the paper currency reserves were exhausted. The present circulation of rupees is estimated at between 155 and 160 crores, or about £100,000,000.

The banking of the country is carried on by institutions of the same character as those with which we are familiar in England, and also by native moneylenders, who charge high, often exorbitant, rates of interest, but run risks and lend money where no others would, and supply capital in small doles for agricultural operations. They are the bankers of the small farmers of India, though the Government grants loans for improvements, and for the purchase of seed and cattle, and makes advances in years of scarcity. Co-operative credit societies are also being introduced and encouraged by legislation, institutions of the same character as the agricultural banks of the continent of Europe, designed to encourage thrift, promote the accumulation of loanable capital, and reduce the interest on borrowed money by a system of mutual credit. Post office savings banks are also encouraged, the amount to credit of depositors being not far short of £9,000,000 sterling. The Presidency banks at Calcutta, Madras, and Bombay are joint-stock companies regulated by an Indian Act of 1876, at which Government keeps a portion only of its headquarter balances. There are also eight exchange and eight local European banks, and the total capital available for financing the larger operations of commerce is about £10,000,000 sterling. The Government, however, is the great Indian banker, which holds most of its own cash balances, has sole control of the paper currency, and through its transactions with the India Office controls the rate of exchange. The Presidency banks are, however, debarred from raising money in the English market, a restriction the removal of which has been, and even now is, under consideration. Mercantile opinion favours the view that existing banking facilities are not sufficient to adequately deal with the requirements of commerce, and the official opinion is that existing banks would suffice, if they were so managed that their resources would be free for the convenience of merchants in seasons of commercial activity. Whichever view may be correct it appears desirable that such further facilities as may be practicable should be afforded, and access to the London market might fairly be allowed to the Presidency banks.

CHAPTER VI

NATIVE STATES

Powers and Limitations—Historical Survey—Political Agents—The Foreign Office—Its Relations with Powers and States outside India —Persia, Arabia, Afghanistan, Tibet

THE Census report of 1901 estimates the aggregate area of the native states at 679,392 square miles, or 38 per cent. of the 1,776,597 square miles which make up the Indian Empire, the population of which is 62,461,549, out of 294,361,056 inhabitants of India, in which are not included the inhabitants of the Shan States of Burmah, the Khasia and Jaintia Hills, Manipur and Bhutan, while the area and population of Nepaul have not been properly ascertained. The native states thus comprise more than a third of the area, and support considerably less than a quarter of the population. In 52, 53, Victoria, cap. 63, it is provided that the expression India shall mean British India together with any territories of any native chief under the suzerainty of her Majesty, exercised through the Governor-General, or through any officer subordinate to him. This suzerainty, in the case of 175 states, is exercised directly by the Government of India, and in the case of 500 through provincial governments. Sir William Lee Warner explains that the generally accepted view is that suzerainty is divisible between the British Government and the ruling chief, and that, of its attributes, the right to make war or peace, and the right of foreign negotiation lies with the Government, while the right to make laws and administer justice resides in the ruling chief. No chief can therefore be properly described as independent.

By including areas left out of account by the Census Commissioner, but which for present purposes may properly be included, the area of India outside direct British dominion is upwards of 824,000 square miles, and the population 68,000,000. The size of the native states varies from that of Hyderabad, which is rather larger than Great Britain, to petty possessions of 20 square miles. The fact that in some parts of India, as in Bombay, native states are extremely numerous, amounting to 354 in number, whereas in other parts, like Madras, there are only 5, is accounted for by the conditions existing at the time the British power was consolidated. In the south, the Nizam of Hyderabad, the Nawab of the Carnatic, the Sultan of Mysore, and the Maharaja of Travancore, had swept away, or bound up into one unit, many petty chiefships and small states before the British power was established. In Bombay, on the other hand, the power of the Peshwa had been weakened, and territories were changing rulers up to the time when the Mahrattas were overthrown by the English, and the latter power recognised the *status quo*, and confirmed the holders of the moment in their otherwise precarious possessions. Most of the native states, however, are of modern origin, the most ancient being those included in Rajputana. Central India, on the contrary, is chiefly occupied by Mahratta chieftains, who were not attracted by the deserts of the Rajputs. As they moved from the Mahratta country towards Delhi, Sindhia, Holkar, and others settled at convenient stations on the way.

The Nizams of Hyderabad were already practically independent when the Emperor fell into the hands of the Mahrattas, and Mysore may be regarded as a revival by the favour of the British of an ancient Hindoo principality. Travancore and Cochin are old-world Hindoo states, which existed, as they are now, before the struggle between the French and English in the south. The Mogul emperors had not been satisfied with suzerainty over the numerous native states which existed in their day. What they desired was dominion, in the quest of which they were led to destroy the Mahomedan kingdoms of the Deccan, which, had they been preserved, might have warded off the fatal onslaught of the Mahrattas. The latter, in turn, simply desired to levy as blackmail the fourth part of the revenue of all weaker powers, and they evolved no real policy in regard to the native states before the ruin of the confederacy on the field of Panipat in 1761.

In South India, warfare with the French, and local intrigue led to the like relations with the native princes, but with the fall of Tippoo Sultan at Mysore, the Nizam and the British became united in a lasting alliance. Bengal had become part of British India with the grant of the Dewani or fiscal adminstration in 1765, and Oudh was for a time the buffer state between it and the Mahrattas. The establishment, by the Treaty of Bassein in 1802, of British influence at Poona led to war with Sindhia and Bhonsla, which was followed by a breach with Holkar, and subsequently with the Peshwa, and by the suppression of the Pindaris, at the conclusion of which, in 1818, Rajputana, Gwalior, Indore, and Nagpur were brought under the British Protectorate. The war of 1814-1816 left Nepaul independent as to its internal administration, but under the control of the Government of India in respect of its foreign relations. Sind was brought into the Company's net in 1843, and the year 1849 saw the annexation of the Punjaub. At first, the British policy was to restore conquered territory, merely retaining sufficient for their own purposes, and for the payment of expenses, but since the phantom Emperor fell under the control of the Mahrattas they ceased to acknowledge his authority, and, in the time of Lord Hastings, adopted the policy of maintaining that the British held the suzerainty of India. Between 1813 and the Mutiny, most of the existing treaties were concluded with native states, and in 1891 the British Government laid it down, in the case of Manipur, that it is its right and its duty to settle the succession in protected states. This did not, of course, imply any reaffirmation of the doctrine of lapse, the exercise of which is generally allowed to have been one of the causes of the Mutiny. It is now clearly established that the rights of chiefs as rulers will be respected, but that the British Government alone shall act for them in dealings with foreign powers and with other native states, that the inhabitants of such states are subjects of their own rulers, and that rulers and subjects are alike exempt from the laws of British India. The internal peace of the native states is also secured, and they are forbidden to employ, without permission, subjects of other European nations, while their subjects, when outside their own territory, become practically British subjects. As states which cannot make war on other states in the same position as themselves, or on foreign powers, need no army, in most treaties the military forces which they may maintain are restricted, and a provision is inserted to the effect that no factories may be erected for the production of guns and ammunition. Native states are, on the contrary, bound to render assistance to the Imperial forces. Since the time of Lord Dufferin, several of the larger units have maintained Imperial service troops which number nearly 20,000 men in all. These are under the inspection of British officers, and when placed at the disposal of the British Government are available for use in the same manner as British forces, though they belong to the states, and are recruited from its subjects. They have already done good service in China, and upon the north-west frontier. In spite of the internal independence guaranteed to the states the paramount authority claims and exercises the right to interfere to correct serious abuses, or even to administer for the time being, when sufficient reason arises. Thus the late Gaekwar of Baroda was deposed, and other instances of similar action are not wanting. The powers of the Governor-General in native states are exercised through political officers, generally called Residents, who are the sole channel of communication, and the political service is recruited from the Indian Civil Service, and from the Indian army. Residents, however, are usually appointed to native states in political relations with local governments from their own local civil service. Officers of the regular political service, having had experience in one native state after another, better grasp the fact that interference in the ordinary administration is neither desirable nor permissible, than officers appointed from the local civil service. The latter almost invariably endeavour to reproduce in the native states to which they are appointed the conditions of the British districts in which they themselves served, and they review the administration of their state as if it were a Government department of which they were the responsible heads. They are prone to establish a regular system of receiving petitions against the decisions of the officers of the state, and, in short, there is much ground for thinking that with the permission, express or implied, of the local government, they wittingly or unwittingly defeat the object of Government in preserving native states, by impairing their individuality, and, insensibly, their qualified independence. Even where the subjects of the state are prosperous and contented, officers of the character described are far too ready to regard the state as a field for the exhibition of their own administrative powers, and for the introduction of reforms. The case is still worse where it happens that the right of the chief to choose his own minister is practically taken from him, in consequence of advice tendered by the Resident or by the local government. There are always factions at these courts, one or another of which frequently gets the ear of the political agent, and able officers of the state, well fitted to become ministers to their Maharajas, may not be popular with the little European clique at the capital. The craze for reform after British patterns, whether or not required, is such that it ever points towards the expediency of bringing in outsiders. The officer thus introduced, almost invariably a capable Brahmin, who has eventually to revert to British employ and knows on which side his bread is buttered, immediately proceeds to justify his appointment by the introduction of wholesale changes in the administration, or of ambitious schemes which dissipate the cash reserves of the State, and do not necessarily add to the happiness of its inhabitants. It is of the greatest importance that the right men should be appointed to political charges, and probably few people are less suited to these offices than the ordinary collector and magistrate from British India, or the heads of the Police or Education departments, or the like, under local governments, who cannot resist the temptation to introduce into native states those principles of administration which they have always practised, at any rate to their own complete satisfaction. When once this spirit is introduced, it is most difficult to exorcise, and the ruling chief, who probably dreads its spread, is himself precluded from raising objections by the approval granted as a matter of course by the local government to every reform, which substitutes for native, British Indian methods of management. Viceroys may, and do, one after another, lay down the proper limits within which the activities of the political agent should be confined, but, however much these homilies may be taken to heart by those who have to look to the Foreign Office for promotion, they become pale and ineffectual long before they have filtered through a local government to the political agent who works under its direct authority, and need care nothing for the Foreign Office at Calcutta. It is a matter of infinite concern to those who value the precious individuality of particular states, their historic continuity, their associations, and economic and social characteristics, to see all those distinctive features which never can be restored, year by year obliterated, and everything painted a pale red colour. The education of chiefs, moreover, has not been conspicuously successful, because youths have been brought up to be English rather than Indian, and to hanker after visits to England rather than residence among their own people. The chiefs' colleges do good work, and the establishment of the Imperial Cadet Corps, though an extremely limited measure, is yet a step in the right direction. The visits of Viceroys to native states are of course most desirable, but nothing less than the strictest instructions to local governments to order their political agents to let the native states alone, and thus get the instructions of the supreme Government in this behalf carried into effect, will avail to relieve the chiefs from interference such as was not contemplated by treaty, and is not desired by the India Office or the Viceroy, to judge from the speeches, for instance, of Mr Morley and Lords Dufferin, Lansdowne, Elgin, Curzon and Minto.

The Government of India has, besides relations with the native states, foreign relations proper, which are alike dealt with by its Foreign Office. It has for instance such relations with Turkish Arabia at Baghdad, with the fortress of Aden, with Muscat, the islands of Perim and Socotra, the Persian Gulf, and parts of Persia, Afghanistan, Tibet, Siam, and China. The possession of Aden connotes control over the neighbouring Arab tribes, which is acknowledged by the Turkish Sultan, and with the Sultan of Muscat engagements have existed since 1798. Treaties also exist with the Arab chiefs who dwell upon the shores of the Persian Gulf, wherein the British put down slavery, and wherein they have an interest of a character owned by no other power. The Sheikh of Koweit is under a treaty of obligation with the Government of India, and the contemplated construction of a railway from Asia Minor to the Gulf, by Baghdad and Busra, renders the possession of, or suzerainty over, his small territory of great importance. A political resident is maintained at Baghdad in order to look after Indian interests in and around the Persian Gulf and in Turkish Arabia. Britain has also preserved the independence of the Sheikh of Bassein, the centre of the famous pearl fishery, who has entered into a perpetual treaty of peace and friendship with us. Persian affairs are now under the control of the British Foreign Office, and though the mission to the Shah's Court was at one time maintained out of Indian revenues, after various changes, in 1900 the Royal Commission on Indian Expenditure récommended that the charges for legations and consulates in Persia should be evenly divided between India and the United Kingdom. The Protectorate over Beluchistan was established in 1855, and in 1857, after the despatch of an expedition under Sir James Outram to the Persian Gulf, the Shah of Persia undertook to resign all claims on Herat or any part of Afghanistan, and in the event of differences arising with the Amir to refer them for adjustment to the British. Under this agreement, the frontiers between Persia and Beluchistan and Afghanistan have been delimited. Of all the foreign relations of the Government of India, those with Afghanistan are of the greatest importance. The late Amir enjoyed a personal subsidy of twelve lakhs* of rupees

* A lakh of rupees is £6666.

a year, to which six more were added when, in 1893, the Durand agreement was negotiated which, like all others, has been continued with Abdul Rahman's son and successor, Habibullah. An Indian Mahomedan represents the Governor-General at the Court of the Amir, who in turn sends an envoy to the Government of India.

Tibet is under the suzerainty of the Chinese Government to which a nominal poll-tax is paid, but the government is in the hands of Buddhist ecclesiastics, who forbid any foreigners to settle in the country. In 1888, a collision occurred with the Tibetans, and in 1890 a convention was concluded with China providing for commercial facilities, subsequent to which, in 1895, delegates were appointed for the demarcation of the frontier, to which the Tibetans declined to submit. After much negotiation Colonel Younghusband, the British Commissioner, proceeded to Khamba Jong, but the Tibetans resisted his progress. In 1904, however, the expedition advanced to Gyantsi, where the Tibetans attacked it, when the fort was captured, and Sir F. Younghusband advanced to Lhassa, where a treaty, to which China assented, was signed in 1906.

The long land frontier between Burma and China necessarily leads to communications between the two Imperial Governments concerned. Since 1875, the Home Government has paid two-thirds of the cost of this diplomatic intercourse, and now a fixed contribution is annually made on this account by India. As to our boundaries with Siam, a joint commission in 1892-1893 settled the frontier line from the Mekong to Victoria Point, and Great Britain and France agreed to respect the integrity of the central districts of Siam in the Menam Valley, France recognising Great Britain's influence in the territory west of the basin of the Menam, in the Malay Peninsula, and over the adjacent islands. Foreign possessions in India are now limited to five small settlements belonging to the French, of which Pondicherry and Chandernagore are the chief, and three small settlements of the Portuguese, of which Goa is the most important.

CHAPTER VII

RUSSIA IN THE EAST

In Central Asia—In the Middle East—North-West Frontier of Lord Curzon—Of Lord Elgin—Anglo-Russian Convention—Tibet Affairs—Baghdad Railway

IT is now nearly seven years since an English translation was published of the record of the Eastern travels of the present Czar, when Cesarevitch, in 1890-1891. I was familiar with the Russian original, and was surprised to see that so frank a revelation of Russian policy was, after some delay, published in English. The powerful Minister Li Hung Chang, at the instance of the author, Prince Esper Ukhtomsky, telegraphed to the late Czar, expressing the gratitude of China at the action of Russia in permitting the Emperor to resume the civil government of Manchuria under Russian protection. Events have marched since then, but Manchuria was held at that time to have already undergone a process of painless identification with Russia. Prince Esper was well known in Petersburg to have the ear of the Cesarevitch, now Czar, who after he succeeded to the throne is reported to have said: "People begin to recognise the merits of Ukhtomsky." What then did Ukhtomsky say in his record of the travels of the heir-apparent? In Benares his prophetic eye saw "the religious centre of an independent India, of federated states, which would have been the outcome of Mahratta supremacy but for the action of a handful of strangers from the West, in consequence of whose predominance the peninsula lay crushed and dumb under the burden of exotic universities, and extensive social and administrative reforms carried out with all the blind energy of self-sufficient ignorance." There is something in this, though the Congress critics would not agree to the condemnation of the universities, for their only objection is to the standard of education being kept up to an inconvenient pitch. "To the English," it seems, "the spiritual life of the races they govern, remains, and must always remain, a sealed book. Russia, in reality, conquered nothing in the East, but only knitted closer the bonds between them and what, in reality, was always theirs!" The Prince pities the women of India, who are sufficiently unfashionable to be contented with their husbands and their lot in life.

Already, in 1890, he praises the Bengalis for their conscious resistance to an inimical foreign culture, which, on the contrary, we know they rapidly assimilate without digesting, and he noted that though "lying crushed and dumb" they had a wholesale permission to think, speak, and write what they pleased, which would strike anyone familiar with life in St Petersburg as extraordinary. Prince Esper, however, foresaw that in the future "Asiatic Russia would mean all Asia." He did grasp, as some of our critics do not, that irrigation was being gradually brought to perfection, though he "reflected with sorrow on the abnormal and ephemeral predominance of a single power in the submissive East," and he looked forward to a process of painless identification with Russia, spreading southward from China, but to no invasion from the north-west frontier, for, said he, "no one has any intention of attacking England in Asia." However unjust he was to the British, he saw some things clearly, and urged that the introduction of progressive and purely Western ideas into the social system of the natives would only be prejudicial to them, and to the prestige of their guardians. Again and again he denies that Russia has any designs upon the north-west frontier of India, in spite of England's cherished, deeply-rooted, though totally unfounded conviction on this point. "But what calls up a smile to Russian lips appears a real threat to Albion and is of some advantage to Russia." It is indeed a disadvantage to Indian finances, upon which an inroad is made, whenever a fresh attack of what used to be called nervousness seizes the British Government or the British people.

The Japanese already in 1890 seemed "very unconscious of the spiritual relationship of Russia with all the peoples of the East," but Ukhtomsky predicted "that they would soon doff the mask of friendship with the English. Russia alone could protect Corea and save China from dismemberment and there were no bounds to Russian dominions in Asia but the boundless sea."

While the Prince actually told the world the literal fact that China, and not the north-west frontier, was the Russian objective, and while, like all his countrymen, he erred as regards the future of Manchuria and Japan, he has probably told the truth regarding Russian designs upon the north-west frontier, and he certainly was right in saying that "all goes well in India when no one interferes with the life of the people, and the natural course of events is left to itself," babudom not being such natural course, but the irregular flight of the product of ill digested university teaching. When he inquires whether our military charges are not too high, seeing that no one has any intention of attacking us in Asia, he asks a question that is being put by a great many Englishmen, who may say, *fas est et ab hoste doceri*, though the present situation in India does not lead prudent men to think that it would be safe to reduce the white garrison below the standard fixed after the Mutiny. But what has Russia's progress been in Central Asia? Ever since the Khan of Khiva placed himself under her protection in 1740, she has been marching towards India and Afghanistan, but it was upwards of a century later that her soldiers constructed Fort Perovsk, commenced hostilities with the Khan of Khokand, and seized Tashkent. In 1868 General Kaufman occupied Samarcand, the most famous city of Central Asia, and the valley of the Zarafshan, the gold scatterer, or Eastern Pactolus.

Prince Gortchakoff explained in 1864 that Russia in Central Asia was a civilised power, in contact with half-civilised tribes, over which it was compelled to exercise ascendency; that expeditions thus became unavoidable, and if the Czar were content with chastising the freebooters, and then retiring, the lesson would be soon forgotten, retreat being ascribed to weakness, for Asiatics respect only visible and palpable force. This was the truth, the whole truth, and nothing but the truth, and it would have been better if we had realised it more fully ourselves. At the present moment we are paying allowances, which are regarded by the recipients as, and really are, blackmail, to practically every tribe dwelling on the Indian side of the Durand boundary line; and after every punitive expedition, followed by a retreat, the allowances of the offending tribes are raised to encourage others to do likewise. We are responsible for all territory up to the Durand line, and we should sternly repress every rising upon our side of it, and in no case ever increase the allowances of any of the tribes. As lately as 1897 it took 60,000 of our best troops to re-establish order on the frontier, and we have no guarantee whatever that the tribes we subsidise with Indian gold would keep the march for us if they were offered better terms elsewhere. We do know something about "Afreedi, Hazara and Ghilzai who clamour for plunder or bribes," we know that we can never engage their affections, and we should frankly adopt as our motto, *oderint dum metuant*.

To return to the Russians. In 1873 Count Schouvaloff assured our Government that they had no intention of taking Khiva, which immediately afterwards was taken. The Central Asian Khanates were thus absorbed. The Russians realised the necessity of inspiring fear among the natives, and their ruthless conquest of the Tekke Turkomans probably caused less loss of life in the long run than our policy of butcher and bolt, for in every one of our punitive expeditions the women and children, who are sent up into the hills, suffer untold hardships. Nothing is so humane as severity leading to fear and peace, nothing so inhuman as weakness resulting in slaughter. When the frontiers of Russian Turkestan were bounded by Persia, Afghanistan, and Chinese Turkestan, that stage in the expansion of Russia was reached at which demarcation of boundaries became necessary. The determination of the Afghan frontier by a joint commission in 1885 proved a difficult business, the

Russians being determined to push down from Merv to the slopes of the Paropamisus, and the neighbourhood of Herat. It is probable that Britain has been, as she had so often been before, bluffed by Russia over the Panjdeh incident, but at any rate no serious differences have occurred since the settlement then effected. Nor, since we have again and again made remonstrances, without any intention of backing them up by arms, a practice no State is powerful enough to indulge in without falling into contempt, was it surprising that the Russians marched at will almost within sight of the holy Persian city of Mashad, of the key of Afghanistan, Herat, to the banks of the "broad and yellow Oxus," and right up to the roof of the world in the Pamir steppes, and into the most fertile valleys of Kashgaria.

Mr David Fraser, who has lately travelled along the marches of Hindustan, has collected some valuable statistics in regard to the population, acreage, and economic conditions of Russian Turkestan. He finds the population of the five provinces and the two native states, Bokhara and Khiva, to be in the aggregate 8,470,000, and the acreage under cultivation 7,400,000, of which 1,500,000 are under cotton, the growing of which, in Central Asia, Russia encourages, herself supplying from Orenburg grain, of which there is insufficient in Turkestan. Besides the 7,400,000 acres (or 11,000 square miles) under cultivation, there are 140,000 square miles of indifferent pasture land, and 700,000 square miles of irreclaimable desert. It is, therefore, economically speaking, a very poor country.

Mr Fraser also supplies the latest statistics of the military strength of Russia in Turkestan. He writes that Kushk, the most forward point of Russian territory, is equipped with a special transport corps and a siege train, and that the total of the Russian troops in Central Asia is a peace strength of 57,787, and a war strength of 99,247 men, consisting of infantry, cavalry, horse, field, and mountain artillery, sappers, fortress companies and field guns. But the size of the army maintained is not so much a matter for consideration as the strength of the army which Russia could send to, and maintain within, her territories in Central Asia. The railway from the Caspian Sea to the Persian frontier passes through an arid desert, but water is obtained by distillation from the Caspian, and after running along the frontier from Askabad to Kiakhta, the line passes over two streams before reaching Merv. The railway between Samarcand and Tashkent, and Tashkent and Orenburg also suffers from want of water supply. Without these railways the transport of troops in sufficient numbers to menace Afghanistan would be impossible. In existing circumstances, armies could be placed on the Afghan frontier, only limited by the carrying power of the line, which is estimated to be double that of the Siberian railways, by which hundreds of thousands of men were placed in the field in the war with Japan.

From Krasnovodsk on the Caspian to Orenburg the railway is 2300 miles long and a branch runs from Merv to the hills commanding Herat, as well as another branch to Andijan near the frontier of Chinese Kashgaria. A fourth branch has been surveyed, and it is believed can be laid down speedily and without difficulty, from Samarcand or Bokhara, to Termes on the Oxus, close to the Afghan provincial capital of Balkh. At Orenburg, the railway system is joined up with that of Russia, and with the trans-Siberian line, while at Krasnovodsk it is in steamer communication with Baku, the Caucasian garrison, and the railway to Moscow. The new Orenburg-Tashkent line doubles the strategical strength of Russia in Central Asia, and, though the lines are single, all the stations, which are about fifteen miles apart, have double sidings, so that pairs of trains can be run. Mr Fraser estimates that as many as thirty-six trains per day could possibly be passed through from Krasnovodsk and Orenburg to the point of concentration if sufficient rolling stock were available. It would, however, be absolutely necessary, in order to send a large army to the Afghan frontier, to supplement the Merv-Kushk line by a railway such as that from Samarcand to Termes. The standard upon which depends the question of Imperial defence for Britain is practically decided by the number of men required for the protection of India, so that this problem is one which immediately affects Great Britain, though the fact is little appreciated by the people of this country, who regard, or affect to regard, problems of Indian defence as isolated and remote. Yet the Russo-Japanese War taught us no lesson of so much importance as this, that Russia, quite unexpectedly and without preparation, plunged into war, ten months after its commencement had upwards of 400,000 men in the field in the Far East, and that these troops had been transported and maintained, in practical efficiency, by one thin line of railway of enormous length. At the lowest computation, not less than 25,000 men, with the necessary stores, per month must have been despatched from Western Russia to the Far East, and no less than twelve pairs of trains every twenty-four hours were successfully forwarded over the line. Russia's offensive power on the Afghan frontier would be at least double that which enabled her to maintain gigantic armies in the Far East, and the distance to the point of concentration would be about one-third of that which intervenes between the Ural Mountains and Manchuria. Evidently then, Russia could easily maintain an army of 400,000 men on what, after all, is practically the Indian, and not only the Afghan, frontier. She could take Herat whenever she pleased, and no man could safely prophesy what, in that contingency, would be the attitude of the Afghans and the frontier tribes, or even of some of our subjects in India.

The portfolio of the Foreign Department of the Government of India is always held by the Viceroy, and during Lord Curzon's practically double tenure of office many important events occurred in this domain. Lord Lansdowne had strengthened the defences of the north-west frontier, had encouraged the native chiefs to institute and maintain Imperial service corps, and he was able to maintain peace by skilful, tactful, and straightforward diplomacy. In Lord Curzon's term of office, the death took place of the Amir Abdul Rahman, which was followed by the peaceful succession of his son, Habibullah, and in his time the Seistan boundaries, and those of Aden hinterland were delimited. Lord Curzon frustrated the desire of France to obtain a coaling station at Muscat, and of the Porte to extend Turkish authority over the chiefs of the Hadramut, and over the Khan of Koweit, whose territory will become of great importance if the Baghdad railway ever becomes an accomplished fact. However Koweit and Mohammerah are now safe. Lord Curzon also recognised that various influences were undermining the British position in South Persia, and he broke new ground by making a tour in that direction. Those who can see no good in him or his works allege that, had he not opened the Quetta-Nuskhi route to Seistan, Russia would have let the Gulf alone. However that may be, they despatched battleships to the Gulf, appointed consular agents, and drew up a new tariff with no friendly intent towards us, and no doubt they had a coaling station in view, notwithstanding Lord Lansdowne's spirited and satisfactory pronouncement, that such would be regarded as an unfriendly act.

The Middle Eastern question, to use Mr Chirols' now universally adopted designation, formerly concerned Afghanistan and the Central Asian Khanates. It now includes the contest for political supremacy over Tibet, and the integrity of Persia, as well as the everlasting question of the north-west frontier, for it is hardly possible for the Government of India without loss of respect supinely to ignore everything that happens immediately outside its own administrative boundary. The exigencies of the party system in England perhaps inevitably commit them to the policy of endeavouring to cultivate friendly relations with the tribes, however difficult of attainment this may be, and at any rate to the avoidance of all aggressive measures towards them, from which it follows that it is desirable as far as possible to police tribal territory with local levies, under the command of British officers.

Lord Elgin claimed to have followed a policy of non-annexation and non-interference, in order to avoid any extension of administrative control over independent tribal territory. In his time, the Government of India was committed to a policy involving a large outlay for fortifications, and the extension of garrisons at forward stations, but Lord Curzon's Government adopted, with the approval of the India Office, a policy of which the three cardinal principles were to avoid locking up regular garrisons in costly fortified positions away from our base, to interest the inhabitants of each district or base, whence such garrisons were withdrawn, in their own defence, and to establish a lien on their loyalty by enrolling them as tribal forces for local garrison work, to maintain a movable column ready to march to the relief of the tribal garrisons, on or near the administrative frontier of India, and to connect the frontier cantonment with each Indian garrison, by light railways pushed forward from the existing railway systems. This policy, unpopular with the more ardent military spirits, but grateful to the taxpayer, was successfully followed, and intimately connected with it was the creation of the North-West Frontier Province. In describing his policy, Lord Curzon wrote: "It may be said that every change in the frontier of India subsequent to 1877 has been dictated, not by considerations affecting the Punjaub Government, but by Imperial considerations, and by them alone." He no doubt used the word "imperial," in this instance, in its Indian, and not in its all-British aspect. The Indian and the British budgets are distinct, and the question will some day arise whether India is always to pay the bill, as frontiers are pushed farther and farther west, after so much of the Afghan Hills has been annexed, and Beluchistan added to the empire, when the flank has been turned, and the frontier appears still farther west in Seistan, in Fars, in Arabistan and in the Persian Gulf. What battleships, floating batteries, and repairing docks might have been created with the money poured out uselessly, as might now be urged, in fortifying the already naturally fortified Quetta! What valuable aid has not been thrown away by the wanton insults unceasingly and causelessly hurled at Mahomedan sovereign and subjects in Turkey! Not only does our policy need definition, but our public men and Members of Parliament need disciplining, if we are to continue to hold our lofty position in the world. No nation can afford to wantonly alienate its neighbours, least of all a nation ruling over many races of many religions.

As to a Russian invasion through Afghanistan, the great Napoleon thought it impracticable, and the Duke of Wellington said that troops would force their way through this wild country, only to find the commencement of their difficulties. Sir Neville Chamberlain, Sir John Adye, and Sir Donald Stewart have expressed the same opinions. We have more reason to fear the economic invasion of Persia by Russia, which is stimulating the import of Russian goods by a system of bounties of 15 to 20 per cent. *ad valorem*; has conceded to them special rebates and railway rates, and has succeeded in ruining the promising trade by the Quetta-Nushki route to Seistan and Eastern Persia. In 1903 it was apparent that Russia already dominated Northern Persia, and had been steadily advancing while we were marking time, in some, and retrograding in other, quarters: that she was furnished with well-trained agents, and encouraged acquaintance with native languages, which the Government of India does not particularly favour: that Russia's commercial, was equal to her political, progress, and that each subserved the other; that it past, would prove equal in the future, to safeguarding our interests, while European populations seeking an outlet increased in numbers, and naval states waxed strong and prospered; that Persia rather than Afghanistan was the danger point, that it was necessary to show that the south and east of that country were within our exclusive sphere of political influence; that the assertion of political predominance in south, south-west, and particularly south-eastern Persia was an object of Imperial significance, and a proper call upon Imperial funds, that our position in the East Indies, including the Gulf, required a larger squadron and repairing yard, that the maintenance of a supremely powerful navy was all important, since the defence of the coast and of the land frontier depends on the navy, which must keep open communication and bring reinforcements, and by which, in fact, and not by individual battles in India, as is generally represented, our eastern empire was won, and by which it must be retained.

It was in consequence of considerations such as these, or at any rate of some of them, that the Anglo-Russian Convention, if not the Anglo-Japanese Alliance, was effected. Russia was established on the glacis of the natural mountain fortifications, and on the bank of the river boundary of our Indian Empire and its protected neighbour. Persia, suffering from internal disorder, frontier disputes, and political unrest, might at any moment call for, or offer an opportunity for, armed intervention; the position of Russia in the north of that ancient kingdom was already assured, and it was our obvious interest to make an agreement recognising and prolonging existing conditions, while Russia, weakened by her reverses in the Far, had

The hour was propitious, and the Convention was signed on 31st August 1907. It contained arrangements on the subject of Persia, Afghanistan, and Tibet, important in each case, satisfactory in some, disappointing in other, respects, but on the whole proved to be a valuable instrument, and, provided it always has a sufficient backing of battalions and battleships, one which should conduce to peace and progress. Since it has been evident, as it has been for some years, that Russia's plan was to turn the flank of our north-west frontier by the peaceful penetration of Persia down to the Gulf, the Afghan Frontier has ceased to be the storm centre it was, and the provisions of the Convention regarding Persia must be regarded chiefly in the light of Indian frontier interests, though a trade of £4,000,000 sterling a year is affected, and by no means favourably affected, by the terms secured. It is characteristic of the prevailing extraordinary want of elementary comprehension of our position in the East that this aspect of the case has attracted least attention in England, and even well-informed and able critics like Colonel Yate and Mr Lynch appear to attach perhaps overdue weight to the Persian provisions, as if they were the terms of an isolated agreement, and not part of a whole. As an agreement regarding Persia only, it would be impossible to approve its provisions. The shores and hinterland of the Gulf, in which we are as well established as Russia is in Northern Persia, are not retained within our sphere of influence, nor the important trade routes which directly or indirectly serve Southern Persia, the Kermanshah-Hamadan and the Korun-Mohammerah approaches to the Tigris and the Gulf. Ispahan should have been neutral, Shiraz ours, and a line from east to west should have given us what is south, as Russia has what lies north, of the salt desert. But we are by treaty assured of equal commercial opportunity, for what such a provision is worth, and it hardly appears that the delimitation of spheres leaves our trade at the mercy of Russia in neutral zones, wherein either power merely engages not to oppose the grant of concessions to the other's subjects. Nor as regards railway concessions can we be placed in a worse position than we already occupied. It is certainly unfortunate that our position in the Gulf is not a feature, and the chief feature, and in part the *raison d'être* of the Convention, though it is mentioned in the Parliamentary paper that the Russian Government in the course of the negotiations explicitly stated that they did not deny the special interests of Great Britain in the Persian Gulf, which were not mentioned only because the arrangement was limited to the regions of that country touching the respective frontiers of Great Britain and Russia in Asia. But by the Convention the integrity and independence of Persia are guaranteed and this in itself is a feature of paramount importance, and should stay the completion of the already far advanced Russification of the country, which we had found ourselves powerless to prevent. It is difficult to deal seriously with objections raised to this Convention by politician's, who claim for Great Britain a right to influence the internal administration of independent countries, or to determine that we should not enter into engagements with such countries, unless in their opinion they reach certain ideal standards of humanitarianism, or display a proper preference for that form of Government which happens to suit ourselves, but as to the adaptability of which to Russia and Persia those acquainted with these countries entertain considerable doubts. At any rate it can hardly be gravely contended that empty solicitude and cheap sympathy are worth paying for by the loss of engagements making for the material benefit of ourselves and of the other parties to the bond. It makes no difference to us whether Persia and Russia are autocracies or democracies provided they keep the peace and do business, and it is not clear what we obtain except the hearty dislike of other nations by assuming that none of them are equal to the task of managing their own affairs, and that all of them are wanting in ordinary humanity. The great point is that Russia's march towards the Gulf through Seistan is stopped short, and so long as the spirit of the present agreement is observed, and the assurance regarding the Gulf itself remains effectual, the danger of having the flank of our north-west frontier turned is averted. It is a painful process to try to bring home to the British electorate that Eastern policy is not a matter of the pomp and circumstance of war, but of preserving in the Middle East and in India those markets upon which we are so dependent, and of keeping the peace, with which the amount of taxation we have to pay, is so closely connected.

As regards Afghanistan the Convention can hardly be attacked with success, for the country is recognised as outside the sphere of Russian influence, and a favourable verdict on this score must cover the Persian sub-issue. Objection has been taken to the grant of equality of commercial opportunity, which certainly is the last thing we get from Russia, but neither political party could be expected to insist upon a reciprocity in Asia which does not exist in Europe. It is, of course, in some sense disappointing that we exact no better terms from Russia than we should have considered fair had her career of conquest continued, but all agreements must be construed in the light of existing facts, and she never relaxed a sinew in Central Asia, through the desperate and disastrous struggle with Japan. The inhabitants of Russian Turkestan have been let alone, not over-taxed, over-sanitated, or over-occidentalised, and they have shown their gratitude recently in an unconventional manner by offering to massacre an energetic minority of revolutionaries, which desires to force upon them the suffrage and autonomy. One of the latest, and by no means the least capable of writers, Mr Angus Hamilton roundly declared, in 1905, that Russia was already the supreme and dominating factor, not only along the northern, eastern, and western frontiers of, but throughout, Afghanistan, and that Russian trade, thanks to good roads, railways, protection, low customs, rebates, and special rail and steamer rates, had everywhere crushed out British competition. Surely, if this be only partially true, as it no doubt is, or was, the Convention concerning Afghanistan is eminently satisfactory, and it is impossible to agree with the Bombay press that we have lost much (in Persia) and gained nothing (elsewhere), though it must be admitted that the regions defined to lie within our sphere of influence in Persia are such, that few indeed are the concessions which are likely to be sought within their limits.

It was anticipated as regards Tibet that the Convention could and would only confirm the policy of Mr Balfour's Government, which decided to veto the appointment of a Resident at Lhassa, to recognise the suzerainty of China, and to pledge itself to the evacuation of the Chumbi Valley. Lord Curzon indeed has characterised as a novelty in international diplomacy the neutralising pledge made by two Powers, one of which is, and the other is not, contiguous with Tibet, which is not a buffer state between Great Britain and Russia. Russia is, however, contiguous with the Chinese Empire, of which Tibet is a vassal state, though it may readily be conceded that her interests are small compared with our own. The Convention gives away, however, as regards Tibet, nothing which had not previously been abandoned, in which are included most of the fruits of the expedition. That much-criticised operation had at least this justification, that Tibet refused to observe the provisions of a previous treaty granting certain trading facilities to British subjects, and it is common ground that the Dalai Lama, or the Junta of Buddhist monks, of which he is the nominal head, wished to cut the country clear from China, to have no communication with India, and to enter into closer friendly relations with Russia, the special mission to which, of 1901, was explained to have no political significance. When the Viceroy complained of the non-performance of the previous treaty the Dalai Lama returned his letters unopened, and refused to negotiate. Lord Curzon therefore despatched a mission to Khamba Jong across the border, and, as no satisfaction was offered, it advanced to Lhassa. Now that holy city is the very heart of the religious life of vast regions in Central Asia, and its rulers possess in consequence a very great political influence notwithstanding the degraded and debased kind of Buddhism of which they are the official representatives. Nor is this influence confined to Central Asia. It is felt all through the Himalayan region, in Nepaul, Sikkim and Bhutan, states in which we are in varying degrees interested, and the first of which supplies us with 20,000 first-rate soldiers. Though the ruler of Nepaul is Hindoo, Buddhism is the traditional religion of the people, the tie with Tibet is strong, if sentimental, and our relations with this state forbid our being indifferent to what passes in the latter state, especially when a nation nominally Buddhist has become the most powerful in the East. Japan and China are hardly Buddhist nations, but they are Buddhist enough to feel some sense of solidarity with Lhassa. Nor was it by any means clear that the Russians were not establishing their influence in this hermit kingdom, in which all that is required is maintenance of British influence and prestige, a task which is not rendered easier by the pledge the late Government gave, and the present administration necessarily has repeated, not to send a representative to Lhassa, than which the maintenance of a trade agent at Gyantse is a matter of less political moment. Not that Tibet is by any means a despicable commercial asset. It is, rather, full of potentialities and possibilities, and with a better Government would inevitably take a very different place in the world of trade. The population was once greater than it now is; there is abundance of pasturage, and much business might be done in wool, cattle, hides, and minerals, and already the total trade with India is valued at £250,000 a year, and the Government of the latter country is actively occupied in improving communications with its hitherto isolated neighbour. It was not to be expected that the present Government would undo that which the last administration had done, but the few facts above recorded will suffice at any rate to expose the folly of the accusation brought against the Indian Government, which was unanimous in approving the despatch of the mission, of having attacked Tibet in a spirit of wanton aggression or vain Imperialism.

The Convention was generally well received by the press of foreign countries, that of Germany holding that the commercial interests of their country are by it in no way prejudiced. Nevertheless, Great Britain was accused of endeavouring to convert the Gulf into a second Suez Canal, and Koweit, and the Euphrates region, with the Baghdad railway, into a second Egypt. The last-mentioned project is one of very great importance. The Germans having a concession for the construction of a line from the Taurus to the Persian Gulf, Great Britain had assented to an increase of three per cent. in the Turkish customs duties, most of which will fall on her own trade, for the ostensible benefit of Macedonia, the empty sympathy of the Powers with which province only serves to inflame the natural resentment the Turks feel at such interference, and to turn it upon the head of their subjects. There is no guarantee that the money thus raised will not liberate other funds so as to enable the Porte to give the desired kilometric guarantee, and to pay interest on the capital required for the construction of the next section of the line. In any case, if the money is found, German though the concession be, and, non-English as the capital may prove, it should be a *sine quâ non* that England should have the control of the Baghdad-Gulf section, or that the whole line should be internationalised. The case is, in fact, political rather than commercial, and care has been taken in the concession to provide against the construction of the Gulf section except as a part of, and subject to the same conditions as, the rest of the railway which is to be taken up section by section in consecutive order. If once this line is made under German control, Germany might turn the flank of our north-west frontier defences, just as Russia contemplated doing before the execution of the recent Convention stopped further railway construction on her part towards the Gulf. Sir Edward Grey admitted last session that this was, or might become, a subject of considerable importance to all those Powers which have possessions in the Middle East, but he was not prepared to make any statement on the subject. For the present the project hangs fire, but it is one which will need constant watching, and the desire of Germany to develop and consolidate her already great influence in Asia Minor will not be in any way lessened by the agreement just concluded with Russia in respect of Persia, in which she has at present no such great interests as to justify her in taking any exception to an arrangement to which she is no party, but which may be regarded by her as in some measure excluding her future participation in Persian commerce and politics.

CHAPTER VIII

UNREST

Our System of Education the Chief Cause—The Defeat of Lord Curzon over the Army Question—The Appointment of the Police Commission—The Support of the Home Branch of the Congress and of Members of Parliament, and of certain British Newspapers—The Plague—Preventive Measures—Prohibition of Religious Fairs—Acquittal of Murderers of Mr Blomfield—The Partition of Bengal —*Svadeshi* and *Svaraj*—*Bande Mataram*—Mr O'Donnell—Sir H. Cotton—Mr Keir Hardie's Visit

OF all the causes of the unrest which has of late unhappily prevailed in India, the chief, of course, is the system of education, which we ourselves introduced—advisedly so far as the limited vision went of those responsible, blindly in view of the inevitable consequences. It is not too much to say that in our schools pupils imbibe sedition with their daily lessons: they are fed with Rousseau, Macaulay, and the works of philosophers, which even in Oxford tend to pervert the minds of students to socialistic and impractical dreams, and in India work with far greater force upon the naturally metaphysical minds of youths, generally quick to learn by rote, for the most part penniless, and thus rendered incapable of earning their living, except by taking service of a clerical character under rulers, whom they denounce as oppressors unless they receive a salary at their hands.

The malcontents created by this system have neither respect for, nor fear of, the Indian Government. Nor is this surprising, for the literature upon which they are brought up in our schools is fulfilled with destructive criticism of any system of Government founded upon authority, and the encouragement given in many quarters to the Congress has necessarily confirmed them in their contempt for a system which fans a flame intended to burn it to ashes.

Happily, however, it is not the case that educated Indians, as such, are necessarily hostile to the British, though when subjected as they are, and all India is, to Brahminical influences they are liable to become, and too often do become, actively disloyal, the voice of the educated classes and of the Brahmins being practically one and the same thing.

Various other occurrences tended to intensify the feelings of disaffection engendered in the manner above described. For the first time in British-Indian history the Viceroy and Governor-General, hitherto regarded as the all-powerful agent of a sovereign ruling by divine right—for Indians recognise no mere parliamentary title—had engaged in a pitched battle with the Commander-in-Chief of the Forces, and had been beaten. More than that, his correspondence with the Secretary of State on this subject had, to the general astonishment, been published, so that all might know exactly what had occurred, and, incidentally, the administrative partition of Bengal had been mentioned in such wise as almost to justify those who resented this measure in thinking that the Home Government had sanctioned it, at least as much because Lord Curzon desired to bring it about, as because they were themselves persuaded of its necessity.

Then Lord Curzon's Government had, with the best

intentions, and perhaps upon sufficient grounds, taken a step which inevitably increased the prevailing disposition to disregard established authority. He had appointed a commission to overhaul the police, who are after all the outward and visible signs of authority, in vast areas, for instance in the greater part of Eastern Bengal, in which a British soldier is never, and a sepoy rarely, seen. The police are by no means an ideally perfect body. There must be among a large force, necessarily receiving small pay, some, perhaps many, black sheep. Still, they are probably on the whole by no means unsuitable for the work they have to perform, and their delinquencies have been grossly exaggerated by the classes, who have used them as a pawn in the game of disaffection. To appoint a commission was to publicly allow that in the eyes of the Government they needed radical reform, and did not possess the confidence of their masters. So another proof of law and order went by the board in popular estimation.

Nor were causes wanting in England. No sooner was the General Election of 1906 over, than a meeting was held at the instance of Sir William Wedderburn to reconstruct the Indian Parliamentary Committee, and to consider "what action might be taken in the new Parliament to advance the interests of the Indian people." Sir William spoke of their great dissatisfaction with their condition, and said the way to improve matters was to work upon the lines of the Indian National Congress. Sir Henry Cotton, not to be outdone in misrepresenting the position, said "the election of an overwhelming Liberal majority had roused in India hopes and aspirations, and the people were trembling in hope that due consideration would now be given to their wishes." He advised his friends to go on agitating, but to adhere to constitutional methods. But the grave anxiety, which speeches such as those have not tended to alleviate, is lest these methods, whatever they may be, should pass into a dangerous phase of discontent and disaffection. The advice of Sir W. Wedderburn, the extra-parliamentary chief of the Congress party in England, has been taken, and a few members of Parliament who serve under this banner have left no opportunity unused in order to promote the aims and objects of the Congress.

For instance, they voted against Mr Morley and the Government on Mr Keir Hardie's motion that the salary of the Secretary of State should be brought upon the estimates, and persistently questioned Mr Morley regarding the deportation of Lajpat Rai to which of course, they objected, asked for the repeal of the Regulation of 1818, as inconsistent with the principles of Liberalism, and for the appointment of a royal commission. The Regulation was denounced as wholly unparalleled in the British Empire. As a fact, however, in the East Africa Protectorate an order in Council authorises the deportation of any person who, in the opinion of the administration, conducts himself so as to be dangerous to the peace, and good order of British East Africa. In native states in India such power is always taken, and not infrequently exercised, an instance having occurred quite recently in Hyderabad. The brothers Natu were, moreover, dealt with under this Regulation not many years since in the Bombay Presidency, and it will probably be found that in the agency tracts of the Madras Presidency instances of its use have recurred at irregular intervals to the close of last century.

Strong attacks were also made on Reuter's Agency, which the agitators in India were unable to muzzle, and which has done good public service by faithfully reporting events from Calcutta. Mr Morley refused to depart from the attitude he had taken up regarding Lala Lajpat Rai, and said that he saw no cause for apology in the use made of the Regulation of 1818, though he would be the first to rejoice when its application would no longer be necessary, and as a fact he released the two agitators, Lala Lajpat Rai and Ajit Singh, when they had been detained for about six months.

Nor were the anti-British agitators without support in England other than that afforded by the British branch of the Congress, and their supporters in and out of Parliament.

At Oxford a University India Society has been formed, one of the objects of which is the discussion of the advisability of introducing representative government. At its meeting, addresses were delivered by Sir W. Wedderburn and Mr Gokhale, when the latter said that "if the Indians had to choose between gratitude for the past and duty to their own people there could only be one choice." This was mild for the speaker, but it would do him good to try the effect of a speech on similar lines at a Russian university. At Cambridge also there is an Indian Club, which is believed to be none too loyal, and the same may be said of Edinburgh, where till now Indian students have been left like lost dogs to wander at will, a state of affairs which an influential committee now seeks to amend, by providing a club under responsible and respectable management.

In Dublin and elsewhere violent attacks were

published upon the Government of India, which in September prohibited the introduction into that country of *Justice*, *The Gaelic American*, and *The Indian Sociologist*, the last-named organ at any rate richly deserving to be excluded, whatever may be the character of the other two. The editor, an M.A. of Oxford, is described as the President of the Indian Home Rule Society, which is no doubt some association designed to tamper with the loyalty of young Indians in this country. Inasmuch as this person has, of course falsely, described himself, because he is a subject of a native state, as owing no allegiance to Britain, it is to be regretted that he is not deprived of the hospitality he abuses, by being expelled as an undesirable alien.

Mr Morley has appointed a committee to consider what can be done to afford to Indian students protection from agitators, who lie in wait for them, and provide them with lodgings, the atmosphere of which reeks with disloyalty to the British Crown.

Among other causes of the unrest must also be reckoned the measures taken to stamp out plague in Bombay Presidency and the prohibition of the holding of great assemblages of pilgrims at religious shrines during the prevalence of cholera. It is not the case that the salt-tax, lately twice reduced, provoked opposition, for it is no new thing, but was an important source of revenue under the Moguls. Its levy therefore is not resented and illicit manufacture and smuggling have declined, while consumption has increased, so that the tax evidently does not press hardly upon the people, though the Deccani Brahmin, and the Bengali Babu naturally say it does, in order to discredit the British Government, who get little else by way of revenue from many millions, who profit by its existence.

Among the agricultural population there is as yet no serious discontent; it is among the town dwellers and the artisans that the seditious speakers and writers find support, and only among Hindoos in the towns. There is, however, and must always be, a certain solidarity of Indians against Europeans, which Brahmins can easily divert towards disaffection, and though they are the natural and intellectual leaders of the people they have now joined hands with anti-Brahminical societies, such as the Arya Samaj, which was at the root of the agitation in the Punjaub. This sect or society accepts the Vedas as the only, and when rightly interpreted the infallible, revelation, but rejects all the accretions and additions to the sacred texts and all the corpus of rites and ceremonies, which now forms the actual working religion. The Brahmins once in supreme power, would, however, make short work of the innovators and heterodox sects by whose help they had reached their goal.

It is the fashion to speak of want of sympathy as one of the causes of the unrest. Sympathy without sentiment is indeed a great gift, though ill-regulated sentiment is necessarily either foolish or mischievous, or deserving of both epithets. It is easy to prescribe the treatment, not so easy to apply it, when sympathy with one exposes the sympathiser to the suspicion of another race, caste, class, tribe, sect, or religion. Rigid impartiality does not make for effusive sympathy—the two things are hardly compatible, and the first is essential.

No doubt, however, the rank and file of the European industrial army are often guilty of arrogance, and generally of ignorance, in their life and conversation among the natives, though, as their numbers are not large, they may be dismissed as other than a serious factor in the situation. The planters, on the other hand, are an important and a wholly beneficial element. Behar, alongside Bengal, and well in touch with Calcutta, the capital of Babudom and India, is prosperous, contented, and without a particle of sympathy with the agitators. This is due in a great degree to the fact that it is, and has been for over eighty years, the home of large numbers of European planters, who are respected and beloved by those whom they employ, for whom they care, as it is feared few Indian employers of labour care. A similar state of things may be observed in other planting districts, with many of which I am intimately acquainted, and the planter keeps touch with the people, not with the English-speaking upper castes and classes, with whom, and not by accident, the official is almost exclusively associated.

The European planter is a most useful auxiliary and a most valuable adviser to the administration, to whom he can impart information by which the latter can otherwise hardly come. It is difficult here to avoid reference to the recent judgment of Mr Justice Mitra, in regard to the murder of Mr Blomfield by a gang of coolies, which has given rise to natural apprehension amongst the planters of Behar. To the lay mind it appears that the learned judge laid it down that a sufficiently large number of men may, without committing murder, kill a solitary victim, provided no one blow dealt by any one of the gang was sufficient in itself to cause death. It is not surprising that the planters have memorialised the Secretary of State, and, though it is difficult to see what he can do, the effect of such a judgment cannot be other than disastrous, and it may be permitted to hope, at any rate, that in no long time it may as a precedent be superseded by another in which equity may subsist alongside law.

Such are some of the chief causes which have enabled disaffected Bengali Babus, with the aid of a licentious press, to work up anti-British feeling in Bengal. Upon this or upon any question, however, it is well to see ourselves as others see us, and a representative critic is M. Raymond Recouly, the well-known French publicist. Writing in the *Revue Politique*, he admits that the English, wherever they go, take with them peace, justice, and material prosperity, born of commercial and industrial development, but holds that they do not understand how it is precisely this material prosperity which gives rise to new aspirations and desires. In proportion as people acquire material well-being so do they exact more liberty. Then, to point the moral, the writer adds that Lord Curzon was too stiff and unbending, too full of Cæsarism in his external and internal policy. It is not clear what the writer would have us do. Should we cease to bring about material prosperity, or should we regard it, when created, as an extinguisher of the benevolent power which gave it birth?—and in that event what becomes of the masses, who have profited by this regeneration? Are they to be handed over to the classes, whose sole aptitude is for destructive criticism, and whose wish is to govern the masses in the stead of the creators of prosperity at whose success they carp, whose methods they criticise, and whose success they, for their part, deny.

The so-called partition of Bengal was, of course, one

of the chief causes of the unrest, though it rather focussed disaffection which had previously existed among the Bengali Babus, than was itself the cause of the agitation.

The whole movement originated, to a great extent, with a small society of the literary, or, as they are called in Russia, the intelligent, classes, who desire to retain a monopoly of the Government appointments, which, with the exception of those enjoyed exclusively by the Imperial Civil Service, they had hitherto enjoyed in the undivided province of Bengal, and who saw in the partition an attempt to break Hindoo predominance. The members of this small society control the native press, by means of which they established at once a paper boycott, a paper national fund, a paper national unity, and a paper home industries association, as a result of which no English goods were to be imported into India. Although the latter, commonly called *Svadeshi*, has upon the whole failed, not without, however, having inflicted great loss and suffering upon innocent people—chiefly Mahomedans—it is yet capable of mischief, for the party which promotes it now asserts that imported British goods are tainted like the greased cartridges, that European salt is purified with blood, and sugar with bones, and that European piece-goods are sized with the fat of cows and pigs. Moreover, *Svadeshi* was merged into *Svaraj*, or independence, and denunciation of British goods eventuated in the condemnation of British rulers. Unchecked by Government, as for a long time they were, the agitators next endeavoured in vain to undermine the loyalty of the army, but it gives occasion for thought that this agitation, which only began in the middle of 1904, has been spread throughout India, by means of the vernacular journals, with a success which an electioneering agency in England might well envy.

Lord Minto, following upon utterances by his predecessors to the same effect, said in one of his speeches that a genuine *Svadeshi* movement would always have the support of the Government of India. The word itself means "own country," and it in no way connotes a boycott of foreign goods, fomentation of labour troubles, and seditious disorder. Agitators had induced large numbers of people to make a vow to purchase only home-manufactured fabrics, but no effort was made in Bengal to initiate or develop industrial enterprise, in respect of which this province has been surpassed by most other provinces. Its jute mills are controlled by Europeans, while the cotton spinning and weaving industries of Nagpur, Ahmedabad, and Bombay have been chiefly carried on with Indian capital. It is in Bombay at present that real efforts are being made to develop a true *Svadeshi* policy, and an Iron and Steel Company with a large capital has recently been floated there by the sons of the late Mr Tata, who founded the Institute of Science at Bangalore. This new company will be financed by Indians, managed by Indians, and the iron ore used will be Indian. Great preparations are being made for the works, which will be situated on the Bengal-Nagpur Railway at Sini, and the plant to be erected will have a minimum capacity for the annual output of 120,000 tons of pig-iron, two-thirds of which will be converted into finished steel. The Government of India is giving this great enterprise very practical assistance.

Another great scheme projected is the utilisation of

the rainfall of the Western Ghats for the generation of electric power to work the cotton mills of Bombay city. These schemes illustrate what Lord Minto describes as the true *Svadeshi* movement, and Bengal will be searched in vain for any proof of the existence of this spirit.

The policy of *Svadeshi* has already proved a failure, the people declining to taboo foreign goods, which till now are cheaper and better than those produced in their own country. The policy of *Svaraj* must also fail so long as England has a spark of spirit left and continues, for India's good, and for her own, to govern the latter country.

Notwithstanding a judicial pronouncement to the contrary, the word *Svaraj* can only mean, and of course is only intended to mean, independence. The pretence that it means self-government under the dominion of another power, impossible where half the world intervenes, and the self-governed are 300,000,000, as against 40,000,000 of the dominion holders, is altogether too thin. No such form of government as that indicated has ever been known to Asiatics, nor is any such form of government possible. Those who cry out for *Svaraj* want to be rid of British administration, and all they would retain that is British is the protection of the fleet and army, for which a new generation of Englishmen, madder than their predecessors, would pay, while all the appointments and all the power in the protected continent would fall, not to its inhabitants, but to one small oligarchy of Brahmins, who despise them.

Intimately connected with *Svadeshi* is the boycott movement started in 1905, which has been practically confined to Bengal and Eastern Bengal, and in spite of which the imports of cotton goods and sugar have concurrently grown in volume. There has been talk of starting *Svadeshi* cotton mills, and of other *Svadeshi* enterprises, but it has had no result. The agitators never calculated their requirements in men and money, but they have been vociferous in speech, and the anniversary of the movement is held in Calcutta, where Mr Surendra Nath Bannerji harangues a crowd composed chiefly of students and claims great things for his policy. Meanwhile, in *Bande Mataram* readers were reminded that the independence of America first found expression in the boycott of British goods, and that India's position was similar to that of all subject nations in the initial stage of their struggle.

Lest there be any mistake as to the attitude of the boycott towards the produce of Britain, let me quote the *Sanjibani*: "Oh, brothers, we will not pollute our hands by touching English goods. Let English goods rot in the warehouses, and be eaten by white ants and rats."

The mention of the *Bande Mataram* newspaper suggests a word upon the signification of this now famous expression, which is translated: "Hail, motherland!" whenever the object is to give it an innocent and commonplace meaning. The words however mean not: "Hail, motherland!" but "Hail, Mother!" "I reverence the mother"—that is to say, Mother Kali, the goddess of death and destruction. The word *mataram* is never used in the sense of the mother country. I have, myself, never come across it with this signification, neither has Mr Grierson, who at any rate is a great authority. The expression, in fact, is on all fours with the cry: "Victory to Mother

Kali!" which is associated with many scenes of riot and bloodshed.

It is an appeal to the lower instincts and ideals of Hindooism in its most demoralising aspects. Students now shout the cry into the ears of passing white men far more aggressively than Chinamen exclaim, or did at any rate twenty years ago: "Fankwei," or foreign devil, as an European passed them in the street.

Again consider the origin of the phrase. *Bande Mataram* is the rebel national song. It was put by Babu Bankim Chandra Chatterjee into the mouths of Hindoo Sanyasis who rebelled against their sovereign lord, the Nawab of Bengal, in the eighteenth century. The novel "Anandamath" was published in 1881, and of course, owing to its origin, the phrase Bande Mataram is peculiarly obnoxious to the Mahomedans. It is now habitually used with the intention of conveying an insult to them and to the English, and so kills two birds with the one stone, while boycott and *Svadeshi* were both alike intended to further the anti-partition policy, upon which the efforts of the agitators in Bengal and Poona were concentrated.

The case for partition is seldom or never stated, and the fact is always overlooked that it had already been decided by Lord Elgin that Bengal was too large, and that division was necessary.

The political agitators, who organised and maintained the anti-partition movement, and control the Bengali press, are for the most part journalists and schoolmasters—the latter being very frequently politicians,—barristers, and pleaders, whose interest it is to concentrate their legal practice in Calcutta, and zemindars with large estates in Eastern Bengal, who, living by choice in Calcutta, find it convenient to have their Government headquarters there, instead of at far-away and provincial Dacca. Others who are in the same position in this behalf are the landlords, who saw their interests attacked, and the ascendency of Calcutta and of the Bengali-Hindoo element threatened, by this division of Bengal. False stories were accordingly circulated to the effect that the object of the Government was to raise the taxes, to deport coolies, and such like rumours. All through the campaign Hindoo schoolboys and students have been urged into the front of the battle, while the real protagonists have been hidden away in the background, and many of these youths have been ruined for life by being implicated in criminal cases, for which they have to thank their Babu tutors in the arts of agitation. A circular was distributed through the agency of the bar libraries in Eastern Bengal, calling the English "lying cheats, who are ruining our life in the world, ruining our industries, and importing their own manufactures, plunder our fields, and throw us into the jaws of fever, famine, and plague. It is our blood they are sucking. Shall we bear it any more? These Feringhees have divided our Golden Bengal into two parts. Swear in the name of Kali that we Hindoos and Mussulmans will serve our country united, and will behead anyone who obstructs."

If the Bengalis had been anxious to prove that there were good reasons for decentralisation of the administration, rather than for concentration at Calcutta, they could not have been more successful than they have been. Partition of course affects the ascendency of the educated Bengalis, and therefore the interests of the lawyers, schoolmasters, journalists, and others whose prosperity depends upon the continued influence of Calcutta over the whole of Bengal. Partition moreover dealt a blow at the political influence they were acquiring by simulating and stimulating the sense of national unity amongst the Hindoo population of the province. Bengalis themselves have no particular claim to be regarded as a nation, and, as shown elsewhere, they are by no means the most educated people in India, indeed, the masses of the province are steeped in superstition, and the proportion of Bengalis educated, in the European sense, is admitted to be about one per cent. of the population. This small minority, however, has been very effectively occupied in debauching the loyalty of the student class, prone in every country to revolutionary feelings, *cereus in vitium flecti*, and flattered at being treated as a political power.

In and around Dacca, the capital of the new province of Eastern Bengal, the centre of a most prosperous country, and of the jute industry, there has been in the past, until the constitution of the new province, very little, far too little, European supervision, and the local landowners, moneylenders, and their agents have acquired great, nay, excessive, influence. These are the classes known as Babus, and with their aid it was possible to turn the *Svadeshi* movement into new and extended channels. Everywhere the people were told that the English were exploiting and ruining the country. The national Volunteer Movement, which was originally a harmless physical exercise and athletic club sort of association, was, after the model of the "Boxers," pressed into the service, and since the Mahomedans are two-thirds of the population of Eastern Bengal, and one Mahomedan is equal to at least three Hindoos in fair fight, and since the former naturally approve of the elevation into a Lieutenant-Governorship of the province in which they are in the majority, the national volunteers had a very moderate success. Nevertheless, they tried to force the Mahomedans to join them in the anti-partition demonstrations, which led to riots at Jamalpore, among other places. One Hindoo was shot in the thigh, and an old man and a boy were beaten to death while engaged in loot, and a few Hindoo widows were carried off by Mahomedans, who, unlike their own males, have no objection to relations with them. Naturally, this riot, which the Hindoos, and not the Mussulmans, provoked, was exaggerated into a terrible onslaught by the Mussulmans upon the peaceful Hindoo population.

It may fairly be said that the boycott and volunteer movements have failed in Eastern Bengal to do more than produce a feeling of unrest, and to undermine the discipline of the students' classes, and it is admitted that the deportation of the two agitators in the Punjaub produced an immediate effect for good upon the agitation in this far-distant region.

Nothing is too unlikely for the supporters of the anti-partition movement to urge. Thus we find Sir Henry Cotton writing in an English provincial paper "that the leaders of both sections of the community in Eastern Bengal are, for the most part, united in condemning partition, but that the ignorant and unruly masses of the Mahomedans have been roused to acts of violence by fanatic emissaries. Vain efforts were made to show that certain Mahomedan leaders did not approve of the partition, but they completely failed." Had any disproof of Sir H. Cotton's allegations been needed, it was afforded by Rafiudden Ahmad,

President of the Mahomedan Conference, held at Lucknow, to adopt the address to Lord Minto, who wrote to *The Times* to say that each member of this deputation was asked his opinion, and that all were unanimous in their approval of partition, and indeed the Mahomedans had already, in each province, passed a resolution in favour of the change—a fact well-known to Lord Minto, who, in answering the address, thanked the Mahomedan community of Eastern Bengal for their moderation and self-restraint. Mr Rafiuddin Ahmad further said, what is notorious to all who have any acquaintance with the subject, that the partition agitation is engineered in England, and kept up in India, owing to the hopes which certain members of Parliament hold out to ignorant people in Bengal that Mr Morley will yield if sufficient pressure were brought to bear upon him. Thus, Mr O'Donnell, M.P., for instance, wrote to Mr Bannerji:

> "Keep on agitating and do so effectively, large meetings are the most useful, you have the justest of causes, and I hope you will make your voice heard. Everything depends on you in India, and remember a Whig does nothing unless pressed. Have mass meetings by the dozen in every district, indoor and out of doors. Morley will yet yield."

Such encouragement produced no little effect, for Bengalis are notoriously more excitable than the more staid and phlegmatic followers of the Prophet. Moreover the Hinduism of Bengal is of a peculiar type, more morbid and emotional than elsewhere, and as Mr Oman, a very well-informed and recent writer held, more calculated to effeminate the race. It is among the Bengalis that the most popular worship is that of Kali the eponymous heroine of Calcutta, the mother of *Bande Mataram*, the goddess, who loves, and exacts, bloody sacrifices, in our day, of goats, but before it, of human beings, as well as of animals. It is among the Bengalis that licentious rites are usual at the Durgapuja festival, and it was in the temple of Kali at Calcutta that seditious meetings have of late been held. It is in Bengal alone that the Kulin Brahmins practise a peculiarly bad form of polygamy. It would not become a subject of the British Empire, and I at any rate would never suggest, that we should exact in Bengal the ethical standard, or rather ideal, which obtains in Britain, but that this is polygamy *in excelsis* is evident from the fact that the partisans of the Babus have endeavoured in vain to deny its existence, including an ex-official of the Bengal Government, who has thrown in his lot with this party, and actually went so far as to say that Kulinism was extinct, until his solitary voice was drowned in a dissenting chorus of unimpeachable authority.

It is partly owing to this emotional and excitable temperament that the Bengalis have easily been induced to imitate, and take part in, attacks upon Mahomedans. Nevertheless the participators in such disorders have been almost exclusively dwellers in towns who have come under, or were originally under, the influence of the Babu element. The ordinary Bengali villager is a peaceable and estimable person, and he and his representatives have lost no opportunity of manifesting their disapproval of the anti-partition agitation. It is, however, the case that in the large towns classes which have hitherto been loyal and orderly in character have been guilty of riotous conduct. For instance, in the riots which occurred last year at Calcutta on October 2nd and 3rd, while the charges against the police were proved to be grossly exaggerated, the Government of Bengal discovered the fact that the disturbances took their origin in the conduct of a usually orderly class of people, from which it drew the conclusion that they were the outcome of the writings and speeches of agitators. The Lieutenant-Governor, Sir Andrew Fraser, warned the Government of India of much more serious possibilities, if a naturally turbulent class followed this example, as a direct outcome of the persistent campaign on the platform and in the press, carried on with the object of bringing constituted authority into contempt, and encouraging resistance to the police. Few will be of opinion that Sir A. Fraser spoke too soon.

In like manner unusual and unfortunate features distinguished the assaults committed by Hindoos on Mahomedans at Comilla in March last year, when the former, incensed by a meeting held by the latter religionists in support of the partition, attacked the Nawab of Decca, assaulted his private secretary, and killed and wounded some of his followers.

Among the leaders of the anti-British faction are men of considerable ability—for instance, Mr Bepin Chandra Pal, who has fully expounded the gospel of the new movement. He, like the writer of these pages, was present when the first Congress met in Madras in 1887, and he again visited the southern capital last year, and explained that the British had not kept their promises, and that he had lost faith in them.

He denounced Mr Morley's statement that so far as his imagination reached, so long must the Government be personal and absolute, and, unlike some adherents of the Congress in England, he admitted that there could be no constitutional agitation in India. He referred to a full revelation of the policy of self-government which was proclaimed by Mr Dadabhai Naoroji at the Congress of 1906. Good government, even if the British Government became good, was no substitute for self-government. India could not be kept by the sword, the army was not big enough. It was the natives of India now who governed India, the British only stood at the top and took the biggest pay. The British incubus once removed, prohibitive tariffs would be imposed on Manchester and Sheffield goods, and English trade with India would soon be a thing of the past. Englishmen would be refused admittance to the country, and British capital would be rejected. If the revolution in India were permitted to be peaceful, the United States of India would be evolved and the ægis of Britain might be left till a conflict arose. If the situation then called for a dictatorship, the Amir of Afghanistan was a man with a headpiece on his shoulders, and it was not merely due to love of gaiety that he made a visit to India. Mr Naoroji is claimed, not without reason, as a sharer of these views, and he is regarded as a Moderate Congressman, and is one whom Englishmen in high places, whether wisely or not, go out of their way to honour. Few who know Orientals will think it is expedient to kiss the rod, and until India turns Christian, and probably after, it will be better not to condone openly avowed disaffection.

Again, Babu Bepin Chandra recommended vast quasi-religious meetings, at which white goats should be sacrificed. White goats probably means Europeans. The Government would not prohibit such assemblies, and the holding of such midnight ceremonies at regular intervals would have great meaning, and might, like the chupatties, work wonders. This reference to the mysterious circulation of cakes just before the Mutiny frightened the Babu, when he saw it published in his own paper, *Bande Mataram*, and the newspaper subsequently more or less repudiated its own report. Babu Bepin has, however, as a consequence of other proceedings, made the acquaintance of the inside of a jail.

Late in 1907, when agitation in Bengal was subsiding, came the visit of Mr Keir Hardie, M.P., leader in Parliament of the Labour party, who, before leaving England, had said : "A lying press campaign is being waged to bias the people of this country against the natives, and make it difficult for Government to do anything to break down the official caste, under which we hold them in the bondage of subjection. I may be able to let a light in upon the dark places of Indian government. Needless to add I go as a warm supporter of the claims of the people. My time will be brief, but with the aid of friends I hope to turn it to good account." Such words bespeak, perhaps, an impartial attitude and an open mind. At any rate, Mr Keir Hardie travelled about Eastern Bengal with Mr J. Chowdhury, a Bengali barrister, connected with the *Svadeshi* agitation, who explained in the press that he was not Mr Hardie's secretary, but served him out of love and admiration, without any intention of prejudicing him against any sect or class he interviewed. Thus he accused and excused himself, while Mr Hardie spoke at Barisal, a local storm centre, and is reported to have said he would do his best to make India a self-governing colony like Canada, as what was good for the Canadians must be good for the Indians, a statement which defies criticism, and, as Mr Morley observed, is as reasonable as to hold that because a fur coat is good to wear in Canada it is good to wear in India.

Other statements attributed to Mr Hardie, in which exceedingly strong language was used against the Government, he repudiated, and of course his disclaimer must be accepted, but the Bengali press described his advent as the act of God, in order to the demolition of a gigantic conspiracy against the Hindoos. The cry that Russian methods had been adopted in Eastern Bengal apparently originated in the conviction of Surendra Nath Bannerji, who was fined 400 rupees (£26) for breach of the police regulations for the conduct of processions, the Babu having dexterously persuaded the police to arrest him, to the profound annoyance of the editor of a rival Bengali newspaper, which protested that Babu Bannerji had no right to selfishly take all the glory to himself. It appeared that Mr Hardie's known views on Asiatic labour in British colonies were not such as to commend him at the outset to the Bengali Babus, but they overlooked this objection in their anxiety to aid him upon his impartial quest after truth. The Labour party, he said, was intensely anxious to see a much larger share given to the natives in the government of the country. Mr Hardie compared *Svadeshi* with Sinn Fein, but one of the Indian weeklies, *The Spectator*, unkindly reminded the Bengalis that he had protested in Parliament that Indian manufacturers should not have the benefit of long hours of work in addition to cheap labour.

The Indian papers report that Mr Hardie cried: "*Bande Mataram*," or Hail, Kali!" at Barisal, amid the lusty cheers of his audience. Nothing could more aptly have illustrated the extraordinary position in which a stranger is placed who, ignorant of India, puts himself in the hands of the Babus. The leader of Labour in England, the denouncer of Indian labour in the Colonies, cries: "Hail to the goddess of destruction! in Bengal!" The utmost sincerity, the most anxious endeavour to get at the truth, the sublimest impartiality, would not suffice to save a man in such a situation.

The Amrita Bazaar Patrika kept records of Mr Hardie's words and of his interviews, with the aid of interpreters belonging to the disaffected faction, with petty cultivators and shopkeepers. Mr Hardie was horrified, it was said, at the contents of a native hut, and was evidently unaware that the owners of palaces have as much, or rather as little, furniture in the rooms in which they actually live, in the East. A low standard of wants does not necessarily evidence poverty. A punkah is a luxury, but it is a far greater luxury not to need a punkah.

From representative Mahomedans Mr Hardie was unable to learn anything, owing to his being under the guidance of a prominent Calcutta agitator, Mr J. Chowdhury, and, on his arrival at Calcutta, the editor of *The Englishman*, Mr Duchesne, questioned him upon the reports of *The Englishman's* correspondent at Barisal, but he gave no information regarding the Mahomedans he had interviewed, or the interpreter who had communicated between him and them.

He thought, however, that while Government interpreters often made mistakes, his own interpreter was exempt from this failing, and indeed it is probable that the latter made no mistake in carrying out the duty entrusted to him. Mr Hardie seems to have accepted anything the Hindoo agitators told him of the truculent and immoral character of Mahomedans as the truth, the whole truth, and nothing but the truth, and he prescribed freedom, such as is enjoyed by Australia and Canada, as the remedy for all the ills to which Indian flesh is heir.

This interest in India on the part of Labour members—or Labourites, as they are called in the Indian press, probably following the analogy of the familiar anchorite—is a new development, and it is not a little extraordinary to see an honourable member of Parliament, with the utmost sincerity and purity of purpose, dancing to the tune set by the Congress as the representatives of the Indian upper and aristocratic classes, and repeated in England at the expense of landlords, against whom the British Government had had by repeated enactments to protect their tenants.

CHAPTER IX

UNREST

The Press in Bengal, in Bombay, in the Punjaub—The Bar Libraries—Deportation of Laj. Patrai—Punjaub Colonisation—Agitation in Madras—The Partition of Bengal—Proofs of Loyalty to the British Government—Remedies for Unrest

IT is now seven years since, in *The Nineteenth Century*, I urged that the newspapers published by Indians for Indians, whether written in English or in the vernacular languages, deserved more attention than they received; that they were the sole means whereby the inhabitants of India learnt what was going on in their own and in other countries; that to them exclusively educated Indians owed their news, and from them they took their opinions. I testified to the ability of these journals, upon which it was one of my official duties for many years to report, and gratefully acknowledged their loyalty during the dark days of the war in South Africa. *The Bengali*, now so vituperative of, and hostile to, Britain, and British administration, then quoted Skobeleff's statement that "England is a vampire seeking the last drop of India's blood," and added, "India thinks otherwise. Russian rule would blast our hopes of political progress, and advancement, and destroy our dreams of self-government." *The Amrita Bazaar Patrika*, now another enemy in Bengal, then wrote: "If the English proposed to leave, the people would entreat them to remain." *The Mirror*, however, said: "The spirit of rationalism and criticism evoked by Occidental influences has undermined the foundations of Aryan faith and religion."

That was a true word, and the agitator found out long ago that contempt for the religion and customs of his country cut him off from the masses of the people, and began to mend his ways, so that at present beef-eating, England-visiting Bengalis are lecturing on the impurities of sugar and cotton sizing, as practised by the irreligious Englishmen to the destruction of the sacred caste of the Hindoo purchaser.

The Tribune of Lahore, not London, thought seven years ago that the people of the West had outgrown Christianity, wanted something more ethereal, more potent than what was presented by Jesus to half barbarians like the Jews, and offered a local prophet to supply the want. *The Hindu Patriot* at that time deplored the manner in which legislation affecting the social institutions of the country had been forced upon an unready and unwilling people, and instanced the Civil Marriage and Age of Consent Acts. That *The Patriot* was right I have never doubted, and alone among those who wrote on the subject I condemned the latter Act in *The Nineteenth Century*, and predicted that the results would be disastrous. True, the act has been a dead letter, but none the less the Hindoos do not forget that at the instance of a Parsee gentleman, backed by philanthropists and others, their British rulers made an offence of one of their cherished customs, because it offended against their own ethical ideals. Indeed I firmly believe that the action then taken is one at least of the reasons why the Indian press at the present day manifests a far less satisfactory, and the Bengali press a downright seditious and hostile, attitude towards ourselves, and our Government in India.

Not that the Indian press as a whole can by any means be condemned as seditious. Take, for instance, recently published passages from *The Hindu Patriot* and *The Hindu Mirror*.

The former, the oldest native paper in India, wrote :

"It is self-advertisers who are at the bottom of the mischief, and these people ought to be kept out of all serious movements, for then the chances of ugly incidents occurring would be reduced to a minimum. It is easy to assume the leadership of men, but not so the task of rightly leading the people. . . . Only such men as have been found fit to guide and control the masses, and whose tried ability and wisdom are a guarantee that they will not lead their followers astray and ruin the cause they have taken up, should be admitted and recognised as leaders."

The latter joined in condemning the extremists, and its attitude may be gathered from the following passage :—

"There is nothing in the national awakening of India to lead one to suppose that it is inconsistent with the maintenance of British rule. It is British rule which brought about this awakening, and through it alone can the ideal of an Indian nation be fulfilled. For over a century and a half England has been the model for India. Japan cannot thrust England out of her place. . . . We want a practical spirit in all our national work. The extremists think they can conquer India by obstreperous noisy agitation. Well, they have not done so yet. . . . Internal reform and development are the two things essential to the real growth of Indian nationality."

Indeed, most of the journals in other than Hindoo hands are well disposed, such as the Parsee papers of Bombay, *The Lahore Observer* and *The Moslem Chronicle*, and papers edited by Hindoos cannot at all be comprehensively classed as disaffected, though the epithet applies pretty freely in Bengal.

In *The Parsee Chronicle* the opinion was expressed that the cardinal mistake of the Government had been to remain indifferent to sedition until the bitter seed had borne poisonous fruit, whereas the application of the ordinary law at an earlier period would have met the requirements of the case. It was pointed out that in native states the vernacular press is only allowed very moderate criticism, in spite of the theories of liberty and autonomy of which so much is heard from the agitators in British India. Even in Baroda, it was suggested, the windows were, with the help of Mr Dutt, dressed for advanced Indian and European admiration. Parsees were genuinely alarmed for trade lest the flow of British capital to India should be checked, and their organ pointed out that in the course of national evolution social and industrial progress is the prelude to political rights. The so-called drain, said the *Chronicle*, was entirely due to the fact that rich Indians would not use their own wealth in productive industries. The English Radical newspapers, which published effusions from youths at college, were severely criticised as having contributed to the creed that the Liberal Government would yield to any demand, however unreasonable, for anything called, however erroneously, popular rights.

It would be difficult to state the case better, but *The Parsee Chronicle* is not concerned to conciliate those who regard a fur coat as equally suitable for hot and cold climates, and the liberty of the press to libel the Government as one of the essential virtues and necessary features of British rule in all parts of the globe.

The native newspapers in Bombay are to a very small extent Mahomedan, but chiefly Mahratti and Gujerati, the former, which is entirely under Brahmin management, being violently anti-British, and the latter fairly moderate, in tone and character. The Brahmins who control the press are here, as elsewhere, lawyers, landlords, writers, moneylenders, priests, clerks and Government servants, and the Mahrattas are landlords, cultivators, traders, and followers of other professions and callings. The Brahmins, who live in Poona, and exercise such journalistic influence, are often described as Mahratta Brahmins, but they are of course not Mahrattas, and do not represent the Mahratta race, or any race. They represent their own caste, the most exclusive and aristocratic in the world, the pretensions of which they have persuaded socialists and democrats in England to champion, a proof that the Brahmin's right hand has not lost its cunning.

The papers they inspire breathe fire and slaughter against ourselves. The editor of *The Vehari*, for instance, taking a poem by Mr Wilfrid Blunt as his text, said that India had fallen into slavery, and that the ultimate means of acquiring independence was by the sword, which must eventually be unsheathed.

The High Court of Bombay sentenced him to two years' imprisonment, and he had previously described the empire of the Feringhees (Europeans in India) as "Hell on Earth," and "the English as surpassing Nero, Nadir Shah, Tamerlane, and even Satan in cruelty. The whole world hated the English, and the mercifulness of God was being doubted because success was being granted to them." For these mild expressions of party feeling he had been bound over to be of good behaviour, but this was asking too much of a Brahmin in command of a Mahratti newspaper, and he soon again offended.

The Deccan Herald printed a manifesto calling on all honest Bengalis to rise and throw the Feringhees into the sea, killing 50,000 of them, and the proprietor and editor of *The Punjaubi* newspaper of Lahore were deservedly sent to jail for the publication of an article in which it was practically stated that all Englishwomen who frequented dances came thither for purposes of prostitution.

In the spring of 1907 *The Punjaubi* accused a European officer of wantonly shooting a policeman for some trifling offence. There was no shadow of evidence to support the story, and the two journalists concerned were convicted, the convictions being confirmed, though the sentences were reduced, in two successive Courts of Appeal. The men were treated as martyrs; an explosion of anti-British feeling took place as they were removed to prison, and the usual complaints were made in the House of Commons that liberty of speech and of the subject was being endangered in India.

But while the Bengali Babus were sowing sedition amongst the Hindoos of the Punjaub, and seditious editors found support in the British Parliament. Mahomedans in Ludhiana were petitioning the Lieutenant-Governor for Europeans to replace the Hindoo personnel of the administration, and at one of the towns they erected a triumphal arch for His Honour, on which was inscribed: "For God's sake save us from the rule of our fellow-countrymen."

The editor of the *Hind Swarajya* of Bombay was bound over to be of good behaviour, over-lenient treatment, surely, for publishing an article headed, "Do that which has to be done." In this precious production it was stated that the English led the Indians along the path of sin, and took away their arms in order artificially to keep up British rule. By their teaching, adultery had begun to spread in Indian homes, and women, becoming independent and pressing men down, had begun to be led along the wrong path. The Indians should engage in battle against the enemy.

But though a Bombay paper is not by any means incapable of disaffection, the *Bengali* press leads the riot of disloyalty and no one more richly deserved the punishment he received than Bepin Chandra Pal, who last autumn got six months' imprisonment—a sentence which the High Court of Bengal considered upon appeal not too severe, in view of the deliberate attempts this Babu made to frustrate the administration of justice. He had refused to be sworn and to answer questions in the prosecution of the conductors of *Bande Mataram*, and ostentatiously demanded the martyr's crown at open-air meetings of students. He announced that he had ceased to edit, and though he was believed to be still closely connected with the conduct of the paper, this was so managed that responsibility could not be brought home. A barrister, Mr A. N. Bannerji, who subsequently apologised and was released, was also arrested for making seditious speeches, and a youth who had been birched for participation in a riot was presented with a gold medal by Mr S. N. Bannerji, whose relations with the *Bengali* were similar to those of Babu Bepin Chandra with *Bande Mataram*.

Bannerji had been a member of the Bengal Civil Service, which he left in 1874, in circumstances into which it is unnecessary here to enter, at a time when Lord Northbrook was Viceroy, Sir George Campbell, Lieutenant-Governor of Bengal, and Lord Hobhouse, legal member of the Council.

About the time the Indian Budget was discussed in the House of Commons in the Session of 1907, the Government of India warned the *Bande Mataram* newspaper that it would be prosecuted for sedition, unless it mended its ways. Babu Bepin Chandra Pal was believed to be the writer or inspirer, and he was, at any rate, the editor, of articles designed to create prejudice and dislike against the English Government, and the English people; and assailing Mr Morley's declaration that British rule will continue, ought to continue, and must continue, with bitter criticism as being fatal to the great issue of Indian self-government, though elsewhere the Hand of God is traced in Mr Morley's blindness, and the text is then *Quem Deus vult perdere*. The reception of that speech in the House of Commons, said the *Bande Mataram*, saved the Indian nationalists the trouble of further argument, and proved the delusiveness of the prevalent faith in the ultimate sense of justice of the British people. Babu

Chandra Pal urged Mahomedans and Hindoos to join in finding a leader and suggested the Amir of Afghanistan. He said India was destined to be a republic with an Upper Chamber of feudatory chiefs, and a Lower Chamber of the common people ; than which no greater nonsense, even from the Congress point of view, could well have been conceived.

The *Yugantar* of Calcutta cried: "Revolution is the only salvation for an enslaved society. With a firm resolve you can bring English rule to an end in a single day, dedicate your lives as an offering at the temple of Liberty, without bloodshed the conquest of the goddess (the mother of *Bande Mataram*), will not be accomplished, let the heads of their intruders be given as an offering, let 70,000,000 hands take up the sword, beggars, and fakirs (religious mendicants) have distributed pamphlets among the native army in Rawal Pindi, the cup of the English is full." At the same time a personal canvass of the troops was attempted, and the prevalence of the plague in the Punjaub was a valuable makeweight, indeed, it was actually alleged that the British introduced this scourge, and the tone in which questions on this point were put in the House of Commons almost suggests that there are in England those who believe this extragavance. It was only an additional charge that the Government were also accused by secret slanders of poisoning the wells.

In the pamphlet supplied to the troops, Sikhs, Punjaubis, Mahomedans, and Rajputs are asked why they fight for the English, and why they accept lower wages than the British soldier, when the negroes in the American army are paid at the same rate as their white comrades. The writer also states that the Russians in Central Asia treat their Mahomedan subjects as equals, and sepoys are adjured to understand that they are eating their own salt, not the salt of the English. The leaflet was published in a journal called *India*, and purported to be a letter from a frontier soldier in America to a native soldier in India. It was arranged that 100,000 copies should be printed for private and free distribution to the troops, in languages which included that of the Ghurkha regiments, and the organisation of the Arya Samaj, of which Lajpat Rai is alleged to be the leader, was believed to be actively engaged in this transaction. At any rate there is doubt that bar libraries have been particularly active in the propagation of seditious sheets, and there is nothing surprising in this in view of the fact that lawyers are at the bottom of the agitation and unrest, and are the most influential element of the Babu class.

While seditious utterances in the Bengal press were unfortunately by no means without precedent, a new and more serious aspect of the unrest was the appearance of the like discourses in the newspapers of the Punjaub.

Were it not that the press of that province is under the control of Bengalis, it would be extraordinary that the latter should exercise so much influence over races who regard them with ill-concealed dislike and contempt. The leaders of the Bengali clique had set before them the necessity for constituting themselves leaders in the Punjaub, and the Arya Samaj and the native press were the weapons to hand. The Arya Samaj is at present chiefly a political society, the ethics of which have been widely adopted in the educational establishments of the

Punjaub. It aims at the amalgamation of reformed Hindooism with the new forces developed by the spread of education. No law is binding in their eyes unless its source be the Vedas. They have the legal element wholly on their side, and it is this class, here as elsewhere in India, which has provided the leaders of the agitation, and has established vernacular journals to aid its propaganda. The forbearance of the Government was mistaken for weakness, and the students as usual were brought up to do the shouting, and to persuade the peasants that the Government was not treating them fairly in the matter of water rates and assessments. The deportation of Lajpat Rai and Ajit Singh scotched the agitation, but the Arya Samaj is still there.

The arrest and deportation of Lajpat Rai and Ajit Singh put an end to open agitation, and plainly showed that the political propaganda of the Arya Samaj inspired the whole movement, the Arya Samaj being itself a society which had its origin in Bengal, from which province agents had been despatched to the Punjaub in order to sow sedition and foster ill-feeling against the Government. The object there, as in Bengal and Poona, and wherever the Congress agents are active, was to obtain control of the administration for the English educated classes, to secure an India preserved from the attacks of other nations by the British army, but from which the British themselves should be excluded. The warlike character of the people of the Punjaub, our partial dependence upon it for the raw material of our best soldiers, the chance of exciting disaffection in the army where it would be most dangerous—these were considerations present in the minds of those who selected the Punjaub as the scene of active agitation. They reckoned without the firmness and absence of panic which distinguished the treatment of the case at home and in India, but the germs of disaffection proved disappointingly easy to plant, and the situation needs, and at the hands of Sir Denzil Ibbetson's successor will receive, the utmost care and attention.

The Regulation III. of 1818, under which the agitators were deported, provides that reasons of State embracing the security of the British dominions from foreign hostility and internal commotion, occasionally render it necessary to place individuals under personal restraint, and in 1897 the Natu brothers were arrested under these powers at Poona, besides which they have been used in order to incarcerate certain dangerous Moplah fanatics in Malabar. In native states such powers are, as has been already said, freely exercised, and last year the Nizam of Hyderabad expelled the head of one of the great families of the state, Nawab Syed Jung Syed-ud-Doula, for writing to him or of him in an impertinent and offensive manner, to the prejudice of good government, and proper respect for the ruler of the state.

It is urged by the Congress critics that these powers were given before legislative councils were created, but that does not in any way prove that they are not as necessary at the present day as they were when no one would have thought of questioning the right of the state to act in this manner.

In November, Lajpat Rai and Ajit Singh were released, after being detained for about six months, whereupon *The Bengali* expressed a fear lest the policy of conciliation should do harm to the new spirit of national consciousness, the comments of other journals of the like character being less ingenuously disaffected. Efforts were also freely made to represent the order for release as the personal act of the King-Emperor, who desired to right the wrong done by his agents. The action of Government met with general approval as it was taken at a time when the extremists had fallen into disrepute and the agitation was subsiding, and only those from whose sails a certain amount of wind was taken, adversely criticised the course taken by the administration.

Other than domestic causes contributed to the success of the agents of the Bengali agitators in the Punjaub, among the warlike races of which province the Russo-Japanese War has no doubt quickened the ever-present martial spirit. The defeat of Russia has inspired the Babu classes with the idea of a United India, wherewith to replace the previously existing Congress programme, while the establishment of the Duma in Russia, and of a Parliament in Persia have also somewhat stimulated vague aspirations of an aristocratic oligarchy for independence. Meanwhile the Bengali anti-English policy, which was transplanted to the Punjaub not two years since, first fastened on the Land Alienation Act, which traders dislike, but agriculturists rather favour, and next attacked the Punjaub Colonisation Bill. In the last twenty years, rainless tracts in the desert have been irrigated and populated by means of magnificent canals, upon the banks of which colonies have been planted, which extend to over 3,000,000 acres of irrigated land, and have a population of upwards of 2,000,000. These were controlled by colonisation officers, who endeavoured to perform practically all the functions of Government in their own persons, till this Bill was introduced to legalise existing conditions and the powers they exercised. Unfortunately, however, some of its provisions gave colour to the charge that the conditions of land tenure were being somewhat altered. The most was made of this, but the Bill was altered and passed by the Punjaub Government, which was falsely accused, by the newspapers edited by the Bengali Babus or their agents, of having broken faith with the occupiers of the colony lands. Though the Viceroy subsequently disallowed the Bill, the mischief had been done. In like manner, the riots which occurred at Rawal Pindi were due to discontent promoted against the new land settlement. As was stated in the chapter dealing with the land system, settlement in the Punjaub is effected for twenty years, at the expiration of which period the assessment is generally raised, because prices usually rise and the revenues of villages automatically increase near great towns like Rawal Pindi. Most of the land belongs, however, not to agriculturists, but to traders and Babus, who at once seized the opportunity of persuading the peasants, who hitherto had had profound faith in the district officer, that rents were to be doubled all round. As a fact the increased assessment in the Rawal Pindi district was due to the greater area under cultivation, not to excessive enhancements. The revision of the water rates upon the Baridoab Canal, which was also attacked, was carried out in the interests of the general tax-payer, who was getting insufficient return from irrigation works constructed out of taxes collected from his pocket, and similar revisions had been made in respect of other Punjaub canals, without any objection before the Bengali agitators came upon the scene.

Nevertheless, there can be no doubt that the seditious propaganda of the Bengal agitators has worked great mischief, amongst the martial races of the Punjaub, where the Government can only last as long as the people believe it to be strong, and the same may be said in a greater or less degree of every part of India.

No doubt the revenue system of the province is somewhat inelastic, and the Punjaub Alienation Act, intended to relieve the peasants from the yoke of usurers, has not been much welcomed by the Sikhs. On the other hand, Punjaub Canal Colonies have been a marvellous success, and it is the irony of fate that the enemy should have found in them an occasion to blaspheme.

In Madras the agitators met with scant encouragement, though the visit of Bepin Chandra Pal was followed by insubordination in the Rajamundry College, which however speedily subsided, without being elsewhere imitated, when the Government supported the Principal in the disciplinary measures he thought it advisable to take.

It is without surprise, however, I see that Sir H. Cotton has stated "that Madras is disturbed and unsettled in sympathy with the feelings of other parts of India." The fact, of course, is that this sober and well-doing province has exhibited no particle of such sympathy, but has been a sad disappointment to Babu Bepin Chandra Pal and his friends. An article recently published in a Bengali paper sadly acknowledged the fact, and ended by exclaiming, more in sorrow than in anger, "Alas! for Madras." Neither has the southern province, or satrapy, as Sir Mountstuart Grant Duff used to call it, contributed to any great extent to the war chest of the Congress, though among the local lawyers are some who speak and write on its behalf, and, being as rich, and capable as any men in India, could give pecuniary assistance if they chose.

The press, then, of Bengal and Poona, and in a less degree of the Punjaub, has contributed in no small degree to the present situation, and the partition of Bengal was invaluable as a magnet to which all the disaffected were drawn, though the charge brought against the Government of India of having rushed the matter through without inquiry, and without any regard to the feelings of those concerned, is wholly untenable.

The question was thoroughly and publicly discussed, but no division would have satisfied the Congress party, who see in a divided Bengal a weakening of the influence which that overgrown province was in a position to exercise. The Mahomedans, two-thirds of the population, are notoriously in favour of the change, and the anti-partition movement is, in point of fact, nothing but an anti-British agitation. It is quite untrue that the majority of the Bengal Civil Service was opposed to the measure, and the Lieutenant-Governor, Sir Andrew Fraser, strongly supported it, saying that amongst the senior offices of the province, with the exception of one, there was complete unanimity in accepting the proposal. The suggestion that Behar and Chota Nagpur should have been, and wanted to be, made into a separate province, is negatived by their memorial protesting against separation, and the obvious line to follow was that previously taken when the Assam Chief Commissionership was formed out of Eastern Bengal in 1874 by making a separate administration of Assam and certain Bengali districts. It followed, almost as a matter of course, that any further subdivision of the overgrown and unwieldy Government would be accomplished by the addition of more Bengali districts to the little province previously carved out of the big Presidency. The Bengalis are not in the English sense of the word a nation, and such solidity or nationality as they now possess is mainly the result of British education and British government. That nationality, however, such as it is, is in no sense impaired by the levelling up of Assam with the districts previously transferred in 1874, and with the districts since transferred in 1905, into a Lieutenant-Governorship, that is to say an administration of exactly the same grade and character as that of the Lieutenant-Governorship, which once included the whole area. The two divisions of Bengal are administered by the same civil service, and subject to the same rules, laws, and regulations, and Eastern Bengal is in no way altered except in so far as it receives the undivided, instead of the divided, attention of a Lieutenant-Governor. The scheme, be it good or bad, was not, as is often asserted, the invention of Lord Curzon, nor is it true that the creation of a Lieutenant-Governorship of Behar and Chota Nagpur would have been acceptable to those concerned. On the contrary, the press of Behar protested against any such proposal, and the press of Behar is as good as the press of Bengal, and better in that it is loyal and moderate in tone. The people of Behar no more favour this proposal than the people of Eastern Bengal object to partition. Indeed, the *Amrita Bazaar Patrika* ungratefully threw overboard the Congress representative, Sir H. Cotton, who advocated the creation of a Behar province in Parliament, saying,

"We trust he and his friends made it quite clear the movement was initiated without the knowledge of the leaders in Bengal. As a matter of fact there is a vast number of people in Bengal and Behar who are very much opposed to separation from Bengal."

No individual can speak to the opinions of many millions of illiterate peasants, but it is possible for them by mass meetings to give expression, to some extent, to their opinions, and the Mahomedans, two-thirds of the population, have expressed their strong approval of the creation of the new province. In like manner the Hindoo tenants of the landlords of Eastern Bengal have met and protested, not against partition, but against the agitation against partition, and against the boycott, which was enforced for a time, to the extreme inconvenience of the population, and to the prejudice of British trade and British goods.

Whether or not it was wise to subdivide Bengal is an open question, and had the results been foreseen the measure probably would never have been carried through. However that may be, the objections raised have been purely factious and artificial. But the English-educated and English-hating Babus were far too shrewd not to see how this change affected the unduly privileged position they had gained as a result of excessive administrative concentration at Calcutta. They hoped to bring pressure to bear on the authorities by injuring the commerce of the capital by their *Svadeshi* and boycott policy, and at the same time, by the same measures, to coerce the Mahomedans into opposing partition, or to force the Government into opposition to the Mahomedans by involving them in riots and disturbances which they themselves, not without success, set to work to provoke.

It will be asked, then, Is there nothing in the objection raised to the so-called partition? There is. The landlords of Bengal are the successors in title of those farmers of the revenue whom Lord Cornwallis created landlords after the English pattern. They are high-caste Hindoos, and their tenants are either Mahomedans or high-caste Hindoos, and the British Government has been occupied ever since Lord Cornwallis's time in protecting these tenants against these British-created landlords, who occupy in some respects much the same position as landlords do in Ireland. Indeed, the tenants have numbered among their most able champions Sir Antony MacDonnell, no oppressor of subject peoples. To this body of landlords it is no doubt a blow that they should cease to have as their local capital Calcutta, which is also the capital of India, and the seat during the cold weather of the Viceroy, and of the great officers of State. Journalists, students, and lawyers also, for obvious reasons, bitterly resent losing Calcutta, and it is true that the solidarity of these classes, as distinguished from the masses, is somewhat impaired. On the other hand, the Mahomedans, the Hindoo tenants, and the native Christians have protested at mass meetings against the reconsideration of an Act of State which has endowed them with a Lieutenant-Governor of their own and has created their districts, which with Assam have a population of upwards of 30,000,000, into a separate Lieutenant-Governorship. The landlord class, of whom the Bengali Babus are the typical representatives, have money. They can and do agitate. They have a violent and vituperative press at their disposal, a press which does not hesitate to say that the object of the agitators is to turn the English out of India. Those who adopt this attitude ask us to believe that the late Viceroy acted for the purpose of destroying the political solidarity of the Bengalis —for it must be remembered that the rest of India takes no kind of interest in the question and, indeed, is not favourable to Bengali pretensions—they ask us to believe that a further extension of administrative changes effected without comment in 1874, and approved by three Secretaries of State, with their Councils of experienced officers, and approved by two Governments of India, consisting of many officers representing all parts of that empire, a measure expressly and enthusiastically approved by the masses immediately affected, is an insult to Bengal, a blunder, and an odious and oppressive act. The peculiar irony of the situation is that the Bengali press, and a few travelled and English-educated Bengalis, who no longer represent the feelings of the Indian people, succeed in persuading the electorate in England and their representatives in a democratic Parliament to take the side of the classes against the masses, of the high castes against the low castes, of a small denationalised group against the uneducated and unsympathising multitudes. I would fain enlarge on this subject in the interests of inarticulate masses, who are grievously misrepresented by men, who may be, and often, but not always are, disinterested and impartial, who may be, and generally are, able and eloquent, but who, if they were angels from above, could not fairly represent people whose manners, customs, feelings, religions, social prejudices, and prepossessions they have abandoned.

The Indian masses care as little for these orators and agitators as they do for representative government, of which they have never heard, but for which, by monumental misrepresentations on the part of the Congress, they are said to be raising vain cries to unanswering heaven.

Again it is untrue, though often asserted, that the judges of the High Court opposed the measure; indeed the change in no way affected them, for they continue to have jurisdiciton over Eastern Bengal. The Chamber of Commerce, too, indignantly protested, by telegraph, against the statement of Mr O'Donnell to the effect that they were opposed to partition; nor was the measure even nominally that of Lord Curzon, for it was actually settled while he was in England in 1904.

That it will, however, in the end increase the expense of administration I believe, for in time the new province will want a Chief Court, or High Court of its own and the new constitution actually has led, as a matter of course, to the entertainment of a larger staff of civil officers. The management of affairs will no doubt be more efficient than before, but whether India wants administration more efficient than Eastern Bengal previously had, I doubt. It is our fault, as I think, that we are for ever pursuing progress after our own pattern, without duly considering whether those we seek to benefit want it, or indeed regard it as progress in a direction in which they wish to proceed.

If, however, British administration of the standard type be good for India, and it is, though something less scientific would be more suitable, then the more efficient that administration is the better, and therefore the so-called partition of Bengal was a desirable measure. Many, however, will think, as I do, that when the people are contented, and ask for no more management, it is well as a general rule to let them alone.

But if proof of sedition, disloyalty, and disaffection has unfortunately been forthcoming in the press of Bengal, the Punjaub, and Poona, gratifying expressions of loyalty have been by no means wanting.

The nobility and gentry, to use their own phrase, of Bengal deprecated the wild and mischievous anti-British agitation, and the Talukdars of Oudh took occasion to issue a similar loyal manifesto. Those who signed the latter pronouncement rejoiced that they were free from the evils of a press which seemed to stir up race against race, class against class, and creed against creed. They deplored the existence of agitation which sought to embitter the people against their rulers, held that the interests of all men of experience and moderate views were identical with the interests of a Government which earnestly sought the welfare of its subjects, and realised that improvements to be effectual must be of natural growth, and that all classes must participate in them.

Maharaj Kumar Sir Prodyot Tagore sent Mr Keir Hardie a copy of an appeal to the loyalty of noblemen and zemindars of Bengal, and referring to Mr Hardie's statement that there was only one people in India, pointed out to him that "India is a great conservative land, and was even more so under Eastern monarchs, with a mass of different races with different religions, opposing constitutions, and separate manners and customs, which go to make it extremely difficult to bring harmoniously together the different elements constituting the people. . . . The British Government and the British race of commercial men have developed the country in such a way as no other nation or Government ever did in the past, not for their own interests only, but also for the benefit of the people."

That is a very fair statement of the case, and is equally remote from the false and odious creed of the anti-British group, and the cant of those who pretend that the British differ from all other people in desiring nothing but the good of other people.

The Behar Landholders Association in turn passed a resolution expressing gratification that efforts to create disaffection had failed in that part of India, and an appeal promoted by the British India Association, and signed by large numbers of responsible inhabitants of all parts of Bengal called on the people to discontinue to give the slightest countenance to wild and mischievous propaganda which tend to create disloyalty to British rule, and feelings of animosity between different classes of the communities of India. The manifesto contains the following passage:—

"We venture to assert that the bulk of the people of the country are loyal and law-abiding. We now appeal to our countrymen for the display of the practical good sense, which some of our critics deny us. We must not forget that, whatever its shortcomings, it is to British rule that we owe the present security of life and property, the spread of education, and the progress, that India is now making according to modern civilised ideals. This is emphatically the worst time to encourage unworthy sentiments and rancorous ill-feeling. No true patriot will hesitate to range himself with us on the side of law and order at the present juncture."

Nawab Mosheen ul Mulk, who has succeeded Sir

Syed Ahmad as the leader of Moslem thought in Upper India, very plainly informed Mr G. K. Gokhale, who was endeavouring to obtain the co-operation of the Mahomedans in the agitation with which he is so intimately connected, that he would not be able to express his opinions as freely as he now could, under any Government, indigenous or alien, by which that of Great Britain could conceivably be replaced, and, he said that the gulf between Hindoos and Mahomedans was being widened by the present political agitation. Mr Gokhale in return urged that the interests of the Mahomedans and Hindoos were identical, but in fact he and his cause suffered a serious rebuff at Lucknow.

While the agitators were actively engaged at Lahore and Rawal Pindi, the Maharaja of the neighbouring state of Kashmir issued a proclamation prohibiting all forms of agitation against the British Government, an agent of the agitators was promptly ejected from his well-governed state by the Maharaja of Travancore, and the Government of Mysore publicly rebuked a journal which had made unsustainable charges against the British Government.

The Maharaja of Bikanir wrote to *The Times*, in July of last year, to answer for the loyalty of his order, which indeed the rise of British rule saved from extinction by the Mahrattas. Maharaja Sindhia, the Maharajas of Idar, Patiala, Cooch Behar, Dholpore, Jodhpur, and Ulwar, who have given, and others who had no opportunity of giving, practical proof of their devotion, are well aware of this fact, and the ruler of Bikanir pointed out that acts of Bengali agitators were in no sense those of the Indian peoples, and that the ruling chiefs were truly loyal, though self-interest might be a factor in their attitude—which surely is matter for satisfaction, not regret.

Upon the return of the Maharaja to his capital his people expressed their warm approval of his loyal letter to *The Times*, while he in turn congratulated them on having abstained from taking any part in anti-British agitation and urged them to maintain the like prudent course in future.

The Nizam of Hyderabad, one of the three premier princes of India, and the ruler of the largest state, assured Lord Minto last November "that the traditional friendship of his house to the British Raj was fully reflected by his people. They were loyal to him and, like himself, faithful to the British Throne. He did not believe a single man could be found among his subjects whose disposition towards the British Government was unsatisfactory. Every Indian endowed with the least sense knew thoroughly well that the peace and prosperity which his country had enjoyed under the benign protection of his Majesty and his august mother would disappear the moment that protection was withdrawn or weakened. From his experience of twenty-three years as ruler of that state, he could say that the form of government was far less important than the spirit of its administration. The essential thing was sympathy, on which the Prince of Wales, with the truly Royal instinct of his race, laid stress on the conclusion of his Indian tour. Sympathy for the people had been a marked characteristic of the Government of India, and the steps now being taken to associate the people more closely with the administration could not fail to bring that sympathy home to the Princes and people alike."

Peculiar significance attaches to his Highness's repudiation of the charge that the Government of India and its servants are unsympathetic, and those who are acquainted with the Nizam know that he is no princely sycophant, but a man who speaks outright that which is in his mind.

As a set off to the cheap denunciations of Mr Bryan, who published as his own opinion the articles of the Bengali Babu's faith, may be taken the evidence of Mr Niels Groïs, a graduate of Harvard University, and a student of international affairs. He was struck by the fact that the Congress at Calcutta was a collection of office-seekers, not of patriots, and in a speech delivered at Boston last year he explained the special opportunities of studying Indian problems he had enjoyed, and compared the disloyalty of the educated classes with the devotion of the masses, who realised that their safety, and in fact their entire well-being, depended on the continuance of British rule. In spite of this obvious, undisputed fact it is the disloyal who are accepted as witnesses, and it is the most satisfactory feature of the projected reforms that another and a far different class will be enabled to give evidence in future.

I have now given some account of the causes which led up to the prevailing unrest, and these have been well summarised by Sir Edward Law, late Finance Member of the Government of India. He attributes it to a faulty system of education, to the liberty accorded to a licentious press, to the lowering of British prestige, and to the want of touch between Government officers and the people. His criticisms as regards the administrative failings of our education system are those which led Lord Curzon's Government to make the reforms he introduced, which, however, will need strong backing, if they are to be maintained. Sir Edward thought the press should not be allowed to publish vituperative or seditious articles, and he deemed it necessary to bring it completely under control. He further held that assaults on European British subjects and British soldiers should never go unpunished, a view which I have urged in the House of Commons on many occasions. Sir Edward was also of opinion that the prestige of the British local administrator should be increased by wholesale decentralisation. In fact, the British Empire was made by men, and not by mere routine administrators, and report writers at the end of a telegraph are not men after the pattern of aforetime.

It is easier, however, to locate the causes of the unrest than to prescribe the remedies, some of which, however, are sufficiently obvious, whether or not they are likely to be applied. And the first of all is to give up the pretence that democratic government is good for, or possible for, India, and to admit and act on the admission that the agitators are, as the masses know, unfit to govern Bengal, or any other part of India; the second is to acknowledge, and act upon the acknowledgment, that an aristocratic basis of Government is natural to the Indian continent, and that the people only really revere their own hereditary leaders, who should be confirmed and increased in power and place. They would develop indigenous constitutions, like the village arbitration courts, so infinitely superior to our own tribunals, which act solely as promoters of litigation, sedition, propagators of disloyal lawyers, and as irritants and solvents of the solidarity of Indian society. Mercifully, reforms are now under consideration which give to the leaders of the people the place from which they have been well-nigh ousted by the lawyers and other products of our educational system, who bite the hand that feeds them. Technical education, village and co-operative banks have already been mentioned, and in decentralisation lies a remedy than which none is more potent. It has often been pointed out that there is too much secretarial government in India, and a good secretary may know, and often does know, nothing of the languages or of the people of the country. All the Congress influence tends towards centralisation, and that influence itself is very much the creature of this dread bacillus of Indian administration, which but for the spread of the English language, had never been born.

One of the chief planks of the Congress platform is the separation of administrative and judicial functions, which means further centralisation and another blow to the influence of the district officer. True, this change would provide a great many more appointments for graduates of the agitator class, and more particularly for lawyers, who are the soul of the agitation, and its most able exponents. These men are, of course, capable of fulfilling most offices as far as intellect and education go, but the masses do not want them, do not like them, and do not trust them. They appreciate village arbitration, or failing that, adjudication by the impartial English officer, be the matter one for revenue or magisterial court.

The power of the district officer should be increased, not, as the Congress wishes, further impaired; the right of appeal should be largely reduced, not, as they wish, extended, but after all the evil can never be fairly righted till Western literature ceases to be general food for the vulgar, and is taught only in quarters wherein it is likely to be understood in its relation to countries and peoples to which its lessons in different degrees apply. India is a country of caste and class, and education should be suited to those educated, and not thrown headlong at the hungry. The local governments, too, should be free from interference on the part of the Government of India, and, except in respect of matters of Imperial concern, they should be masters in their own house.

The Indian Congress should be brought under regulation, and the danger of alienating the Mahomedans, of all classes, and the Hindoo masses, who are loyal, by yielding to the Babus and Brahmins, should be more thoroughly appreciated. Frequent prosecutions for sedition have of late been instituted, and sentences of some severity have been passed; but the licence of the press should be curbed by binding over editors under heavy penalties to good conduct at the first appearance of sedition in their papers, and of enforcing their recognisances whenever they next offend. The Indian Press is not as that of England, and may enjoy the same liberty when it shows the same sense of responsibility. The Government must regain the confidence of the masses for the local officer, and inspire a feeling that its strength is equal to its justice. Not that the Government has been unmindful, of the responsibility which rests upon it, at this juncture.

In November (1907) it passed an Act for "the prevention of seditious meetings," which enabled provincial administrations to declare any part of their territories proclaimed areas in which no public meetings are allowed without permission under penalty of fine and imprisonment. Mr Gokhale opposed the Bill in the Viceroy's Council, and urged that the agitators were few in number, which indeed is true, and is a useful admission. Would that they possessed powers for evil only in proportion to their numbers! Lord Minto freely allowed that there was no disloyalty among the Indian masses, but he could not minimise the significance of the Lahore and Rawal Pindi riots, the insults to Europeans, the assaults, looting, and boycotting in Eastern Bengal, nor forget the seditious addresses, newspapers, and leaflets, designed to inflame social feeling, and—fortunately, all in vain—to seduce the Indian army from its loyalty. At the same time he disclaimed any intention of checking the growth of political thought, which the Government only desired to direct into beneficial channels. The new Act was at once put into force in one district of Eastern Bengal, but up till now in no other locality. It had previously been found necessary to promulgate an ordinance for regulating public meetings in Eastern Bengal and the Punjaub, and as the necessity for such regulation continued, it was considered desirable to pass this permanent Act.

The position of the Mahomedans, and the necessity which exists for giving them representation having some proportion, not to their numbers, but to their weight, character, strength, and influence, can never be overlooked when the remedies for unrest are under consideration.

While the Congress and Babu factions perpetually importune the Government with various demands, the Mahomedans stand aside, having confidence in the impartial justice of their rulers, an attitude which is almost inconceivable to those accustomed to English party government. There is no doubt, however, that the opinion is widespread that agitation pays, and the writer has frequently heard the honours list discussed by Indian gentlemen with the remark, "only the natives who worry and oppose the Government are remembered by it on these occasions. Loyalty does not pay." The Mahomedans have always refused to have anything to do with the Hindoo Congress, and have invariably given the Government silent but effectual support, and in view of the occurrences of 1905, and the manner in which their approval of the partition of Bengal, of the population of which they form two-thirds, was concealed and denied, they thought it necessary to consider their position. They had organised a great demonstration in favour of partition, which they abandoned at the express desire of the British officials, lest it might result in a breach of the peace, and they never concealed their regret at the resignation of Sir Bampfylde Fuller, or their resentment at the manner in which certain members of Parliament of the Congress group "unwarrantably took upon themselves to speak on behalf of the millions of India." They accordingly sent a deputation to the Viceroy urging the Government to take more efficient measures for finding out the opinions of their community, and for giving it due representation in any scheme of reform, which might then, or at any later date, be under consideration.

That this desire has not been overlooked will be apparent from the account of the reforms now proposed, which is given immediately after a short notice of the Congress, which, because of the part it has played in the recent history of India, is deserving of a separate chapter.

CHAPTER X

THE CONGRESS

Sir W. Hunter's Opinions—Lord Cross's Act—Mr Gokhale—Babu S. N. Bannerji—Mr Naoroji—Mr Tilak—Parties in Congress—Babu B. C. Pal—Mr Subramania Iyer—Sir H. Cotton and the End of British Rule

SIXTEEN years have passed since Sir William Hunter wrote that the India of that day was the India of the national political Congress. He said one of the chief results of the reorganisation of Indian education, and the throwing open of the Government schools and colleges to all Indian subjects, irrespective of their race, creed, or caste, was to convert what was formerly a hostile, into a loyal, India. We now know, however, that the result has been to create an English-educated class, which can hardly be described as conspicuously loyal. But if Sir William Hunter was wrong in his forecast, in so far as it related to the Congress, it is well to remember that he was right as regards the masses, and in reminding his readers that India had, nearly up to the time at which he wrote, been more or less hostile, and that the Company's servants failed in a policy of conciliation. Hunter confidently answered in the affirmative the question, Can we conciliate India? He said that the desire of the classes, we sometimes hear spoken of as the troublesome classes, is no longer, as in Lord Metcalfe's time, to get rid of our government, but to be admitted within it to a larger share.

It would be hard to say this of the Babu agitators and their dupes at the present moment. If words mean anything, they do wish to get rid of us, merely retaining our army to keep them in the seats of the mighty, from which, without it, they know they must inevitably, and amidst universal rejoicing, be ejected. Yet it is true that in 1885, and during the Afghan War and the war in the Transvaal, satisfactory proofs of loyal friendliness were forthcoming from most quarters except Bengal and Poona. Even from Bengal came reassuring notes, for perhaps the Babus dreaded the shadow of the realisation of their dream. The feudatory princes have most nobly vindicated their claims to be friends and allies of the Empire, and the masses of the people are quite loyal and contented.

Sir William Hunter describes the Congress, called by its members the Indian National Congress, as a most conspicuous outcome of the new sense on the part of the people of interest in the Government. It might be objected that the Congress is not Indian, and is not national, inasmuch as it is not by any means supported by all the nations in India; but, however that may be, it consists of delegates whether or not elected, from the various provinces, who have annually met together for twenty-two years in order to discuss what in their opinion are the political interests of the country, and every year they pass practically identical resolutions. They complain of the administration of the Excise, and of the Arms Act; they ask for a reduction in the salt-duty, so largely decreased in the last few years; for further employment in the public service; that the House of Commons should exercise more control over Indian revenues and expenditure, and that the natives of the country should have a more effective voice in making their own laws. At present, the chief legislative authority is the Viceroy's Legislative Council, which makes laws for the whole empire. It consists of the Executive Council, with additional members who are selected from the influential classes, and from the British mercantile community, and also other additional members nominated by the governments concerned to represent the great provincial governments, of which latter class the writer of these pages was a member. The natives of the country were well represented among the additional members, and a great many of the Congress guns been have been spiked, since the administration of the Excise has been improved, the salt-tax has been largely reduced, the employment of natives of India increased, and the legislative Council reformed in the direction, if not to the extent, desired, for Lord Cross's Act provided for the annual discussion of the Indian expenditure in the Viceroy's Council, for giving members the right to ask questions, and for the increase in the number of the members of the Legislative Council.

The moderate wing of the Congress is understood to favour a gradual development which in the end will make India an autonomous member of the British Empire, and Mr Gokhale is regarded as a member of this branch. Certainly in England his utterances have been such as are well within the purview of such a programme. But there are others who desire to separate from Britain at the earliest possible opportunity, and to this end pursue a persistent campaign of misrepresentation. Of this school is Mr Tilak, the extremist nominee for the Presidentship in 1906, who was convicted some years ago of attempting to excite disaffection, but it is only recently that politicians of this type have had a preponderating influence in what was formerly, upon the whole, regarded as a moderate and well-affected association. The Mahomedans, however, who have good reasons for, and good opportunities of, being well posted as to its objects and intentions, have always regarded it with distrust and suspicion. The partition of Bengal was a godsend to the extremist section, which, encouraged by the attitude of certain politicians at home, in and out of Parliament, made the most of the not unnatural objections raised by the Babu class to this administrative measure. Day by day the virulent abuse of Government gathered volume.

Soon even Babu S. N. Bannerji, whose hatred and resentment have been sufficiently pronounced, was surpassed by Babu Bepin Chandra Pal, the editor, till a prosecution was launched, or part editor, or proprietor, or part proprietor of *New India* and *Bande Mataram*. The latter paper plainly states that "our British friends should be distinctly told that their point of view is not ours, they desire to make the government of India popular without ceasing in any sense to be essentially British. We desire to make it autonomous and absolutely free of British control. We must go to the hamlets." And they have gone to the hamlets, to debauch the loyalty of the peasants, and they are endeavouring, with as small prospect of success, to capture the Congress caucus, the chief obstacle being the opposition of the moderate men of means, who supply the sinews of war, and have no idea of generally running amok, and losing all that they have in the resulting disorder. Then the peasants, and the masses generally, have no sympathy and no concern with the movement, nor the old-fashioned Hindoos, nor of course the Mahomedans, who have publicly recorded their disagreement whenever opportunity has offered. They have indeed recently started a Congress of their own, called the All India Moslem League, as a protest against the assumption by the Hindoo Congress of the epithets Indian and National. Among the objects of this league are the promotion of loyalty to England and of an attitude of readiness to fight for the British Government.

In the end Mr Naoroji and not Mr Tilak was nominated President for 1906, but the victory really lay with the extremist party, whose views he expressed in a speech, asking for self-government like that of the United Kingdom or the Colonies, and denouncing the present government of India as a barbarous despotism unworthy of British instincts, principles, and civilisation. He further advocated the raising of a corps of missionaries to go to the hamlets and preach this creed under the supervision of the Congress caucus, which, as has been already remarked, maintains a branch in England.

The two parties in the Congress are now known as the Moderates and the Nationalists, the latter having taken their title from the Irish party, whose organ, *The Freeman's Journal* of Dublin, has published various articles in favour of an autonomous India. A nice dispute arose between these two parties as regards the place at which the meeting for 1907 should be held, and as to the President who should preside, and finally Surat, and Dr Rash Behary Ghose, were declared the winners. Dr Ghose is accounted a Moderate, and no doubt he may well be so described in comparison with some of his competitors for the post of President, but it should be distinctly understood that though there may be two factions in the Congress, both of them are now associated with disloyal propaganda.

Nevertheless the Congress is not sufficiently extreme to satisfy these extremists, for *The Amrita Bazaar Patrika* has published a series of articles entitled, "How to make the Congress useful." In one of these it is admitted that the association consists merely of English educated middle-class men, and that to make it really national, zemindars, merchants, and representatives of the cultivators of the soil should be included within its ranks. The reason why they keep aloof is well known, for the Congress only interests itself in political matters, and it is an open secret that zemindars and men of higher rank, though they may not join it, provide it with the sinews of war. *The Amrita Bazaar Patrika*, however, in an unwonted burst of candour, asks its readers to remember "that many of our wants and grievances are of our own making, and that it is within our power to remove them without any official or outside help. No nation has ever been able to regenerate itself by relying on others. It is impossible for the Indian National Congress to bring about the salvation of India so long as it does not teach the people self-reliance. The Congress to be of any use should teach the people to arrange for their own education, to cease quarrelling amongst themselves, to develop their industries and agricultural resources, and to learn the art of self-government."

It has been mentioned that a schism arose regarding the appointment of a President last year, and that the extremists wanted Mr Tilak, whom they described as a hero and a martyr, because he was sent to prison ten years ago for good and sufficient reasons. There are degrees amongst the agitators, Babu Surendra Nath Bannerji being regarded as more moderate than Babu Bepin Chandra Pal. Bannerji is, however, sufficiently hostile, and, though he is believed to have renounced Hindoo orthodoxy and prejudices, in his speeches he generally appeals to them in order to arouse enmity against the Government. It is far too readily assumed that the railway strike which has lately taken place has not been fomented by these agitators, for it is well known that their emissaries have been exceedingly active amongst the employees of the East Indian Railway, and most disgraceful speeches have been made at important stations on the line.

Mr Skrine, who compiled a very interesting life of Sir William Hunter, probably altogether overestimated his hero's influence when he wrote that whatever result the Congress achieved was due to the interest of the latter with the British public. However that may be, Hunter's support was of that discerning and moderate character, which the Congress, now become a society dominated by the anti-British damned-Barebones school of controversialists never appreciates. It is more accurate to regard the Congress as one of many results, not as one of the chief causes, of the unrest in India, to which, however, it has of late most actively contributed, while, since it has declared the boycott to be a legitimate weapon, it has committed itself to open defiance of the law. At its meeting in 1906 resolutions were sprung and passed without any real discussion, and votes were not taken, so that it is impossible to say how far those present concurred in what are put forward as its deliberate opinions. In 1907 the meeting broke up after a free fight, and there was not even a pretence of any resolutions. It is, however, highly improbable that the majority really believe that representation after the English pattern could or should be introduced into India, or that compulsory education could or should be forced upon a country so utterly unprepared for so advanced a measure.

As it is of much importance that the facts regarding the Congress should be known, it may be permissible to take two exponents of its policy, one in India and one in England, whereby a fair idea will be gathered of what this movement really means.

Mr Subramania Iyer, a capable Brahmin, lectured at Tanjore not long since, and he is as good an example of a moderate Congressman, as Congressmen go, as could well be quoted, having been for many years editor of one of the best native papers in India, *The Hindu*. He spoke of the short bright interval of Mahratta rule, when the superiority of the Hindoo nation was asserted. Now the main facts regarding this miserable period in the history of India, when the Mahrattas robbed and plundered at will, and attempted nothing like peaceable or orderly administration, will be found in the first chapter of this little book. His review of the religion of the country is so little accurate that he describes temple worship and perpetual widowhood as practices of Buddhism, and the influence of Buddhism on Hindooism as bad, which is entirely contrary to the fact. But "Shadwell sometimes deviates into sense," and Mr Subramania Iyer does point out that prior to British rule there was no political unity and no political consciousness. He regards the Queen's proclamation as extorted by fear, and says the moment the cause for fear was gone the promised reforms were abandoned. Chapters II., III., IV., and V. of this work, which are wholly unargumentative, should supply a sufficient answer to this change.

He then declares that not complete severance from England, but self-government on the Colonial model, is the object set before himself and his friends, and he quotes a judgment which, not without reason, occasioned great surprise, by Mitter and Fletcher, J.J. of the High Court of Bengal, which he describes as a golden declaration, and which certainly gave to *Svaraj* a meaning contrary to that which the word obviously owns. "*Svaraj* then," says the ex-editor, "is our political ambition, and *svadeshi* and boycott are our weapons. India will not be a subject nation for ever, now we have the support of the High Court Judges."

Now, *svaraj* simply means self-government *sans phrase*, and does not connote dependence. On another occasion, these discourses being suited to the audiences, the same speaker said: "What is the result of a century's rule in India? Destitution, disease, physical and moral emasculation." Of course Lord Curzon, who endeavoured to deal with the difficulty at the root, and to amend the deplorable educational system, comes in for unmitigated condemnation for "his reactionary designs and his autocratic manners."

Then take a representative of the Congress in England, preferably a Member of Parliament, either Mr O'Donnell or Sir Henry Cotton, whichever be the leader of the little company of captains which represents in the House of Commons views which are abhorred by all the Europeans in India, civil, military, and commercial, and receives no support from any quarter, other than the Congress, the Babus of Bengal, and the Brahmins of Poona. It may be convenient to take Sir Henry Cotton in preference to Mr O'Donnell for the moment, because, like myself, regardless of the warning of Job, he has written a book, in which he says that "the existence of a Liberal administration compels the adoption of liberal and sympathetic principles in dealing with Indian questions on the spot." Now if there is one thing upon which all sane men are agreed it is that party politics should not be introduced into our Indian Empire, the inhabitants of which regard them in the same light as the Shah, of whom I heard in Persia, who when an effort was made to explain to him what Whig and Tory meant in England, summed up the subject by saying: "Why does not the King knock these madmen's heads together till they do agree." At any rate it is needless to say that the slightest suspicion of party advocacy is forbidden to civil servants, and any infraction of this rule would very properly involve their dismissal from the public service. Indeed continuity of policy has been followed with rare exceptions, and these relate solely to external relations. Again, a complete ignorance of what is common knowledge in India, or an evident desire to obscure the facts, is exhibited by assertions like this: "The Babus rule public opinion from Peshawar to Chittagong." Now the Babus are the most unpopular class in India, and no traveller returns and writes a book without anecdotes which illustrate this perfectly notorious fact. It might fairly be said that the Babus of Bengal and the Brahmins of Poona are the leaders of the English educated anti-British class, but public opinion, thank heaven! is not yet confined to these classes. What is to become of the English, who have made such a mess of the great Indian problem, whose chief success in the opinion of Sir H. Cotton has been the permanent settlement of Bengal, to protect the cultivating tenant against the landlord, under which settlement the British Government has been actively legislating at frequent intervals ever since the days of Lord Cornwallis; whose Indian railways have ruined the carrying trade, just as English railways ruined the stage coaches; whose education is only partially successful because it is not compulsory; whose tea and indigo industries are bolstered up in some manner, of which no one else is aware, by public money, while the estates themselves are watered with the blood and tears of unwilling slaves, who nevertheless cannot be got, at the expiry of their indentures, to leave their prison, in which they settle for life; whose census commissioners are such lunatics that they see in these settlers the salvation of at least one little province? Surely, it would be better that these bunglers and oppressors, the English, should as soon as possible leave the country to be governed by the Babus, and that, it appears, actually is the solution. Sir Henry Cotton positively writes "It is the purest folly for us to continue to rule on worn-out lines only suited to a slave population, and the principal object of the Indian Government should be to apply itself to the peaceful reconstruction of a native administration in its place. The withdrawal of the military support would not be injurious to Anglo-Indians, but would constrain them to adopt a more conciliatory demeanour towards the people of the country. England could withdraw her own standing army, and secure treaty rights for India from the European powers." This she would no doubt do after the abolition of the army and the navy, and with this climax of preposterous politics, quotation from "New India" may end. It will indeed be a new India when these principles are adopted, and yet it is curious to see how, even in a work like this, a residuum of common-sense clings to a man, who has gone through what in most cases proves to be a highly educative experience. It is doubtful whether the Labour benches will altogether agree with Sir Henry Cotton when he writes that "the basis of internal order in India is a patrician aristocracy of indigenous growth trained to control and lead the lower orders." Now such aristocracy would of course govern India, if they had the chance, according to Indian ideas, as the Congress party says, and what are Indian ideas? The rule of caste, wealth, birth, and strength, and of forced labour, which is not exactly the theory which finds favour with those who have been induced to support this propaganda in England. Again, what will the allies of the little Congress party in Parliament say to this: "The maintenance of an hereditary landholding class is the corner-stone of internal political reconstruction. The lower orders stand in urgent need of an aristocracy above them. The prosperity of every country requires that there should exist within it, not only a proletariat, the great body of the people who devote themselves to labour, but also a class of capitalists who provide funds which enable labour to become productive. It is only under the fertilising influence of capital that labour is productive"? This is not quite the note of the speeches which are delivered on this subject by socialists. Nor do they recognise that birth as well as election and nomination is a principle of selection. Mr Ramsay Macdonald, the Whip of the Labour Party, commits himself to the plain statement that capital is the enemy. In short, Sir Henry Cotton can no more than other people run with the hare and hunt with the hounds, and it is impossible to condemn your fellow-countrymen, root and branch, and throw in your lot with hostile and unreasonable critics of your class and calling, and at the same time to obtain credit for retaining some saving sense of sanity upon side issues of the alphabet of economical and political questions. It is of course very difficult to satisfy democrats and socialists in England and an aristocratic oligarchy of Brahmins and landlords in India, and although the latter seems able to persuade the former that all will be right, if they can oust us, as the Peshwas ousted their masters, and ruled in their stead, yet an ex-official turned anti-official writing on this subject obviously occupies so difficult a position as to be entitled to commiseration.

Another ex-Indian civilian and ex-member of Parliament, Sir William Wedderburn, lately publicly stated that the Indian people complained that the masses are in extreme destitution, and that it is owing to the effects of a disastrous administration that the country is scourged by disease and famine. It is a sufficient answer to this that, upon the agitators' own showing, the people of India have no means of making known their feelings; that no such opinions as these are expressed by their hereditary leaders, and that the people repudiate as their representatives the English-educated Babu class, which is practically denationalised, and merely joined for the present with the members of the Brahmin caste because they can, when thus reinforced, more easily harry and harass the administration.

It is of course extremely mischievous that ex-officials should become anti-officials, and lecture about the country that independent opinion is unanimous, that the people think this and think that, and it is worse than mischievous that they should asperse an active and able administration by attributing to its action calamities which it does all that humanity can do to alleviate. Nor is it easy to refrain from noticing that ex-officials who have spent their lives as concurring, and presumably willing, instruments of Government, and who no sooner leave its service than they state that contact between Europeans and Asiatics is prejudicial to the latter race, have to explain why in their own careers they failed so conspicuously to practise what so incessantly and insistently they preach. Hostile though it is to Government, the Congress at first welcomed Lord Curzon, and flattered him profusely, but they roundly denounced him when he declined to be led, and refused to receive the President of one year who wished to lay the resolution of the Congress officially before him. It might, however, lead to the grossest misunderstanding in India if the head of the Government received officially a member of a body which claims to represent 300,000,000 of people, of whom probably 99½ per cent. have never even heard of its existence. Nor would the Viceroy be carrying out his elementary duty if he encouraged anything which admitted the false and fatal principle of party politics into Indian administration.

Partition gave an opportunity to the Congress party of exhibiting their strength, and, successful as they have been in making demonstrations, their success would have been even greater had they not combined with this agitation the policy of *Svadeshi*, which their sympathisers outside Bengal have shown little inclination to accept, and of *boycott*, which has altogether failed from the commencement.

The meeting of 1907, proved altogether abortive, and broke up in confusion, but even then some craft and subtlety was displayed by the leaders in claiming that the Moderates were overwhelmed by the Extremists, the fact being that both wings are hostile to British rule in India.

CHAPTER XI

PROPOSED REFORMS

Advisory Councils—The Representation of the Landed and of other Interests — Past Preponderance of the Legal Element — Official Majority assured—Legislative Councils—Enlargement proposed—Supreme and Provincial Councils — Mahomedans — Electorate—Special Representation—Denunciations of the Scheme—Admissions of its Merits—Sir A. Lyall's Opinion—Judicial Appointments—Civilisation in Bengal—Council of India Act, 1907—The Indian Members of the Secretary of State's Council—Decentralisation Commission

MR MORLEY in his Budget Speech of 1907 announced that, notwithstanding the occurrences to which reference has been made in a previous chapter, the Government proposed to introduce into Indian administration certain changes which had been recommended by the Governor-General in Council, and explained that, in his opinion, to postpone or withdraw reforms which had previously been contemplated, because of the unrest and agitation which had supervened, would have been construed as a triumph for the party of sedition. They had resolved, therefore, to approve the establishment of advisory councils of notables to serve the double purpose of eliciting independent opinions, and diffusing correct information as to the acts and intentions of Government.

The second proposal was the extension of the general principle of substantial enlargement of the legislative councils, both of the Governor-General, and of the heads of provincial administrations. The details, Mr Morley said, had not been considered, but the maintenance of an official majority was a necessary condition. A longer time was also to be allowed in the Viceroy's Council for the discussion of the Budget, and two Indian gentlemen were to be appointed to sit on the Secretary of State's own council, a new and welcome departure from previously existing practice in filling up these appointments.

A circular by the Government of India to provincial administrations was subsequently published as a Parliamentary Paper, and from this despatch it appears that, since the Councils' Act of 1892 was passed, by which the legislative councils were enlarged, and the elective principle was recognised, the number of scholars studying English had risen from 298,000 to 505,000; the number of matriculates annually turned out from 4286 to 8211, and the yearly tale of B.A.'s, from 708 to 1570. The Government of India observed that the ruling chiefs, and landholding and commercial classes, representing the most powerful and stable elements of Indian society, had now become qualified to take a larger part in public life, and it was all important that they should be properly represented in any scheme of reform, the more particularly since the needs and sentiments of the masses must find expression through those who are acquainted with their daily life, and are qualified to speak on their behalf, and the essential condition of all reform was stated to be the maintenance in undiminished strength of the executive authority of the Government.

The members of the Imperial Advisory Council

would be appointed by the Viceroy, and the Council would consist of sixty members, including twenty ruling chiefs, and a suitable number of territorial magnates from each province. Office would be held for five years, and the Council would have no legislative or formal powers, but would deal only with such matters as might be specially referred to its consideration.

The provincial governments also were each to be provided with an Advisory Council, the members of which, as a rule, would represent the great landholders of the province, in which it would perform similar functions to those which the Imperial Advisory Council would discharge in respect of the Government of India. Smaller landholders, industry, commerce, capital, and the professional classes would also be represented, besides non-official Europeans. These bodies would be entirely distinct from the legislative councils, whose powers, of course, are formal, and defined by statute, but they would be consulted on matters in respect of which legislation was contemplated, as well as on other occasions. When the legislative councils were enlarged, under the Act of 1892, it was recognised that territorial representation was unsuited to India, and the electorate was so constituted that all the more important interests were represented. It is, however, hardly disputed that, in the case of the provincial councils, the elective system has proved a failure. Out of 54 members elected by district boards, no less than 36 have been barristers and pleaders, while out of 43 members elected by district municipalities 40 have belonged to the same profession. Out of the 338 non-official members, who have been appointed to provincial councils since the system came into force 36 per cent. have been lawyers, and only 22 per cent. landowners, though between 70 and 80 per cent. of the population are, in some sense, agriculturists. In fact, the lawyers have practically monopolised the representation.

The principle of a standing majority is accepted by the Government of India as legitimate and necessary to the ends and aims of the paramount power in India, and they remark in their circular that this position has never been disputed by any section of public opinion in India which does not dispute the legitimacy of the paramount power itself. They might have said much more than this, for the admission of any other principle would, in the eyes of the natives, make the Government ridiculous and impossible.

It is now proposed that the Imperial Legislative Council should have a maximum strength of 54, including the Viceroy. Of this number, the members of the Executive Council, and the Lieutenant-Governor of the province in which the Council for the time being sits, account for 8, and the intention is to nominate additional officials, not exceeding 20 in number: one ruling chief, and 4 non-officials nominated by the Viceroy to represent universities, or special interests, of whom 2 must necessarily be Mahomedans, 2 experts also nominated by the Viceroy from time to time for special reasons, and 18 elected members. Of the elected members 2 will be chosen by the Chambers of Commerce of Calcutta and Bombay; 7 by the non-official members of the provincial councils of the great provinces of Madras, Bombay, Bengal, Eastern Bengal, the United Provinces, the Punjaub and Burma, and 7 by the nobles and great landholders of the same provinces, excluding Burma, and adding the Central Provinces. The remaining 2 members will be elected by Mahomedans.

Under this scheme the former non-official members now elected for Madras, Bombay, Bengal, and the United Provinces will be raised to seven in number, the privilege of election being extended to Eastern Bengal, Punjaub, and Burma. The Government of India states in its circular to local governments and administrations that it is impressed with the necessity for giving substantial representation to the great landholders, who not only constitute the aristocratic and stable elements in Indian society, but also represent the interest of the landlords, great and small—in short, the landed interest, in a continent in which that interest is paramount among all classes. For it should be remembered that no small proportion of the landlords are holders of quite small estates, whose interests are nevertheless identical with those of the great landlords, the latter not being by any means a class apart from the people, of whom indeed, in this pre-eminently agricultural country, they are the best and, under existing conditions, the only representatives.

It is suggested that the provincial electorate for choosing the seven representatives of the landholders on the Imperial Legislative Council should vary from about 100 to 150 members, and that the amount of land revenue payable to Government, which should confer the right to vote, should be not less than 10,000 rupees, or £666 a year. It is probable that an electorate of this character would be difficult to manipulate, and better calculated than a larger and more heterogeneous body to defy the wire-pulling which has resulted in the almost complete monopoly of representation by the legal classes.

The question of the electorate, however, is left, as indeed are all others, to the local governments, who are desired to inquire, deliberate, and report fully their opinions upon the proposals referred for their consideration. Great importance is attached to the representation of the Mahomedans, who are a factor in India far greater than would necessarily follow from their numbers in comparison with those of the Hindoos. Lord Minto observed last year, in answering a deputation, that any electoral representation would be doomed to failure which aimed at granting personal enfranchisement regardless of the beliefs and traditions of the communities composing the population of the continent, and it is notorious that the Mahomedans have never received representation commensurate with the weight of their community. It is suggested that the provincial electorate for Mahomedans should be differently constituted in view of the fact that not many of their co-religionists are included amongst the great landlords. Of the four seats reserved for them in the Viceroy's Council, two will be filled by nomination by the Viceroy, and two by election in rotation from Bengal, Eastern Bengal, the United Provinces, the Punjaub, Bombay, and Madras. The electorate in this behalf would be constituted partly on the collegiate, and partly on the tax-paying, basis. As regards the provincial legislative councils, conditions vary so much in different parts of India that greater latitude must be allowed to the provincial administrations as regards recourse to the principle of election. At present the larger number of the elected members of such councils, who also constitute the majority of the electorate for the Imperial Council, are chosen by municipalities and district boards, the franchises of which bodies are unduly, indeed extraordinarily, low.

It may be taken for granted that some provincial governments, for instance that of the Punjaub, will consider their territories insufficiently advanced for the application of the elective principle in any form, and that in others a landowning electorate of the class suggested can hardly be obtained, few large estates being in existence. In the former case some kind of collegiate representation could probably be evolved and in the latter the creation of an electorate of smaller landholders would not appear to present insuperable difficulties. Special provision would probably have to be made for the Sikhs in the Punjaub, while the Parsees of Bombay, not without reason, think they should enjoy special representation, to which their loyalty, wealth, and enterprise justly entitle them. They are, however, but 94,190 out of 294,361,056, and it is obvious that the principle of special representation must have its limits, unless something like an Indian parliament upon British lines is to be created. Nor are the Parsees overlooked upon the Legislative Council of Bombay. Indeed the attitude of the Parsee Association in claiming special representation is not universally approved by Parsees, *The Oriental Review* holding that they should throw their lot in with the other Indian communities, though it is pretty clear that what is meant is that the Parsees, who include among their number so many able men, should be persuaded to join the malcontent Congress party, and not accept the proposed reforms. Of that there is, however, no fear; so loyal, intelligent, and sober a community being unlikely under any circumstances to join Bengalis who love agitation for its own sake, or Poona Brahmins whose *métier* it is to hate the English.

As regards native Christians, they are already sufficiently represented by the European official members, who invariably look after their interests in the Provincial and the Imperial Legislative Councils. Nice questions in which they are interested sometimes arise, with some of which, as Additional Member from Madras, I myself was concerned. With one such relating to the law of succession I was able to deal, but another still awaits satisfactory solution—the amendment of the Christian Converts Dissolution of Marriage Act, under which converts to Christianity, who like the early Christians are generally poor, suffer considerable hardships, and particularly the Roman Catholic Christians, because they are, under the combined operation of the above-mentioned Act and the Penal Code, deprived of the benefit of the Pauline dispensation. This privilege of the faith, by the common law and the immemorial usage of the Church, permitted the dissolution of a marriage subsisting between a convert and a spouse who refused to live with him or her, because of his or her conversion, by a simple process, outside the courts, lasting thirty days and costing nothing, whereas the present procedure is, to a poor fisherman for example, only less prohibitive than the private Act of Parliament for divorce procedure, which formerly obtained in England. If, however, this solitary grievance were remedied, little would remain for a representative of native Christians to accomplish. Why this has never been put right I cannot understand, nor could my colleague, Sir Griffith Evans, who said: "The Catholic Christians can get no redress as to the hardship of the marriage laws. Their converts are branded as bigamists, their children bastardised, and their priests turned into criminals."

The Mahomedans lost no time in expressing their gratitude to Lord Minto for his speedy fulfilment of his pledges to the great deputation and their approval of "a sincere and timely attempt to respond to the practical ideals of liberty and progress, which are stirring the natural leaders of all classes and sects in the country, provision being made for due and adequate protection of the great Mahomedan minority in India." They understood that Lord Minto's Government "of its own initiative put forward a scheme which would in the main command the approval of all moderate and sober leaders of public opinion in India." The Secretary of State, too, has taken great pains to explain that the scheme was in part that of the Government of India, which he had approved, but did not originate.

Nevertheless, nearly all the critics affect to consider the contemplated reforms as the personal proposals of Mr Morley. Condemnations therefore of a personal character fall to the ground, and objectors are left to explain why all the members of the Executive Government of India are perverted Liberals or anti-democratic Tories.

No sooner had Mr Morley's speech announcing the proposed reforms been telegraphed to India than open-air meetings of denunciation, chiefly attended by students, were held in Calcutta. Babu Bepin Chandra Pal congratulated his hearers that, though the Congress movement had been unable to awaken enthusiasm, the *Svadeshi* agitation had been more successful. "The English at last were afraid, and were resorting to conciliation. But the people would be satisfied with nothing less than *Svaraj*—self-government. The Feringhees"—a contemptuous name for Europeans—"were fools to think they could check popular forces at the point of the bayonet. Realising the seriousness of the situation, they now took to extending popular powers. They shook in their shoes at the remembrance of the Mutiny, and were mightily afraid of another rising." The speaker was very bold regarding the attitude of his own newspaper, which, however, distinctly moderated its tone after he himself had been warned to amend his ways. The admission that the reforms extend popular powers is useful, and no doubt inadvertent.

The objections taken to reforms of the Imperial Council centre around the provision of seven seats for nobles and great landowners, who, without the slightest justification, are described as well-born sycophants. That there are some of this class may be true, but that this description fits them all is wholly untrue, and Lord Curzon, who was as masterful as a man may be in the Viceroy's chair, did not find the native princes and chiefs very amenable to his endeavour to prevent them from leaving their states or revisiting Europe without permission. Nor do the records of the Government of India show that the upper classes are by any means "master please" gentlemen. It is a very simple matter for the few agitators to describe the many who agree with the Government as interested time-servers, but something more than vituperation is needed when one small class stands against many millions.

It is said that only chiefs and nobles likely to agree with Government will stand a chance of being nominated; that their powers will be vague and ill defined, and that there will be no free and public discussion. One paper asks what opinion can Maharajas give as regards important administrative or legislative questions. Now, Sir Arthur Havelock, who has governed colonies all over the world, and was also Governor of Madras, after meeting the present Maharaja of Travancore, said he was reminded by him of nothing so much as of an exceptionally able and well-informed Permanent Under Secretary of State. The Congress would count no princes and nobles except such as had joined their camp, to which, under the completest possible misunderstanding as to the power and influence of the organisation at home, a few of them unfortunately do belong, or to the funds of which at any rate they subscribe.

Time is lost in dealing with objections to the maintenance of an official majority. Our Indian fellow-subjects, who consider that a ruler patient of any criticism whatsoever is weak, would write down as mad any such who expected to be beaten, and to continue to rule, and the party which wishes to reduce the majority see in this expedient the means of representing that, but for the votes of the sycophants, the opposition would have won the day.

The agitators wish to have their own majority in order to reduce the army, repeal the Army Act, and fill all posts by natives of the country, in short, to be rid of the British Government. The use made of the principle of election in appointments to the Legislative Council is such as no sane administration can afford to ignore. No one at present can be elected unless he is the nominee of the Congress party, though it is notorious that the latter is not representative of the people, but of class and caste interests, and that the Mahomedans, Rajputs, Sikhs, lower caste and class Hindoos are wholly opposed to its policy, and detest the speech-making lawyer and intriguing Babu.

Of course it is the case that under existing conditions, while Indian gentlemen serve as Judges of High Courts and members of Legislative Councils, none occupy executive offices of correspondingly high rank, and consequently few Indians other than those on the Legislative Councils actually take part in the discussion of measures before they become law. It would, however, be a great error to suppose that many such are not consulted, for local administrations are under an obligation to collect opinions from every quarter before they report to the Government of India what is the feeling of the country on any particular legislative project. In fact, no measure becomes law without the most widely extended inquiry, and it is unfortunate that this fact is not better known. The shelves of the Secretariats groan under ponderous files containing innumerable opinions from public bodies and private individuals about every Act which is found in the Statute Books.

It is also true that the proceedings of the Advisory Council will be confidential, but as none of the Congress and Babu parties are likely to serve upon it for some time to come there will be no occasion for the delivery of long speeches addressed to press reporters. Sir E. Law, no Indian civil servant, or sun-dried bureaucrat, but a man of wide and varied experience, observed that members of Council of the Congress party were prone to adversely criticise proposals of Government in long speeches in order to maintain their reputations as political patriots. Such patriots will probably have no opportunity of thus advertising themselves upon the Advisory Councils.

Nor can it be denied that no powers are granted to these councils, and Sir Edward Law has suggested that they should be called together once or twice a year, and that if they object by a majority of three-fourths to any measure on which they are asked to advise the project of law should be dropped. In regard to the first suggestion, Sir E. Law perhaps hardly realises the enormous expense considerations of custom and dignity entail upon native states, whenever their rulers visit the capitals of India; and as regards the second, it would be quite incompatible with the maintenance in undiminished strength of the executive authority of Government that anybody should, in any circumstances, be empowered to override its decisions, or to frustrate its intentions. It is only in a few of the more democratic countries of Europe, if there, that a government can, under any circumstances, be defeated, or can defer to opponents, and continue to exist.

Then objection is taken to the idea of counterpoise, the aim of the Government being, it is said, to create a countervailing influence against the opinion of the (English) educated classes. *The Indian Patriot*, for instance, writes:

"It is useless to pretend that the large landowners, the backward classes, the artisans and traders form or direct any kind of public opinion in the country. That is done by the educated classes, by officials, lawyers, journalists and others, who, because they have an opinion, make themselves felt. The counterpoise is intended to neutralise the effect of public opinion. Backward classes, who are at present incapable of forming or influencing opinion, are to be brought into prominence, so that they may, by their silence or by their adherence to Government in all matters, neutralise the effect of the public opinion which makes itself felt at present by means of press and platform."

It is natural that the agitators and lawyers do not like the idea of being put, as far as may be, in their proper places, but they represent no one of the many classes but their own.

Another journal, on the same side, is sufficiently ingenuous to write:

"The big landowners take little interest in affairs, and where they do the credit is due to the educated classes. At all events the leaders of the Congress movement have been doing their best to create an intelligent interest in them about public affairs, and have spared no pains in securing their sympathy."

No doubt the Congress party has done its utmost to capture the agricultural interest, but so far, fortunately, it has failed.

Sir Alfred Lyall, on account of his administrative experience, his scholarship, and his sympathy with the inhabitants, is one of the greatest living authorities upon India. He says "that those who are pressing for a system which would in a short time put the great power of government, of war, of finance, and the highest problems of administration in the hands of elective bodies, are selecting the line of greatest resistance." Of course moderate reformers in India realise that self-government is a distant ideal, and only desire to take steps now to prepare the way. The recent revolution in Persia is quoted in the vernacular press as a proof that Asiatic nations are not unsuited for representative government, but it is early yet to draw any conclusions from that vexed and distracted land. Sir Alfred was in favour of appointing any native of India, of proved ability, to any office for which he was qualified, and, so far as the writer is concerned, this very much expresses his own view. Nor is it easy to say why the judicial service, even in the grade of district judge, should not be chiefly officered by some of the many admirably qualified Indian lawyers who would be only too glad to accept these offices, though Mr Justice Metra's recent ruling as to the meaning of *svaraj* somewhat shakes an opinion to this effect held with confidence for thirty years. The intellectual gifts of the high-caste Hindoos are, however, not disputed, nor is it for their English rulers to impute to them a want of corresponding morality, or, in a Western sense, civilisation. But if a claim for Western representative institutions be founded, as the Congress seems to hold, on the assimilation of Western civilisation, it is relevant to point out that compulsory widowhood, infant marriage, polygamy, and other practices abhorred of European races, flourish not only unchecked, but with the marked and peculiar approval of the upper castes and classes, who set the fashions others below them follow. Further, these practices are particularly prevalent in Bengal, the province in which agitation and unrest and a demand for a Parliament and Home Rule originated; that in which the licentious Sakti worship chiefly prevails; that in which was manifested the strongest opposition to the

Age of Consent Act of 1891. Some, however, even of the Congress organs in Southern India are "hopeful of good results accruing from the proposed reforms, so far as the Legislative Councils are concerned, as all sections of the community will elect the best men." The Bengalis are more bitter, and no praise can be found in their press.

In one quarter race representation was denounced, and Mr Morley convicted out of his own mouth of inconsistency because he declined, though anxious to appoint Indians, to set up racial standards, when urged to provide in the Indian Councils Bill for the appointment of Indians to his Council. But it can hardly be seriously contended that this position as regards British and Indians in the Council at home has any application to the representation of different Indian races in the Indian continent. In other quarters the justice of special representation for Mahomedans is admitted, even in respect of such as are converts from Hindooism, like the Moplahs of Malabar, and the Labbays of the southern districts of Madras. Indeed in this, as in many other respects, it is to Southern India the inquirer into Indian questions must go for anything approaching moderate and statesmanlike criticism of the very important proposals now under consideration.

While far-reaching reforms have been formulated and are under consideration in India, a useful measure has been passed by Imperial Parliament, the Council of India Act of 1907. This Act contains valuable provisions calculated to keep the members of Council in closer touch with India, and to provide for new blood being more frequently imported. It met with no serious opposition in the House, though an amendment was proposed by Mr O'Donnell. The number of the Council, which had previously been 12, was raised to 14, and it was an open secret when the Bill was introduced that Mr Morley intended for the first time in our history to appoint two representative Indian gentlemen, no condition as to race being part of the past or present law in this behalf. At the same time the salary of the two extra members was provided by reducing the salary of members from £1200 to £1000 a year, a measure to which no great objection can be taken for reasons given in a previous chapter. The period of absence from India before appointment was reduced from ten to five years, so that men fresh from India might be concerned in its government, and the term of office of future members was reduced from ten to seven years, in order that fresh blood from India might more frequently be introduced. Just as the reforms proposed in the councils in India were unacceptable to the Bengal agitators, because they provide for real representation of different races and classes by members of such races and classes, so the reform accomplished in the Secretary of State's Council, which disposes for ever of the charge that Britain considers any office too great for qualified Indians, proved obnoxious to the Bengali agitation because really representative Indians were appointed by Mr Morley. These were a Hindoo, Mr Krishna Gobinda Gupta, and a Mahomedan, Mr Syed Hussein Bilgrami, C.S.I. The former gentleman served for thirty-four years in the India Civil Service, and reached the high position of member of the Board of Revenue in Bengal. He is a man of the highest character, of great ability, of good family, a native of Eastern

Bengal, and has served on various commissions and in many responsible offices. Mr Syed Hussein is the grandson of the Oriental interpreter to Lord Dalhousie, a man of great ability, learning, and literary power, who has served in Hyderabad, Deccan, under Sir Salar Jung, the friend of his own and of our country, as private secretary to the present Nizam, as Director of Public Instruction in the Hyderabad State, and as an additional member of the Governor General's Council. He was a staunch friend of another friend of his, and of our, country, Sir Syed Ahmad, and he possesses the rare distinction of being equally acceptable to Moslems of the old and of the new school. Needless to say, through a long career he has borne a stainless reputation. The Secretary of State was to be congratulated on having obtained such helpers in his difficult task, but their merits were not likely to commend them to the Congress school. *The Bengali* is the organ of Mr Surendra Nath Bannerji, who, like Mr Krishna Gobinda Gupta, began life in the Indian Civil Service—

> "But there,
> I doubt, all likeness ends between the pair."

The following is an extract from the pages of this journal:—

"Indians require an altogether different type of men to represent their interests in the Council of the Secretary of State, and we are afraid that our countrymen will look on this last act of Mr Morley's as another blow to the aspirations of the Congress party."

Again *The Indian Patriot* writes:

"We admit that the appointment of Indians to the

Indian Council is a great step in removing the obnoxious colour bar; but Mr Morley himself spoiled its immediate political effect by nominating two men who are out of touch and sympathy with the people at large, and who are worse than the worst Anglo-Indians in their political opinions."

That is to say, they represent the Hindoos and the Mahomedans, but not the Congress, the Poona Brahmins, and the Bengali Babus.

The Bengali warns the Government that it is playing with fire, that its elections are shams, that the educated classes are ceasing to repose confidence in the Legislative Councils, and will have less faith in them as reconstructed. The constant effort of the disaffected vernacular press is to make believe that the Babus are the representatives of the masses, to whom, however, they are of all classes the most obnoxious. The only interest the Babus and the Brahmins have in the masses is to exploit them, and to keep them ignorant and subservient to themselves. *The Amrita Bazaar Patrika*, the other leading newspaper of Bengal, agrees in condemnation, and objects to any scheme under which the Government majority is assured. *The Hindu* of Madras, so long edited by Mr Subramania Iyer, who has been quoted in Chapter X., holds up the principle of minority representation to ridicule, and obviously, where the majority runs into hundreds of millions, the principle is not likely to be welcomed with enthusiasm.

The Indian *Spectator*, on the other hand, a moderate and impartial organ, thought advisory councils would have a steadying effect upon the pace at which Western ideals were being superimposed on Eastern civilisation. "Our politics have been too much dominated by partisanship. A truly representative government is not synonymous with government by the advocacy of one class on behalf of another class. It must try to secure direct and personal representation of as many classes as possible, and the proposed reforms will be a distinct step in the realisation of a true representative government."

A Royal Commission was also appointed last year "To inquire into the relations now existing, for financial and administrative purposes, between the Supreme Government and the various Provincial Governments in India, and between the Provincial Governments and the authorities subordinate to them, and to report whether, by measures of decentralisation or otherwise, those relations can be simplified and improved, and the system of government better adapted to meet the requirements and promote the welfare of the different provinces, and without impairing its strength and unity, to bring the Executive Power into closer touch with local conditions."

There is no reference to the relations between the India Office and the Government of India, and the direction in which decentralisation is chiefly contemplated is in the relations between the Central and the Provincial Government—a thorny question, because the actual authority of the Government of India over subordinate administrations is unlimited, while in practice its exercise is greatly restrained by the jealousy of interference manifested by the latter, and the reluctance to override them always felt by the former, authority. There is, however, ample room for decentralisation, both in this behalf and in respect of the relations between provincial governments and their subordinate authorities, who are far too much hampered by inspections, reports, and other aspects of the red tape demon, who destroys efficient administration. As regards finance, considerable reform, all in the right direction, has recently been introduced, but it would be premature to hold that even that chapter is closed.

In addition to the above suggested reforms and changes in the administration, the Government of India now proposes that the Budget should be discussed under separate heads, to be explained by the member of Government in charge of the department concerned, after which a general debate would follow—more time than at present being allotted. Systematic criticism cannot exist under the present arrangement, and that some change is necessary will be readily understood by anyone who, like the writer, has been a member of the Council, and has been faced by the alternative of either cutting his criticisms unduly short, or of making the proceedings, which have lasted uninterruptedly from morning to night, unduly long.

In the foregoing pages I have described the character of the proposed reforms, and the manner in which they have been received. But so wholly and completely does the Indian recognise strength as the first requisite of Government, the rest being comparatively nowhere, that it is admitted by the Indian newspapers—let *The Indian Patriot* speak, for it is a fair representative of the more moderate Congress organs—that "No minister ever held a stronger position than Mr Morley holds to-day. He is for the moment more powerful than the most despotic monarch. His methods of administration receive the support alike of Liberal and Conservative members."

So may it always be, and in that event the Congress in India, and its representatives in England, will soon learn to confine their aspirations within reasonable limits, and British rule will be perpetuated to the infinite benefit of the multitudinous masses of the many peoples which inhabit our Indian Empire.

CHAPTER XII

SOCIAL REFORM

Conservatism of Hindoos—Double Life of Reformers—Age of Consent Act—Infant Marriage—Shastras of Antiquarian Interest only—Necessity for Knowledge of Vernaculars—Value of Sportsmanlike Habits—Difficulty of Commensality and Reciprocal Female Intercourse—Domestic Life of Hindoos—Prayer and Praise—Life of Women—Actual Religion of the Hindoos—Caste—Marriage—Drinking—Alcohol and Tea—Death—Character and Position of Men and Women—Evidence of Miss Bhor, Colonel Meadows Taylor, Mr Duff, Abbé Dubois, Mr Crooke, Mr Kipling, Mr Clarke, Miss Noble, and Keshub Chunder—Sir Madava Rao on Hindoo Customs—Hindoo Charity

THE movement in favour of social reform in India has been overwhelmed by political agitation, which alone has of late engaged the energies of the English educated classes. Indeed the agitators have realised the absolute necessity of adopting the conservative attitude which is that of the masses. Ten years ago all those who are now clamouring against British rule in India were eagerly attacking customs which are woven into the very framework of Indian society, and at that time a great deal was heard about the necessity for educating women. Even then, in South India at any rate, where female education is most advanced, the prejudice against sending girls to public schools was somewhat wearing away, partly owing to the parents having become wise enough to see that there is no greater impropriety in girls going to school than boys, and partly because of the substitution, where-ever practicable, of female for male teaching agency. There is no doubt that among Hindoos generally the impression prevails that education is likely to lead women to wrongdoing, and however much the Government, philanthropic, and missionary bodies, and wealthy and generous individuals, may do, to advance this cause, the real spadework must be accomplished, and the greater part of the cost must be borne, by the people themselves, who have the cause at heart. As the eminent Indian educationalist, Mr Raganatha Mudaliar, said of persons of his own position and education, "We feel it to be a grievous sin to marry our infant daughters, but even if we could summon up sufficient courage to set at naught the shastraic prohibition, we succumb to the weeping entreaties and expostulations of our wives. There is a general consensus of opinion amongst educated men in India that widows should be allowed to remarry but such remarriage on a large scale will be possible only when women learn to assert their rights against perpetual widowhood. We would allow the members of each division of a caste," only that, be it noted, not the members of different castes, "to intermarry, but their is no hope of this reform, small as it is, being carried into effect unless our women rise to something like the intelligent level we have ourselves attained." Such was the feeling in Madras, the province most advanced in respect of social reform, and most backward in accepting the Congress political programme.

The subject of social reform is necessarily vague, comprehensive, and ill defined. The Indian masses, it has never been denied, are fulfilled with the conviction that the social customs and institutions which have so long stood the test of time possess peculiar merit, and are superlatively well adapted to their own requirements. The masses in this behalf include all Hindoos who are not, and, off the platform, a great many of those who are, English educated. The people are passionately attached to the simple faith and primitive ways of their forefathers; they are prepared to take what a Brahmin says as gospel, and the women, who are the most conservative half of the population, exercise the strongest possible influence over the men, though the true position in this respect has been obscured and, unintentionally of course, misrepresented, by interested observers, whose field has necessarily been limited to the lowest and most degraded classes.

If any proofs were wanted that the desire for social reform had only touched the merest superficial fringe of the Indian peoples, it would be found in the double life led by most of the reformers themselves. An ardent radical in his domestic life does the very things that in his public life he denounces. He believes in astrology, marries his children in extreme youth, spends more than he can afford on ceremonies, submits to the exactions of the priests, and in general conforms to Hindoo standards.

He is perfectly well aware that if certain texts can be found in favour of remarriage of widows, at least an equal number can be found to condemn this practice, and that custom, which is the real arbiter, has been against it for centuries.

That experienced statesman, Sir John Strachey, in 1899 wrote: "The people of India are intensely conservative, and wedded, to an extent difficult for Europeans to understand, to every ancient custom, and between their customs and their religion no line of distinction can be drawn.

It is, of course, true that no social conditions render it necessary now that the community should be divided into sections, with impossible barriers between them, for the four principal castes do not confine themselves in these days to their proper avocations. The Brahmin is now as much an official as he was formerly a priest; the Vaisya as much a clerk as a shopkeeper; the Sudra as much a peasant-proprietor as a farm-servant, and the Kshatriya, once a warrior, is now anything you please. Not only can no member of one, intermarry with a member of another, of these castes, but there are innumerable subdivisions of each of the actual castes, in respect of which the same disability obtains. Legislation, of course, is powerless to deal with such a situation; if, indeed, legislative interference were desirable, which I, for one, do not think.

The failure of the Age of Consent Act has proved that it is useless to legislate too far ahead of public opinion. As to the practice of infant marriage, the evils resulting from it have been greatly exaggerated. Perverse as such a practice appears to us to be, its moral and social consequences have not been, by any means, as disastrous as reformers pretend. The majority of women in India are probably as happy as women elsewhere. Custom reconciles to any hardships, but such hardships are the subject of habitual and monumental exaggeration. The ordinary Briton is unable to understand the sacramental and mystical conception of marriage as a binding tie for this life and the life hereafter. One of the ablest Hindoo judges who ever sat on the bench in India, Sir T. Muttuswami Iyer, "deprecated any legislation which would involve an irritating interference with the most important domestic event of the majority of his Majesty's Hindoo subjects." The Hindoo system provides every woman with a husband, and every man with a wife, and if in Bengal, where all those customs are most prevalent, 21 per cent. of the women are widows, as against about one half that number in England and France, on the other hand, the proportion of unmarried females is more than twice as great in England as in Bengal. It must also be remembered that cohabitation or actual marriage does not take place until the girls reach the age of puberty, the marriage ceremony, in fact, being nothing more than an irrevocable betrothal. Girls must marry early when they mature early, and as the mean age for married women in India is twenty-eight, and in England forty, there is, in fact, no great difference, when climate and length of life are taken into account, the child-bearing ages in Europe being fifteen to forty-five, and fifteen to thirty-five in India.

It is well known that in old times girls were married after they came of age, that remarriage of widows was once permitted, and that there is no authority in the Vedas for the practice of suttee. Nor in very early times did the system of caste prevail, for it was developed towards the end of the Vedic period, and arose immediately from the fact that all class occupations were hereditary. Soon the smallest difference, as regards trade, profession, or practice, became enough to lead to the institution of separate castes, which are now some 4000 in number. But, of course, it must be understood that existing conditions have obtained for many centuries, and that the Shastraic system is of purely antiquarian and academic interest.

It is one thing to fall back upon the Shastras for historical light, and another to base modern reforms upon these ancient texts. They are worthy of all reverence, as they hand down the traditions of a past civilisation, and no social reformer can neglect or ignore them, but it should be manifest that rules and observances which became men of a bygone age cannot suit people who live in the present day, in different circumstances and environments. The Bible, the law, and the prophets can all be expressed, so far as Hindoos are concerned, by the one word custom.

Upon the much-debated subject of social intercourse, volumes have been written. The fact is that complete fusion, and intermarriage to any great extent, are impossible.

Of all the Hindoos I have seen in India none were more Europeanised, or associated more freely with Europeans, than the late Mr Satthianadan, M.A., LL.M., professor of philosophy at the Presidency College, Madras. He and his wife were both Christians, who habitually frequented the society of the English in the presidency capital, and he, as a high-caste man, possessed particular and, among Indian Christians rare, facilities for noting the feelings of Hindoos of all grades. He wrote: "The educated classes claim to be free from the trammels of caste, but there is glaring incongruity between thoughts and deeds, between public professions and private practice. Much is said against caste, but it still reigns supreme in some form or another even in the most enlightened circles. There is still absence of sympathy between the peoples of India. They are separated by impassable barriers, and, seeing that the points of disparity between the different classes that constitute the Indian population make their cordial sympathy with one another impossible, how can we expect the Indian population, made up as it is of those motley races, to mix cordially with Europeans, a people entirely different from them in creed, colour, customs, and costume. India consists merely of a vast assemblage of races divided into countless unsympathising castes and classes. I admit that English education and Western civilisation have amalgamated to some extent the forces among the Indian population, but greater exertions must be put forth in the castes and classes to bring about a deeper sympathy and more complete union." Then referring to the Briton he quotes Emerson: "Every one of these islanders is an island himself, safe, tranquil, and incommunicable."

But while there can be no fusion and intermarriage, friendly intercourse is by no means difficult, provided always that the Briton can talk the Indian's language.

Of all reasons which prevent free intercourse the chief is ignorance of the languages on the part of the British. It is true that certain tests are exacted from those who enter the public service, but they are of a rather elementary character, and no sooner does the official enter into his kingdom than he finds that everybody about him speaks perfect English, and, though he does not know it, nothing reaches his ears except what has passed through these, generally by no means disinterested, interpreters. The irregular relations which formerly were so frequent between Englishmen and the women of the country led to a complete acquisition of the language in many cases, but the number of Englishwomen in the country has of late so much increased, and any European having relations with native women is so relentlessly persecuted by them, and so disparaged by his fellow-countrymen generally, that this approach to the people is practically abolished.

The pursuit of sport is indeed the only means of access remaining, except for those choice spirits who strike out lines for themselves regardless of the opinion of the little station in which their service is for the most part passed. The freemasonry of sport obtains just as much in India as anywhere else. In the hunting field at home all classes meet upon an equal footing, and this is very much the case in the jungle. Association of this kind leads to a frank interchange of views, and to mutual self-respect and esteem. Statements are often made that Indians will not bring the gun up to an elephant, for instance, but a sportsman who has shown that he himself is dependable will never have occasion to make this complaint. Upon the whole the wonder is, that men unarmed, or if carrying a second rifle inexpert in its use, can be got so readily to put their lives into imminent danger to please a stranger, and for a paltry wage.

The Indian is no more wanting in courage than he is in truthfulness, but unless he knows his man he is always on the defensive, and is ready with some, probably quite unnecessary, wile.

He naturally does not feel at home with a man who cannot talk to him, or, if he tries, will in all good faith, very likely use disrespectful language, and say for "you," "you fellow."

Sir Alfred Lyall explains this matter in a couple of lines as well as could be done in a volume:

"There goes my lord the Feringhee, who talks so civil and bland,
Till he raves like a soul in Jahanum if I do not quite understand,

It is indeed true that want of knowledge is rooted in the want of sympathy. I cannot see that there is anything whatever in the plea frequently put forward that there can be no friendly intercourse until the women on both sides frequent the society of the men. Surely there can be no friendly intercourse unless each side accepts the customs of the other, for which, in point of fact, there are always excellent reasons. At anyrate, to make that a condition on the threshold is to prevent any stepping over it. Nor does the absence of commensality constitute any legitimate ground of complaint. So little is this a bar to social intercourse that I am convinced that any attempt to break it down will set back such progress as has been made. Table manners are a stumbling block of the most mountainous character, and it is not too much to say that different races in Europe abhor the customs of their neighbours in this respect, and that the English are convinced that they are the only clean feeders. Natives of India have wholly and absolutely different standards, and it is exceedingly sound policy for our intercourse to stop short at the table. I have myself seen spirited efforts made to break down these barriers, all of which were foredoomed to failure. Attempts on the part of Europeans to give Indian gentlemen refreshment in separate tents and houses, with cooks and attendants of the proper denomination, have resulted in nothing but misunderstandings. At the first meeting of the Congress held in Madras infinite pains were taken by the Governor of Madras and his staff to entertain the delegates, with, I think, very moderate success.

Unfortunately, it is a fact that Europeans who can really carry on a conversation in the vernacular languages are exceedingly rare. It is the most valuable asset a public servant can have, but it is not recognised in honours and promotions. There is also, unfortunately, some truth in the statement, often repeated, that the influence of Englishwomen in India tends to widen the breach. There are of course many exceptions, but upon the whole there is little love lost between English women and Indian men. Moreover, in spite of speeches, writings, and protestations, extremely little has been done by the natives themselves to bring about what is commonly called social reform, a subject as difficult to define in India as it is in England. Even when some person, greatly daring, marries a widow, he finds that he and his wife are lightly regarded, if not absolutely despised, even by those who have actually urged them to such action. Practically nothing has been done in the thirty years which have elapsed since first the subject was broached, and, instead of adhering to the main lines as laid down by the leaders in this behalf, the reformers of late have occupied themselves with anti-nautch demonstrations and endeavours to prevent dancing girls from taking part in festivals and celebrations. Women of this class are just now strongly denounced, and it is alleged against them "that they have cast down many wounded, yea, many strong men have been slain by them, that their house is the way to hell, going down to the chambers of death." All this may be true, but immorality, like everything else in India, tends to become hereditary, and the position of the temple female attendants no doubt amounts to a publicly acknowledged profession, though it is subject to limitations, and is not on all fours with that of the ordinary prostitute. Objection is now taken to the presence of these girls at the solemnisation of weddings and on festal occasions, though their notorious association with students is an occasion for hard winking.

Originally, they were dedicated as virgins to the service of religion, and they are now the handmaidens of the idols, of which the priests and others have long said with Horace: "*Ne sit ancillæ tibi amor pudori.*" No doubt this custom and others are open to objection, but those who are busily occupied in preaching social reform are too apt to lose sight of what the domestic life of India really is, and from a perusal of tracts and pamphlets it would be readily imagined that it stood in urgent and exceptional need of drastic reform. No doubt it is capable of improvement, but, at the same time, it is probable that in many respects it is superior to that of other countries, and in few respects falls below normal standards. It would be extremely difficult to draw a picture of the family life of Europe, and it is equally difficult to draw a picture of the family life of India, but as a common Christianity imposes standards possessing some similarity in ideal, if not in practice, upon all the inhabitants of Europe, so the Brahminic or Hindoo system conduces to the maintenance among the many peoples and races of India of something approaching a common standard of life and conversation, and, even where customs repugnant to Hindoo ideals exist, the scheme on the whole will be found to be fashioned on the Hindoo or Brahminic system. It is very difficult, almost impossible, to distinguish between caste and Hindooism. The superintendents of the Indian Census of 1901, who reported for the different provinces, are pretty well agreed, where they have to define Hindooism, in saying that so long as a man observes caste rules he may not only do pretty much as he pleases, but may actually offer his individual worship to any god or hero, to any stick, stone, or natural feature, which his own inclination, or the animistic traditions of his village, has endowed with supernatural attributes of a constructive or destructive character.

An accomplished Bengali gentleman, Mr Ghose, who published a life of the Maharaja Nabkissen, a faithful friend of the English in the days of Clive, observes that "there is no fear of English rule going wrong if we remember the principles of Queen Victoria's character, and in respect of reforms follow the English method of evolution, not that of revolution." Nevertheless, our Indian legislature has made spirited inroads upon the principle of guaranteeing to the natives of India their own customs and their own religion, though whenever these have been of a revolutionary character they have been still-born. Such, for instance, has been the fate of the Age of Consent Act, as I anticipated in an article published in *The Nineteenth Century* for October 1890. It is necessary, therefore, in describing the domestic life of a Hindoo family, to take an example from a characteristic area, and it is best to go to the Deccan or South India, for there Mahomedan rule and Mahomedan customs never took root. Even in Hyderabad the people are Hindoos, and the Nizam and his Mussulman lords a mere privileged handful, while on the south-west coast there are states which were completely unaffected by the Mahomedan conquest.

To begin at the beginning, the site must be chosen and the house must be built according to caste rules, in auspicious months; hymns are chanted; saffron, turmeric, and sandal are smeared upon the beams;

flowers are offered, and the edifice is apostrophised according to custom in that behalf provided. The house consists of one or more quadrangles with open courtyards, and a blank wall generally offers to the street. The kitchen is the best apartment, and combines in some respects the characteristics of a chapel and a cooking place. The church in England is often a small affair beside the mansion house, and the missionary's chapel a lowly hut beside his bungalow, but in Indian houses no part should be higher than the kitchen, into which no person of a lower caste than the master may look or enter. The other rooms open upon an inner verandah, in which cows and calves are stabled. There is little furniture; indeed, that actually used consists of a few pots and pans, brazen vessels, and elementary bedsteads, these simple articles being generally collected in a small, plain, unpretentious room. The married sons live under the paternal roof, and an extra man makes no difference, as they all sleep upon the floor, and after all, in many parts of Europe, and at least in one capital, men servants do the same, or use the sofas and chairs. In the centre of one of the quadrangles there should be an altar, on which grows a shrub of holy basil. Suppose the owner to be a Brahmin, and already installed, he must rise before the sun, and repeat texts from the puranas. I give one, and have translated it, as I have others quoted, for the benefit of such as require a translation :

> "Rama, thou givest all good things,
> Who but thyself deliverance brings?
> Thee with one voice we all adore,
> Ah! let me praise thee more and more."

Then comes the rinsing of the mouth, washing of

the feet, cleansing of the teeth with a particular kind of stick never again used, then the bath, prayers, oblations to the sun, and the fixing of the caste marks upon the now purified person ; the salutations north, south, east, and west, and the repetition of the sacred Sanscrit text :

> "Hail earth and sky and heaven, hail kindly light,
> Illuminator of our purblind sight."

Before the midday meal there are more prayers, ablutions, and offerings, and then the male members sit on the floor and eat their rice or other grain, with pickles or condiments, off plates of plantain or other leaves. Food is eaten with the hand, and water is poured into the mouth, so that neither the vessel nor the fluid touches the lips. There are prayers again at supper-time, which comes at sundown in the simple healthy life of the Indian villager, but the perpetual prayers and ceremonies are capable of some abbreviation. No one goes to the temple for service as we go to church, but worship is performed daily by the official priest, just as Mass is served in the Catholic Church, and upon holidays and festivals the people collectively adore the gods. As for the females, it will suffice if they worship their husbands, which is their actual duty, and they are pretty well occupied with bearing and rearing children, and with their domestic duties, and are probably not inferior in domestic virtues to any in the world.

It may be fairly said of a Hindoo wôman, "that the heart of her husband doth safely trust in her, that she rises while it is yet night, and gives meat to her household, that she stretcheth out her hand to the poor, and reacheth out her hand to the needy, that she looks well to the ways of her household, and eateth not the bread of idleness, that her children rise up and call her blessed, and her husband praiseth her."

She is hard at work all day, and in the cultivating classes, helps in the field. At night, when the lamps are lit, she makes obeisance to the god of fire, saying, if the translation be accepted :

> "This flame proceeds from God above,
> This lamp is lit by heavenly love,
> So praise we when each night begins
> The flame which burns away our sins."

Much the same ceremonial may be seen any day in a Russian village, where the peasant bows himself before the eikon and the lamp in the angle of the wall, and, like the Hindoo, he too knows that he is, and that no one else is, orthodox.

There appears to be some doubt as to whether the good deeds of the husband and wife are transferable, but it seems certain that, after her husband's death, she can hasten his final absorption into beatitude by her prayers and penance, which is very much like the doctrine of the elder branch of the Christian Church.

In the lower castes, of course, where the worship is rather demonolatry or animism, the daily ritual amounts to little more than an obeisance to the sun in the morning and to the lamp at night.

There is no consciousness during one life of a former existence, and the average Hindoo troubles himself little about religion, but very much about caste.

Hindoos are divided amongst themselves into non-dualists, who believe nothing has any real separate existence from the one God ; dualists, who hold that the human soul and the material world have a distinct existence, and the non-dualists, who nevertheless ascribe to the deity a twofold aspect: the supreme spirit the cause, and the material universe the effect. All this is to us as real as the difference between the ὅμο and the ὁμοιόουσια, and among the Hindoos common folk are content to worship Siva or Vishnu, whose outward and visible signs are respectively the horizontal line and the trident on the forehead.

Now had Christian missionaries been content that converts should retain these marks, the top knot, and other signs and observances of caste, Christianity might have made more way in India. The Catholics once had a fair hope of the wholesale conversion of the extreme south, where they actually brought over high-caste natives, until the controversy known as that of the Malabar rites was decided against, what was held to be, trifling with idolatry. It is too late now, even if another policy were adopted, for Christianity and low caste have become once and for ever inextricably associated.

All Indian questions are caste questions. No Englishman who had turned Hindoo would be accepted as an authority, even by Hindoos, regarding the religious and social characteristics of the people he had forsaken, but here in England the authorities accepted by the public and the press are almost invariably those who, having been, have ceased to be, Hindoos, or, having a special mission to convert Hindoos, are naturally not impressed with such evidence as tends to show that Hindoos stand in no need of conversion. Yet an ancient civilisation and a faith professed by hundreds of millions are entitled to respectful treatment, and the law-abiding—for with the exception of one class the Hindoos deserve the epithet—to an unprejudiced judgment. Yet I have seldom heard other than misrepresentation on the platform in this country of the domestic life and the character of the people.

It has already been recorded in regard to Hindoo marriages, the evils of which have been so enormously exaggerated, that the actual marriage ceremony is no more than a binding betrothal, and it may amuse the reader to quote from the venerable institutes of Manu the following advice:—

"Let a man not marry a girl with reddish hair or deformed limbs, nor one troubled with sickness, nor troubled with too much, or too little, hair, nor one immoderately talkative." Polyandry is not much practised in India, and it may be worth mentioning, that the Nairs of the Malabar coast are not polyandrous, for though their system allows a woman to change her husband, she is not permitted to have more than one at a time. The instincts of the Hindoo are monogamous, and he rarely takes a second wife, unless the first has no male issue, when the paramount religious necessity for having a son to perform his funeral sacrifices renders obligatory either a second wife or an adoption.

The marriage ceremonies are long, complex, and costly, and eating, drinking, and presents are not wanting. The question is asked and answered, but the garments are tied together in the place of the presentation of a ring, the exact counterpart of which is a gold ornament fixed around the neck. Rice is thrown over the newly wedded, just as it is with us; hymns, feasting, and processions follow, and the bride, who in the case of respectable families is never of a marriageable age, returns to her parents' house to await the arrival of womanhood. Though in many respects these marriages resemble our own, there is no wine, of course, and the feasting is vegetarian in character, for the upper classes never drink wine nor eat meat unless they have received an English education. The lower classes may enjoy flesh and liquor, but they must, and do, approximate to the standards of their betters if they wish to obtain the respect of the public. Pariahs, who are, of course, a caste, though a low one, eat flesh, and that which they do eat is generally carrion, since the cow is sacred, goats are wanted for their milk, and animals generally are too expensive to be slaughtered. Those who have lived in Indian villages will readily understand the feelings with which the upper classes regard the flesh-eaters, who are, it must be admitted, in all respects infinitely their inferiors.

It must not be supposed because they are not eaten, that animals are always kindly treated. True, the Jains, who are a handful, maintain hospitals for sick and wounded creatures, but bullocks and horses exist in conditions which would give the S.P.C.A. a little work, though the interference of such societies is to be strongly deprecated, as an agency foreign to the ideas of the people, and practising that interference with their domestic life which they strongly, and very naturally, resent at the hands of strangers. Yet the Hindoos give their cattle a rest and a feast at the New Year festival, and on other proper occasions, and make offerings to the King of the Snakes, whose worship, in one form or another, and to a greater or less extent, prevails all over India.

Though no wine is drunk except by those who have learnt English habits, it is not the case that the

British introduced alcohol into India, where intoxicating drinks have always been known and used, such use, however, except among the English educated, being confined to the lower classes, and regarded as disgraceful and degrading. Temperance is as distinctly a characteristic of the Hindoos as tolerance, and in both respects they are an example to the nations of Europe. Notwithstanding the evidence of M. Meredith Townsend to the contrary effect, Hindoos, besides dinner and supper, have a light early breakfast of cold rice or cakes. Tea-planters hope that at some future time tea drinking will become universal in India—a consummation to be most devoutly desired, because the drinking of tea involves the boiling of water, and would in India, as it does in China, preserve the people from malarial fever, which, and not cholera or plague, is the real scourge of the continent. The Government should spare no pains to push tea drinking, and it is to the credit of Lord Curzon that he did help the planters, too little encouraged in the past, to sell their salubrious leaf in the country of its origin.

Travellers are allowed a good deal of licence as regards caste rules, which really are the most reasonable in the world, elastic where they cannot be kept, and rigid where they can. Everywhere, however, wayfarers are helped, and to assist the son of the road, as Sadi calls him, is a religious duty.

To quote again from my translation, in the institutes of Manu it is written:

> "Who sends the stranger hungry from his door
> That stranger's sins are added to his score;
> Who entertains a stranger, though his sins
> Are red as scarlet, he salvation wins."

Many ceremonies attend the dead as well as the living, and the sick man in his last moments is carried from his bed to lie upon the earth or beside the river. Thus the house avoids pollution, and nothing can pollute the sacred stream or holy mother earth. The chief mourner, whose claim is decided for the same reasons as obtain among ourselves, performs the sacrifices before the body is borne to the funeral pyre, made up perhaps, in the case of the poor, by contributions of a few sticks from neighbouring houses. He walks three times round the blazing fire carrying a pot of water, which finally he dashes on the ground: "Thus the pitcher is broken, and the dust returns to earth as it was." Some castes, of course, bury their dead, and all do in certain exceptional cases. Ceremonies are less elaborate with the lower castes, and the same distinction applies to the periodical rites for deceased ancestors. As a result of these prayers and ceremonies, the spirits of the departed are provided with a temporary body, while without such they would wander about as malignant ghosts,

"ψυχὴ καὶ εἴδωλον ἀτὰρ φρένες οὐκ' ἔνι πάμπαν."

Next the temporary body is changed for the ethical envelope and passes into the ancestral heaven, there to remain until absorbed, or, as is more widely held, receives judgment according to its works in this world, being reborn after a longer or shorter period spent in the purgatorial heaven or hell, to again accomplish a mortal life in another guise, until at length it qualifies for nirvana, or absorption into the Divine essence, for the Hindoos also believe that each soul is *divinæ particula auræ*. They acknowledge likewise a Supreme Being, the immortality of the soul, and the necessity for, and existence of, another life in which sin and virtue meet with their reward.

In the Sama Veda, the typical man of sin is described. His head is Brahmin murder, his eyes liquor drinking, his face theft, tutor slaying his ears, woman killing his nose, cow destroying his shoulders, adultery his chest, oppression his stomach, while smaller sins are otherwise distributed about his person. He is black, which of course the upper classes of the Hindoos are not, as indeed Hindoos of any class seldom are, and he is bright-eyed and malevolent. In the institutes of Manu the body is otherwise described, and if I may again translate, in this wise—

> "Bones are its rafters and its beams,
> Tendons and nerves its scores and seams,
> Blood is its mortar, and the skin,
> Frail covering, roofs the mansion in.
> Its occupants are age and woe,
> Death and decay, as sure as slow;
> Right gladly should the vital spark,
> The soul, *renounce* a home so dark.
> Birds at their pleasure quit the tree,
> Who leaves the world alone is free."

This is a melancholy picture, but is the Hindoo home melancholy? By no means, nor are Hindoo women miserable. Their lives are made up of light and shade, like those of other races, nor have they less of light. Miss Bhor, a talented Mahratta lady, wrote of Bombay: "In those parts of Western India, where the Mahomedan invasion very slightly affected the old Hindoo customs, the Brahmins and other high castes neither veil themselves nor live in seclusion, and have as merry a time as the men." This of course is equally true of South India, and of all parts of the continent wherein the Mahomedans did not settle in strength. In all such regions, and they are far the greater part, though they do not include the great cities visited by travellers, women wear no veils, and suffer no seclusion, but freely live and move and have their being. Of child marriages the same writer says: "The Hindoo system is bad, but it is worked out on the whole in a kindly and sensible fashion. Marriages turn out happily much oftener than might be thought possible under such circumstances, and as regards child widows, in the working out of this iron caste system there is much real heart and tenderness, which soften its cruel decrees."

Colonel Meadows Taylor, one who knew the Hindoos if ever anyone did, said: "They are as courteous and intelligent a people as any in the world, kind to their children, respectful to their parents, charitable, honest, and industrious, and with such vices as are common to human nature." He denied that they were untruthful, and saw in caste the means of enforcing the, at least outwardly, moral conduct of its members.

In like manner Mr R. C. Dutt, when he leaves the company of the English educated agitators, testifies to the "dislike and distrust the people of India have of the rapid introduction of modern Western methods. Their dislike to the alienation of their chiefs and rajahs, who cease to live and move among, and become strangers to, their own people. There is not, on the whole earth a more frugal and more contented peasantry."

Some day, Mr Dutt, who wields the pen of a ready writer, will explain how such a people can be ground down by the misgovernment of aliens, and how the association of their chiefs and rajahs in the government, which is now proposed by Mr Morley and Lord Minto, can be other than grateful to the people, whose characteristics he, on this occasion at least, so faithfully describes.

Abbé Dubois, than whom no European ever knew India better, but who takes, I think, an unduly unfavourable view of the character of the people of Mysore, writes: "Animated in this behalf by the purest and noblest sentiments, Hindoos consider a man happy in proportion to the number of his children, which are the blessings of his house."

Sir Thomas Munro, Sir Joseph Fayrer, Sir James Malcolm, Sir William Sleaman, and a host of witnesses, have testified to the many and exceeding great merits of the Hindoo character, and with all they say I would, as one who spent a quarter of a century in learning their languages and living amongst them, most heartily associate myself, while compelled, in justice to a people I respect and admire, to repudiate altogether the descriptions of them given by those who, for personal or political reasons, persistently and perpetually misrepresent them. The Dewan, or chief minister of Travancore, which the Census shows to be absolutely the most educated, as it is the most beautiful and most prosperous, region in India, writes: "The Hindoo home is founded on religious principles, the father is guardian, preceptor and patriarch, the woman is protected by her male relations, nor, looking at other countries where celibacy is practised by women, can I consider universal marriage altogether a curse." This is true enough, and I remember what a Hindoo judge of one of the Indian High Courts said, speaking of the difference in the law as regards adultery, which in

India is a criminal offence. He thought "the exigencies of modern European society" hardly allowed of a similarly severe view being taken in Europe of what the Hindoos regarded as a serious crime.

The same Dewan of Travancore wrote, and heaven knows how truly: "There is great misapprehension amongst European nations regarding the purdah, in which there is no slavery or tyranny, but as families rise in the world their females ask for the privileges of the zenana system."

Then Mr Crooke, who takes a very high place amongst those few who are qualified not by platform orations or political agitation, but by personal knowledge of Hindoo life, particularly in Northern India, writes: "The Northern Indian peasant's life is one of ceaseless toil, but it enforces industry and temperance, and is compatible with a ready cheeriness which can find amusement in the veriest trifles. It would be a great mistake to suppose the wife of the peasant to be nothing more than a drudge. Nothing in the house is done without her knowledge and advice, and she is not perhaps worse off than her sister in a similar grade in other parts of the world."

It is curious to find Abbé Dubois, at the beginning, and Mr Crooke at the end, of last century, during the course of which no two men probably knew India better, saying in almost identical words that to imagine that the State can permanently improve the condition of the depressed classes is the dream of an enthusiast. Even a reduction in expenditure and a respite from perpetual increases of administrative charges for the furtherance of progress in Western civilisation, whether needed or not, whether acceptable or not, whether suitable or not, would hardly affect the lowest classes to any great extent. For they do not now groan under an excessive salt-tax and a grinding land-assessment. As has been shown in previous chapters, these are immemorial imposts which the British Government has progressively and enormously reduced. Had they done less in the way of reduction and rigidly abstained from ever levying a new tax their popularity would have been greater, and there would have been less occasion for the enemy to blaspheme. At present, although the total collected is less, it is impossible to deny that there are new cesses and taxes, the inventions of the foreigner.

It is necessary to realise what the domestic life of the Hindoos actually is, before considering what steps should be taken to reform it, though such hesitation would not be tolerated by ardent and professional reformers, who would first of all abolish, and then study any customs which came within their restless and disturbing orbit. Nothing for instance is further from the fact than the assumption, universal in this country, that ladies behind the purdah—who are ignorantly presumed to be the majority of the women of India—are universally ill treated.

How many a missionary or another has stood up in England and said: "I returned and considered all the oppressions which are done under the sun, and beheld the tears of such as were oppressed, and on the side of their oppressors there was power, and they had no comforter." But hear on the other side Mr Kipling: "Even purdah women have always been in touch with a thousand outside interests," or Mr Crooke: "Women exert a wide influence and control, whether within or without zenanas and little that goes on outside escapes their ears." Nor are they neglected by the Government, for they have in many cases special legal guardians in the Court of Wards. Mr Dutt, too, writes: "Purdahs prevail chiefly in the towns of Northern India, where the rule of the Moslems remained for centuries."

Mr S. E. J. Clarke, a man intimately acquainted with Hindoo life, writes of Bengal: "Women of the labouring and agricultural classes move freely about. Girls are by precept, instruction, example and discipline taught a high ideal of womanhood. Even purdah women go on pilgrimage, entertain and visit their friends, and see a great deal of the outer world. I deny that Hindoo women necessarily have a miserable life, and must bear testimony to the happy side." Mr Crooke writes: "There is an utter lack of seclusion except for women of the higher classes," who as has been said, insist on it as an honour due to their rank.

Everything tends to obscure the facts on this subject. For instance, the success of Lady Dufferin's Fund which has been great, and to which I endeavoured in humble fashion to contribute, has not been chiefly amongst purdah women. *The Amrita Bazaar Patrika* wrote: "There is no objection, whatever, on the part of Hindoo or Mahomedan ladies to be treated by male doctors"—and this is, of course, a fact. A Hindoo lately wrote a book called "Kamala's Letters," in which one of the female characters says: "Purdah does not exist in Hindoo society except when wealth holds despotic sway. Where elsewhere it is found, it is due to the new products of English education, who, rising in rank and position under false notions have taken to it."

The same writer adds:

"Though it is the policy of our rulers not to interfere in our social and religious matters, it seems to me they do so when they choose. Much in our system which may appear unreasonable and intolerable cannot be altered without interfering with the very character of our social fabric. There is no commoner fad of the hybrid products of English education than their twaddle about the cruelty of caste."

The writer is believed to be a Brahmin of great attainments and high position in the South of India.

Amongst the Mahomedans, the case as regards seclusion is, of course, different, but even with them the whole question is, and always has been, and no doubt always will be, the subject of monumental misrepresentation.

The extent to which Christian teaching has affected Hindoo domestic life can hardly be regarded as great. Keshub Chunder Sen protested against "the denationalisation so general amongst native converts, who abandon the manners and customs of their country, forgetting that Christ was an Asiatic."

Miss Noble, who has become a Hindoo, and has written interesting and valuable books concerning her new co-religionists, is as good an authority upon Hindoo social life as Indian writers who have become Christians, and she says: "From my own experience, I can refute the charges of oppression of Indian women often levelled against the Hindoos. Such a crime is less common and less brutal in India than in younger countries. Indian national customs need no apology." That, I confess, is my own view, but, as has been pointed out, thirty years ago all the English educated were, by profession, at any rate, reformers, though during the last seventeen years a strong Hindoo revival has set in, the force of which is not yet spent. It is not for us to take any exception to this change of front, though it is due to the fact that the reformers soon realised the hopelessness of attempting to obtain the sympathy of the masses on any other terms, and we may well say, as the *Novoe Vremya* wrote of the Russians in China: "We are strong in these regions in proportion as we do not interfere with the religious convictions of the native population."

It is a curious fact, which Dr Bhandarkar, amongst others, has noticed, that the caste and race spirit seems to increase with the spread of education, which, indeed, the agitators, with accustomed exaggeration, say has produced a solid Hindoo nationality, spreading from the Himalayas to Cape Coranum, and from Kurachi to Chittagong.

The doctor says: "In my early days all classes joined in a public movement. Now Hindoos, Mahomedans, and Parsees act independently, as do even separate castes. There is greater estrangement than existed before social reform was thought of." Significant proof of strength of Hindoo feeling was afforded when the lawyer and Babu classes of Southern India tried in vain to rush through the Legislative Council the Gains of Learning Bill, which would have proved a powerful solvent of the caste system and of the Hindoo home with its joint earnings.

Abbé Dubois believed caste "to be the best part of Hindoo legislation, solely owing to which India did not lapse into a state of barbarism, and owing to which she preserved and perfected arts and sciences, while other nations remained in the same condition." Eighty years later, Sir John Strachey urged that between castes, customs, and religions no line can be drawn.

Novels regarding Indian life are now not infrequently written, and generally a purpose lurks within the narrative, in which fact and theory often fight a hard battle. For instance, Mr Dutt in his "Lake of Palms," an admirable and most interesting picture of Bengali life, makes one of his Hindoo characters say "that the remarriage of a widow is a sin and a scandal, a madness beyond thought," while he represents a pious family as sanctioning such a marriage by the advice of a holy man, who finds no objection in the Vedas! Similarly "social boycott has lost its horrors in India," in spite of which it seems "women of good birth and family dare not ask the married widow to their feasts and ceremonies."

The average respectable Hindoo would regard with contempt and disgust such an advertisement as the following, which is a fair specimen of many which appear in newspapers favoured by the agitators and reformers: "Wanted a young virgin widow to be married to a bachelor of twenty-four, of high prospects, fair and good-looking, object being reformation. Full particulars and personal interview, after approval of photo. Proper party only need apply." Enforced widowhood, as Sir Richard Temple long ago pointed out, "is not nearly so general as is made out by those who would deduce a moral from Indian manners for the glorification of the habits of the Christian." In Hindustan proper, perhaps 25 per cent. of the population prohibit, and 75 per cent. permit, remarriage.

Sir Madava Rao, the famous Indian statesman,

testified to the same effect. He was an advanced thinker and reformer, though he died before reform became associated with agitation and disaffection. He considered the life of a Hindoo girl "as happy as that of a bird or a bee," and wrote: "Many writers on Hindoo social reform have not clearly understood the existing system, which is the product of long development, nor accurately compared it with other systems, before underrating the advantages, and exaggerating the disadvantages, of the Indian system. The great majority of the people who retain their religious beliefs and social usages would prefer non-representation to misrepresentation, by those who have given up those beliefs and usages."

These are words of profound wisdom, and the old statesman might have added that his own people are the most charitable in the round world.

Not only do Hindoos support all their poor relations, but they very generally help pauper scholars. Whether it is to the public advantage that such should be enabled to pursue their studies is indeed doubtful, but the Hindoos think so and say:

> "Heaven's gate is near the sinner
> Who gives the humble scholar dinner."

Nor in England, at any rate in Wales, is a similar belief unknown.

"Charity our household divinity" runs the family motto of the Maharajas of Travancore, and it may be said in varying degree of all his Highness's fellow-countrymen. Such charity is universal, and all embracing, so that it is only when crops have failed over a large area for several successive seasons that the Indian Famine Prevention Code is brought into operation to afford that outdoor and indoor relief which in Europe is necessary even in normal seasons. Perhaps no trait in the character of the Hindoos, who possess so many admirable qualities, is more attractive than their charity, but it must be admitted that what is all embracing must necessarily be, and indeed is, indiscriminate, and possibly demoralising. The able-bodied beggar is relieved as readily as one incapacitated from earning his own living, and of course, feeding a Brahmin possesses special merits, no matter how well able he may be to feed himself. It is true of hundreds of thousands in India that they could work, but to beg are not ashamed.

Such being the Hindoo home, and such being its occupants, few thinking men will agree with those who maintain that India needs a complete upheaval, so that out of social chaos a new and happier dispensation may arise. On the contrary, the cure for such ills as exist must necessarily be exceedingly slow. Education must spread so far and so wide that the cry for reform must come from the fields and the workshops of the artisans, and not only from the lawyer's office and the educationalist's study. Not till then will the time arrive for sweeping changes. Reforms which will probably sooner or later come to pass are these: Intermarriage between subdivisions of castes, the widening of the circle from which husbands and wives may be taken, voluntary renunciation of the habit of marrying infants and of children unable to earn the means of subsistence, reduction of expenses in the celebration of ceremonies and the introduction of some discrimination into the dispensation of charity. But without any of the reforms the Hindoo system is one of which there is little cause to be ashamed.

CHAPTER XIII

ECONOMIC POLICY

Hunter misquoted—Lord Salisbury misquoted—Development of Cotton, Tea, and other Industries — Writings of Mr Naoroji and Mr W. Digby—Their easily exposed Contentions—Average Income of Indian Peasant—Mr Dutt's Charges—Their Refutation—His Experience acquired in Bengal—Mr Hyndman's Position—Labour Questions and Problems—Indians in America and Africa—True *Svadeshi*—Indian Industries—Legislative Interference therewith—Factories Commission—Gold Mines—Wages—Indian not comparable with English System—Different Conditions—Mr Theodore Morison's Views — Comparative Wealth of Indian and other Labourers—Need for British Capital—Congress Agitation keeps such away—Preferential Tariffs—Prosperity increasing—Efforts of Government—Effects of its own *Svadeshi* Policy—Necessity for revising Railway Rates—For using Coal as Fuel—Development of Cottage Industries necessary, and Abstention of Government from Interference with Labour

ONE cause of the unrest is the belief strongly held by three-fourths of the educated classes that the economic policy of the Indian Government is radically unsound and grossly unfair to India. They read and quote Bradlaugh, Digby, and Naoroji, and maintain that the so-called "drain" to England, and other results of our economic policy are the real causes of the poverty of the people, of famine, and indirectly of plague. Here again it is eminently desirable that some authoritative pronouncement of the economic policy of the Government of India should be available, a memorandum showing what it is and what are its results, but none such exists, and even those who desire light know not in what direction to seek it. Sir William Hunter, as usual, is pressed into the service of the detractors of British government in India. Mr O'Donnell circulated in the House of Commons on the occasion of the last Budget debate a memorandum called "Rack Taxing in Rural India," in which he gave a sensational quotation from Hunter to the effect that the "Government assessment does not leave enough food to the cultivator to support himself and his family throughout the year." If Hunter had said this it would not have much mattered, for probably there has never been an Indian civil servant who spent so much time in England, and in headquarter offices, and so little in rural India, as he did, but as a fact he said nothing of the kind. He was writing of a Bill relating to four districts only of one presidency and of these he said: "The fundamental difficulty of bringing relief to the Deccan peasantry, *as stated by the special judge entrusted with this task*, is therefore," and then follow the words Mr O'Donnell attributes to him, and he goes on to say: "*If* the Government assessment reduces the cultivator to this condition," and so on. Such is quotation for the purpose of discrediting the British Government.

The use made of what Sir W. Hunter wrote recalls another, and far more serious, misrepresentation of an able and humane minute penned by Lord Salisbury when Secretary of State for India. Who has not read in the works of the anti-British writers, "India must be bled," the odious admission, as it is called, of one of Britain's greatest statesmen. Now Lord Salisbury in 1875 was very anxious to relieve the Indian cultivator as far as he could, and in a minute on the land-tax wrote: "So far as it is possible to change the Indian fiscal system, it is desirable that the cultivator should pay a smaller proportion of the whole national charge. It is not a thrifty policy to draw the mass of revenue from rural districts, where capital is scarce, sparing the towns, where it is often redundant. As India must be bled, the lancet should be directed to the parts where the blood is congested or sufficient, not to those which are already feeble from want of it."

Of these humane, sensible, and statesmanlike words Mr Dadabhai Naoroji makes use of four, "India must be bled." This is an instance of what I called elsewhere the "damned Barebones" method of controversy, and it is very popular with the bleeding India school of writers. Then considering for a moment Mr Naoroji's writings, which are regarded as a kind of gospel by young Bengal, his "Poverty of India" is a fearsome work of nearly 700 pages, written, as the Indians say without *bundobast*. True, he prefaces most of his indictments by a profession of faith in the British, but this expression can only be looked upon like the Frenchman's "*Que messieurs les assassins commençent*," for he does not scruple to say "that British rule has reduced the bulk of the population to extreme poverty, destitution, and degradation, that it is a new despotism of civilisation, resembling the murder effected by a clever and unscrupulous surgeon, who draws all his victim's blood and leaves no scar," and he does not hesitate to describe the English as "the most disastrous and destructive of the foreign invaders of India." In denouncing the home charges, which, no doubt, should be reduced, as I have said elsewhere, to the lowest possible figure, he leaves out of account the fact that without the home charges there could be no British Government in India. He says nothing of remittances for interest on loans raised for the development of the country towards which the Indians will not subscribe themselves, and of allowances for Englishmen who have spent their lives and health in India. When he calculates the loss she suffers by the excess of her exports over her imports he says nothing of some of the most flourishing countries in the world, which in this behalf are in the same position, or of the approaching ruin of England, as some folk predict, because her imports exceed her exports. It is not serious treatment of a difficult problem to add up the imports for a series of years, subtract them from the exports, and call the balance the life blood drained from India. The greater part of these charges represent interest on capital invested in our Eastern Empire in reproductive works, to the great advantage of that empire, and of its working classes, and most of all of those weaned thereby from petty agriculture, to which alone the masses of the people can ordinarily look for a livelihood. It is difficult to seriously criticise a writer who says: "Foreign trade adds nothing to the wealth of the world, and not a single atom of money is added to the existing wealth of India by internal trade." And what does this profound economist recommend to right a world in which apparently everything is wrong? The further employment of natives in the public service! So he has got no further than the failed B.A., in the study of economics, and it is not wonderful that he should be regarded by that individual as his guide in the sphere of politics and economics. Apparently also, when Indians are employed in offices now held by European civil servants, he would, regardless of the cost, give them pay and pensions at the rate drawn by the alien administrators. Of course Mr Dadabhai Naoroji writes from very little knowledge of the Indian people, he being himself a Parsee whose life has been spent in England. Still, it is extraordinary that a man should be accepted as an economic authority who does not see that the best hope for India lies in developing her resources ; in encouraging her tea industry which pays higher wages than obtained before, and so tends to raise wages all round ; in encouraging the cotton and jute mills, gold and coal mines, and in fact in developing that internal and external trade which he thinks adds nothing to the wealth of the nation, but to which alone others, no less anxious than he is to see India prosperous, look for the further improvement of her patient and estimable population.

The case of the bleeding India school teems with contradictions, and while Mr Naoroji argues in his classical works that India has become poorer because the prices of Indian staples have not risen and bases an immense fabric or fabrication upon this assumption, the Congress journals cry out because the wages of agricultural and other labour have not advanced *pari passu* with the rise in prices, and their premise that prices have risen is of course correct, though they suppress the fact, easily proven by reference to old records, that there has been a more than proportionate rise in the rate of wages.

Next amongst the prophets comes (the late) Mr William Digby, who revels in statistics regarding the bleeding of India, and calculates the amount extracted by the economic drain in the nineteenth century, with the greatest precision, at £4,187,922,732. Like Mr Naoroji, he holds that the influx of imports is of little or no value, while the loss of exports is a fatal wound, and he describes our rule as "naked and unashamed exploitation, outrageous plunder, a mockery and a curse to hundreds of millions of British subjects." To prove this rather comprehensive conclusion he makes elaborate comparisons of the condition of the natives of India with that of the inhabitants of European states. Had Japan, China, Arabia, or some other Eastern nation been taken as a standard, something of some value might have been evolved, but Mr Digby proves too much in showing that all Indians, for instance the powerful Punjaubi, a far finer man than the average Englishman, is habitually starved. He makes much use of the Russian peasant, but I have lived with Russian peasants, I am a Russian interpreter myself, and showed in an article published in *The Nineteenth Century* for October 1902, that if the Russian has ten times the income of the Indian, his board and lodging costs him several times ten times as much, and that the Indians get more comfort from their smaller resources. Space will not allow me here to show as I did in that article how ways and means East and West actually compare when considered with elementary understanding, or to deal with Indian conditions and Indian critics at length as I did in *The Fortnightly Review* for August 1902. So much that is absolutely contrary to fact is taken for granted, such frequent reiteration calls for such emphatic refutation, that considerable space is required for overthrowing the structure, albeit it is founded on sand.

It is, however, unnecessary to repeat what has been said in previous chapters to refute the argument that the British invented famine, which on the contrary they have almost abolished. Mutually destructive propositions are as common as over-confident and unsupported assertions, and the numbers habitually in want of food are calculated to have increased from 40,000,000, itself the mere conjecture of one individual of no special authority, to 100,000,000, while elsewhere it is urged that owing to British maladministration the population has not sufficiently increased. Sir Salar Jung, who raised the land revenue in Hyderabad by 260 per cent., is praised, while the English, who in the same period effected an increase of 25 per cent., as Mr Digby says, are condemned. The profits of the industries are said to go to English capitalists, but does Indian labour take no toll on these profits? The superior merits of the administration of Indian states are extolled, but their complete failure to feed their people in famine days is suppressed.

When family after family is shown to earn too little to support life, it is evident to anyone with any knowledge of the country that the cost of living has been pitched too high, and supplementary sources of income have been ignored. Then official results are repudiated because based upon official figures, but it is an irrefragable merit of Digby's own conclusions that they are based upon such figures!

Then in regard to Bengal, the permanent settlement of which Mr Digby, like Mr Dutt and Mr Naoroji, is bound to praise, for are not the landlords of Bengal the supporters of the Congress, he finds that in that province the average income falls most below the official estimate. This is very likely the case, though it would take a great deal to prove, but if true it entirely shatters the creed that permanently settled Bengal is exceptionally prosperous.

It is hardly to be expected that a writer who ignores the most elementary principles of economics should think worthy of mention the legislation for the emancipation of the peasant from the clutches of the moneylender, the extension of irrigation, the establishment of co-operative agricultural credit, and the industrial eminence of Bombay. In point of fact, it is mere claptrap to say the average Indian got 2d. a day in 1850, 1½d. in 1880, and ¾d. in 1900, and contempt, as I suppose, has prevented the Government from exposing such nonsense. No one knows what the average was in 1850, and it certainly has not fallen since 1900. The Government has at length, after an elaborate inquiry, found the average income per head to be 30 rupees, and reasons have been given elsewhere for thinking that this is as fair an estimate as is likely to be made.

Mr F. J. Atkinson, whose training and experience specially fit him to deal with Indian statistics, calculated that between 1875 and 1895 the agricultural income increased from 26 rupees to 35 rupees, or 39 per cent.; the non-agricultural income from 28 rupees to 34 rupees, or 18 per cent., and, as these two classes were 97 per cent. of the population, that the average annual income of the masses had risen from 27 rupees to 35 rupees, or 28 per cent. Taking into account the remaining classes, he made the income of all three sections to be from 30 rupees to 39 rupees, or an increase in the average income of 29 per cent. These figures are worthy of great respect, though their author does not claim for them scientific accuracy, nor, though an expert, is he capable, like Mr Digby, of calculating a century's drain within twenty shillings. Lord Cromer in his day estimated the average income at 27 rupees, as against the 30 rupees of Lord Curzon's Government, so that there is not, when the difficulty and complexity of the subject is considered, so great a disparity as might be expected.

None of the chief detractors of British rule have explained why, if the land is universally rackrented it happens that it sells for several times the assessment, of which there is proof. Again, it was the same Sir William Hunter, who saw so little of life in India, who was so misquoted by Mr O'Donnell, who dogmatically asserted in 1880 that 40,000,000 of Indians went through life on insufficient food, an utterly unsupported, and therefore mischievous, statement.

More light is thrown upon facts by one entry from Mr Digby's peasants' authentic family budgets than from all his invective and bewildering statistics. The cultivator of 4½ acres provides in his budget an expenditure "of 8d. a month for the small goddess and the local ghost." Starving men do not spend much money on ghosts and goddesses.

Mr Digby complains that the British have drained away all the capital. Mr Justice Ranade, however, who is an authority accepted by the Congress school, says: "There is no lack of capital in the country," and if no Indian can exist on less than 30 rupees per head per annum for food, which is, of course, absurd, how can Mr Digby be right in saying elsewhere that "they can exist, if existence it can be called, on almost nothing." Mr Digby's figures, in fact, are compiled with the utmost levity, and his calculations of the revenue of India are based on the assumption that the land revenue is a certain proportion of the gross produce, which he lays down with confidence, if without knowledge. The lower the land revenue, the poorer the Indian people must appear, according to his method of calculation. It would be easy to show that the agricultural produce of the country is double the figure at which he assesses it, but of course it is not from statistics, but from observation in the field, that the condition of the peasants can be really estimated; nor does Mr Digby seem to grasp the fact, that the ordinary peasant carries on a great deal of his traffic by barter or in kind. In fact, he, like Mr Naoroji, has no actual knowledge of Indian rural life, which is not obtained by editors whose Indian experience is confined to an office in the city of Madras. It is possible that Mr Naoroji may be acquainted with one of the languages spoken in Bombay other than English, but it is certain he has had little or no opportunity of using such knowledge in his life, and Mr Digby, as I know, had no knowledge of the vernacular tongues.

No man, with any practical experience of the country would, like Mr Digby, base an estimate of the wealth of India upon the transparently absurd assumption that the gross produce of "golden" Bengal does not amount to £1, or 15 rupees, an acre. Yet this estimate is accepted in innumerable essays, articles, and pamphlets, and, like any stick, is good enough for the British Government.

If this method of calculation were followed, it would be easy to prove that no person in England had less than £45 a year, and in referring to land revenue as taxation Mr Digby ignores altogether the fact that, where the land is held directly from Government, the land-tax includes what here we call rent, and should be compared with the total burden of the land in this country. Mr O'Donnell repeats the same error, though he must be aware that the two charges are not in the same category.

Mr R. C. Dutt, who arrives at much the same conclusions, is a critic of a different class to Messrs Digby and Naoroji, but he is equally unsparing in condemnation of British rule, and of the civil service, of which he was a member, and he, too, does not hesitate to make sweeping statements as if they were facts of universal acceptance.

For instance: "The poverty of the Indian population is unparalleled in any civilised country." Upon what travel and inquiry is this statement based, and what is it worth, unless based upon comparative knowledge? "The famines of the latter part of the nineteenth century are unexampled in extent and intensity in ancient and modern times." The few histories written by Indians prove this statement is altogether contrary to the fact, and I have in previous chapters sufficiently dealt with this monstrous misstatement: "The finances of the country are not properly administered." If the Chancellor of the Exchequer is a good authority, one may venture to quote Sir Michael Hicks-Beach, who said that "the finances of India were not only better administered, but in a more satisfactory condition than those of Great Britain." Then, "India in the eighteenth century was a great manufacturing, as well as a great agricultural country." True, she had manufactures, though we have yet to learn that she produced more than she does at present, but she was always, and still remains, mainly agricultural. Certain of her industries were, and one industry still is, in some respects, subservient to the same industry in Britain, but in consequence of British rule she has been endowed with many other new industries, which employ at least as much labour. It is impossible to deny that prohibitive tariffs were imposed at one time in England, upon competing Indian manufactures; but it is not in any way proved that the balance of profit was not with India in the whole transaction, or that other European races, one of which was bound to acquire her, would not have imposed equal or heavier tariffs.

Then "the land-tax is not only excessive, but, what is worse, it is fluctuating and uncertain in many provinces." But, as has been shown in previous chapters, it is immensely less than that collected by our predecessors in title. Of course, Bengal the permanently settled is said to be more prosperous than Madras and Bombay, but if Mr Dutt has had any experience of these other provinces, so as to be able to compare conditions, he has omitted to say so in his book. His official services, like those of the other chief supporters of the Congress in Parliament, were rendered in Bengal, the home of the Congress, and the place of origin of anti-British agitation, and he takes no notice of the fact that it is in Bengal that the British Government has chiefly had to intervene to protect the tenant from the landlord, and he has never had the opportunities enjoyed by civil servants in other provinces of seeing the permanently settled system and the ryot-wari system working side by side.

He does not scruple to say that "a special law, called the slave law by the people of India" (query, what people, and in what language?) "still exists for providing labourers for the tea planters in Assam, ignorant men and women, bound down by penal clauses to work in tea gardens for a number of years, for whom the utmost endeavours have failed to secure adequate pay." I was a member of the Select Committee of the Legislative Council which examined this law, and from personal knowledge can contradict the whole of this statement, but perhaps it would be sufficient to refer to the Census Report, which exposes this foolish charge. I have referred to the matter before, and wages in tea gardens are above normal rates, which this industry has thus been the means of raising.

Of course revenue and magisterial functions should be separated, but enough of that elsewhere.

As an instance of Mr Dutt's treatment of historical subjects may be mentioned his account of the Black Hole tragedy: "Siraj-ud-Doulah's prisoners died one hot summer night." Now I do not think it proved that this tragedy was ordered by the Nawab, but this is a strange account of a cruel outrage.

Again, "the reign of Queen Victoria has not admitted the people of India to any share in the control and direction of the administration of their own affairs."

Elsewhere, I have quoted Babu Bepin Chandra Pal to the effect that "we," the Indians, "now govern India." The fact that, except as regards something under one thousand appointments, the whole public service is manned by natives is not worth Mr Dutt's attention. It would be interesting to know where history taught the lesson "that it is impossible to govern a country in the interests of the people without bestowing on that people some measure of self-government and representation." History teaches the exactly opposite conclusion, and self-government and representation obtains to-day amongst a mere fraction of the inhabitants of the world, nor does the system seem to work well at present in regions to which it is being extended in Europe and Asia.

The alliance between the Congress and the socialists in Britain will be severely strained if Mr Dutt expresses the matured opinion of the former, "that the soil was private property in India, as amongst all other civilised nations," but the statement is, if true, not in India by any means the whole truth.

Mr Dutt's work teems with allegations which are erroneous and unsustainable: "Only those who pay light rents are prosperous," yet the fact is notorious that the districts in which rents are lightest have been in times of scarcity most seriously affected, the obvious reason being that there the land is poorest. The Indian cultivator is indeed worthy of all praise, but to single out his "habits of prudence" for eulogy is to indulge in untimely sarcasm.

Mr Dutt's contentions regarding assessments are noticed in Chapter III. He finds that the extension of cultivation has not made the nation any more prosperous—a position which can hardly need serious refutation—and that India is the poorest country on earth. Has he then visited all the countries on earth—and are statistics in respect of all such available? Has he compared them—or are his conclusions the fruits of omniscience? If so let the claim be made, and then ordinary mortals will know how to deal with the revelations. Meanwhile, like any other Congressman, he combines the out-and-out advocacy of democracy and reform with the stoutest possible defence of landlordism and aristocracy, at any rate in Bengal. In one respect, however, he throws over the tenets of his school and of its ex-official, now anti-official, supporters, and admits that there is no strong feeling in India against the opium monopoly.

One fact to be remembered in dealing with the writings of Messrs Dutt, Naoroji, and Digby is this, that statistics are wanting for the first half of last century, that the first regular Census was taken in 1872, and that the Statistical Department at Calcutta was not created till 1880. Never was so vast a superstructure raised upon such pure conjecture as the case against the British Government according to the Congress, which now has the support of the British socialists.

The opportunity of attacking British rule at a time when opposition was displayed in India was too good for Mr Hyndman to lose, and he returned to the charge on his old war horse, frequently foundered, but still propped up with the same bad arguments and sham statistics. Famines have become more frequent, except in native states; the death rate is rising, and it is true that the record is reaching something like a normal figure for Asia; poverty increases; the exports exceed the imports; the imports are dangerously low; the land assessment is raised; Mr Digby's figures are true figures; land-tax and economic rent are confounded; the Indian peoples weep the tears of such as are oppressed, and on the side of their oppressors is power, but they have, other than Mr Hyndman, the Congress, the Bengali Babus, and the Poona Brahmins, no comforter. Of the famines in anti-British days I have spoken, and of the 1¼ millions who died in 1899-1900 most came from native states when past relief to die on British relief works.

To the confusion of Mr Hyndman the last Census showed an increase of 3·9 per cent. in the population of British India and a loss of 6·6 per cent. in native states, the decline being greatest in Baroda, and the states of Central India, Rajputana and of Bombay, in which the failure of crops was as severe in the last famine as it was in British India, while measures of prevention and relief were by no means so comprehensive and efficient. I have pointed out these indisputable facts to Mr Hyndman in *The Times*, but he returns to the charge. Facts are no use to him, and he continues to think the native states are best administered. No one can be more anxious to agree with him so far than an ex-Resident of Travancore and Cochin, but all native states are not as they are, and the truth must be told.

As to the assessment that subject has been sufficiently treated elsewhere, and the figures regarding the death rate only began to be approximately accurate in quite recent years. Competent authorities calculate the rates before 1880 at about 35 per mille, and the figure now is 33, including the loss from the plague epidemic. The folly of accepting 24 per mille for 1884 is apparent when the fact is remembered that few European countries at that time had so low a death rate.

Upon the question of the drain Mr Hyndman, relying on the conjectural figures of Mr Dutt, omitted necessary deductions, which reduced the excess of exports over imports from 30 to about 10 millions, and grossly exaggerated, indeed more than doubled, the amounts paid to Europeans as salaries out of Indian revenues. He treats, and indeed most writers on the Congress side treat the figures of Messrs Dutt,

Digby, and Naoroji as if they came down from heaven, whence indeed they might have come, so little relation have they to the facts on earth.

It must be remembered that none of the papers exposing these figures, none of the letters published from time to time in *The Times*, and holding the field, are ever republished in the native press, which immediately repeats all over India any statement, however false and misleading, made to discredit British administration. The drain, in fact, is an imaginary monster, and in other countries where the like phenomenon exists it is regarded as a proof of prosperity. Everything that goes out is paid for, and in such commodities—for instance, cotton goods and bullion—as the country most wants. Had capital been raised in India for her development, the interest would have been three times that paid to Britain, and as a result of the drain there are hundreds of golden streams flowing from the new trades and industries developed by the foreign capital and the foreign agents. The Statesman's Year-Book shows that in the United States and in Argentine the exports exceed the imports by 74 and 15 millions respectively. Yet they are superlatively prosperous countries, while Persia, Turkey, and China show excess of imports over exports, ranging from 1½ to 14½ millions, and they are not exactly in the van of the world of progress. Suppose India ceased to export so largely. she would in proportion be paid less, and her peoples would accordingly suffer. It is they get the money or goods paid in return, and not the Government. All the raw products, except tea, coffee, and indigo, are produced from native sources, and with native money. What would India do with her excess of crops and products if she did not export them, for there is a great surplus even in famine grass, famine being dearth of money, not, from an all-Indian point of view, and in these days of extended communications, of grain. Surely that this surplus exists is a proof of the wealth, not of the poverty, of India. Trade is not the result of dark intrigue between the Indian Government and the British and foreign nations. The fact is, India pays no tribute to Britain, and her present prosperity and future salvation depend on the development of the industries she owes chiefly to British enterprise, often, like the tea industry, too little rewarded, and too successfully attacked by faddists and theorisers.

The Labour question in Assam arose entirely from the action of the Chief Commissioner, Mr (now Sir H.) Cotton, whose view that the coolies in the tea gardens were underpaid was not shared by the Assam Commission, or probably in any quarter other than the Bengali Babus and agitators, who saw an opportunity of depreciating a British enterprise, to the benefit of which to Assam, and other parts of India, eloquent testimony is borne by the last Census Report, by the condition of the labourers themselves, and by the rate of the wages they enjoy.

Questions regarding labour in India and other parts of Asia have lately received unusual prominence owing to the Chinese Labour question which has excited so great a feeling throughout England, where it is believed on all hands that such labour competes with that of white men from Britain, owing to the first strike which has happened on the East Indian Railway, and owing to the problem of Indian immigration into the Transvaal, and the Pacific Coast of America.

It is hopeless to expect dispassionate consideration of this complicated and, for England most uncomfortable, question, until the irreconciliables learn, as they would learn from actual experience, that Asiatic labour does not compete with skilled white labour, but provides for the latter a larger field. In countries with a tropical climate white men are unable and unwilling to perform the actual drudgery, which in such cases falls to the lot of the Asiatic immigrant. If they could do this work, they would waste their time and lower the rate of wages by so doing, their proper function being that which they always perform wherever white and coloured labour are concurrently employed—namely, that of inspecting and supervising, which is necessarily a more highly paid and more congenial duty than actual manual labour.

The cry for the expulsion of Asiatics from the Pacific Coast is due to fear of competition in labour, to ignorance of, or to perverse blindness to, the fact that the enormous capabilities of a land flowing with milk and honey await just the plentiful supply of unskilled labour which the Asiatics can, and Europeans cannot, supply, and to failure to appreciate the fact that the more Asiatics are employed the more work there will be for white men. The fear of Japan, and the racial feeling of dislike is industriously fanned by the Yellow Press, but it is clear, and it is only right, that the people of the Pacific Coast must acquire their experience, and settle this question, for themselves, while the Mikado's Government manifests no desire to force Japanese immigration upon an unwilling continent.

In the Transvaal excitement has been raised to fever pitch by the passing of the Registration Law. In

Natal, Indian coolies are allowed either to renew their indentures upon expiry, to return to India, or to remain in Natal subject to a special poll-tax, which, in the absence of registration, they generally escape. Large numbers, however, of the superabundant coolies have crossed over to the Transvaal, and without a system of passports and registration the Transvaal Government cannot regulate such immigration. Hence the new law, to carry out which it is also necessary to provide against transference of passports, which are usually passed on to others by their original holders, who have either died or left the country. Hence also the necessity for identification by finger prints, which has been in force some years, although it has been represented as a new and cruel refinement of oppression on the part of the Transvaal Government. A committee was formed in England to conduct an agitation and to rouse public feeling upon the subject. Of this committee I was a member, but I resigned, because it appeared to me, and still appears to me, obvious that the Transvaal Government must have, and will have, its own way in regard to this matter, and that it knows its own business much better than we do in England; that if interference is practised in regard to such details as those of immigration laws, such laws cannot be properly administered, and the consequence will be that Indians, who have already become a rock of offence, will be utterly cast out, like an abominable branch, to their own disadvantage, and to the loss of the Transvaal, where they are a valuable and prosperous asset. Surely it is time to admit the undisputable fact that there is an ineradicable prejudice against the introduction of Orientals into our Colonies, except upon such terms as the Colonies themselves lay down. It is an affair for themselves alone, and no good can come of accusing them of being hard-hearted, arrogant and unjust, epithets in exchange for which they might readily and with equal justice return others, such as ignorant, unpractical, and sentimental. Already the Indians in Natal exceed in number the Europeans, whom, if they were enfranchised, they would outvote. A great deal too much is made of the plea that the injustice, for so it must appear to those who hold that one law is possible all over a world-wide Empire, must prejudice our position in India. It will probably do nothing of the sort. Indians are accustomed to be governed, and are perfectly well aware, from long experience, that there are some Colonies to which they are allowed to emigrate, and others to which emigration is forbidden. They are also practical people, who realise that while they are in a country they must submit to its laws, and the class of Indian which emigrates has made up its mind to put up with any resulting inconvenience.

No one can feel more keenly than I do how unfair it is that our highly civilised, law-abiding, and humane Indian fellow-subjects cannot settle at pleasure in any particular part of the so-called British Empire, but since that Empire consists in a great measure of a loose aggregate of self-governing communities it is far better to acknowledge the fact, than to persevere in petty coercion and moral suasion, which are doomed from the outset to failure, and can only exasperate Colonies, which know how to, and mean to, manage their own affairs. The arguments used by those who conduct this agitation are manufactured for the occasion. The kind of political and social equalities for which they are working has never existed in India between caste and caste, tribe and tribe, people and people, nor does the British Government practise, nor will it ever practise, unless it be in a brain storm, the principles which the committee is now seeking to impose upon an unwilling colony. It is, of course, most deplorable that 2000 Hindoos should have landed last year at Vancouver and have been subjected to inhospitality and ill-treatment, but it is impossible to dictate to white men in any part of the world what shall be their attitude in respect to brown men, or yellow men. How would the English bear to be coerced into accepting Chinese labour? It is not a question even open to argument. The unrest in India has nothing to do with it, and the Bengali Babus and the Poona Brahmins, who are prepared to use this or any other argument, care no more what becomes of the coolies from India, than they do what becomes of coolies in India, or of the British Empire. It is notorious, let Mr Meredith Townsend testify amongst other authorities, that feelings of pity and sympathy do not exist amongst Orientals, though, like others, they may be simulated for purposes of political agitation.

The Colonies think that Asiatic competition is driving out white men. They are as much entitled to their own opinion on this point as labour in England is entitled to the opinion that Chinese competition drives out white labour in the mines of the Transvaal. They are determined to keep their country as far as possible a white man's country, and they have as good a right to do it as Australia. They have an object lesson in Natal, close at hand, where the Indians are already to the Europeans as 13 is to 10. It will be impossible to keep the Colonies if the Home Government endeavours to force them to become a field for Asiatic labour. The Indian question in South Africa is by no means only a coolie question, for Indians compete with European traders with great success wherever they penetrate, and work harder for less profit.

In Canada a similar problem presents itself for settlement. Chinese immigrants have been subjected to a poll-tax which now amounts to not less than £100 per head, but numbers which at first fell off are now rising again, the scarcity rate of wages being so attractive that the immigrants can pay the crushing fine imposed upon them, and the need for them being so great that they can always obtain employment.

There are in Canada around about 15,000 Japanese who are considered as serious a menace as the Chinese, and keener competitors with the working man. That is to say that their wants are fewer, and that they are content with less. The two classes, those who realise the advantages to white labour of Asiatic immigration, and those who are unable to see, or deny, that any such advantages result, are both represented in British Columbia, whither immigrants come from China, Japan, and India. The Western Federation of Miners of the United States controls the situation, and it is opposed not only to coloured, but also to white immigration, labour being paid at present at scarcity wages. Strong objection is taken to the immigration organised by the Salvation Army, and to the arrival of Indians, both of which classes of British subject are quite as unwelcome as the Chinese and Japanese.

Here is a serious situation like that which has arisen in the Transvaal, and it is impossible for the

British Government to impose free trade principles in respect of labour upon self-governing colonies, which, in fact, it does not, never will, and never should, itself enforce.

The strongest Free Traders are avowedly, or otherwise, protectionists as regards labour questions. It seems to me that it is far better to openly take up the position, as I would, that British labour should have open, acknowledged, and undisguised preference over foreign labour, that it should be assisted in every legitimate manner, but that no steps should be taken in obedience to a blind outcry, which proceeds from a want of appreciation of the true conditions of the problem, and probably tends to run counter to the true interests of white labour. Take for instance merchant shipping, in connection with which objections are raised to the use of Lascar labour. It is obvious to anyone who has travelled by our ships to the East that their help is an absolute necessity in tropical waters. Without it our Eastern trade would dwindle to small dimensions or disappear; first of all, because the shipping companies could not without it pay a dividend; secondly, because white labour could not stoke in the Red Sea, or perform many functions which come naturally to the coloured man.

Immediate objection might be taken to this argument, of course, and anyone might point out that the case is given away when it is admitted that the companies would not pay so well if the labour employed was white. But the real fact is that all-white labour could not be got, and if it could be got it could not be paid, and the only result of abolishing Lascar labour would be to destroy a great and flourishing trade, which now employs immense numbers of white men as supervisors and inspectors, by whatever nautical titles known, of coloured seamen.

Few courses are more likely to prejudice the cause of labour in India than the action of the Congress party, which is actively engaged in disparaging British goods throughout India, and it is now asserted by their agents that there is very little cotton in Manchester goods, which, they say, are loaded with china clay, starch, magnesium and zinc.

Under the true *Svadeshi* policy, which Lord Minto enunciated, there would be a great future for India, not only for its textile industries, but for work in gold, silver, iron, copper, brass and wood; in pottery, dyeing, tanning, and leather work; in cane and bamboo; in turning, carving, and embroidery; in sugar refining, tobacco curing, and in oil and flour mills. The raw material for many of these industries is at present exported to foreign countries, whence the manufactured product is now returned to India, where an abundant supply of cheap fuel and cheap labour is alike available. It is not likely, for instance, that India will export oil seed permanently to the value of £106,000,000 and import oil to the value of £22,000,000.

Again, she grows cotton enough for her own consumption, and exports the greater part thereof, and half of her imports are Lancashire cotton manufactures. She is one of the greatest sugar producers in the world, but she imports sugar to the value of nearly £5,000,000 sterling. There can be no doubt that the countervailing excise levied on cotton fabrics and yarns produced in Indian mills of a lower count than twenties, in order to prevent the import-duty acting as a bounty in favour of the Indian manufactures as against those of Lancashire, is regarded as a grievance. This is not unnatural, and it is probable that there are others who, like myself, voted for the countervailing excise in the belief that it was a necessary consequence of India's connection with England, and of the free trade policy of the Empire, and not because it was in itself required in the separate and exclusive interests of India, so far that is, as such can subsist.

It must be admitted that while India is, and it may be hoped will remain, completely independent in respect of her finances, she is, though internally independent as regards her economic policy, subject as regards all matters by which other parts of the British Empire or foreign countries are affected, to the necessity of adopting the principles Imperial Parliament prescribes as affecting all dependencies of the Crown, and it must not be forgotten that the countervailing duty does not affect the still extensive hand-weaving industry.

The Indians are cunning workers in wood and ivory, capital carpenters and good blacksmiths, and as shoemakers they might with education eventually approach the Chinese standard. As weavers they are unsurpassed, probably unequalled, in the world. Gold, coal, manganese, lead, copper and other minerals abound in the bowels of the earth: diamonds and other precious stones are found upon its surface: the forests are full of rare and valuable products, over and above timber, out of which anything can be manufactured from a ship to a match-box. Skins and tanning materials are equally plentiful; alongside cotton and jute grow dyeing materials; the best of carpets are made by the most ordinary prisoner in goal; fibres are positively a drug in the market. At present, Germans and Japanese supply at sufficiently low prices for their clients, furniture, fans, ropes, mats, carpets, baskets, buttons, and a hundred other things, which could be equally well made in the country, not to mention the supply from England of cotton goods, hardware, and other important products. If the proposed University of Research will favour the establishment of new industries, Mr Tata should be admitted at once to the Hindoo Pantheon, without going through the early stages of deification described by Sir Alfred Lyall.

It is in textile industries that India will best be able to compete with European and other Asiatic countries, and it is not surprising that she regards with suspicion efforts to introduce into her mills labour regulations calculated to limit the output, but not to raise wages, nor to render the wage-earners more comfortable and contented, for according to their own standards they have at present little of which to complain. A working day of thirteen hours does not in India by any means signify thirteen hours work. But a short statutory day does mean hard unremitting labour without those intervals for eating and gossiping, smoking, and washing, that go-as-you-please atmosphere which is so grateful to the Oriental mind.

A committee which recently considered textile factories' labour in India has made various suggestions which should be accepted with some reserve, and not without modifications. For instance, improving the homes and home surroundings of the mill hands is a matter outside the conditions under which they work in the factories, and interference will assuredly be resented. Any attempt to secure uniformity in the administration of the Factory Act may be fraught with great inconvenience, and even great injustice, for since climatic conditions are by no means constant in a great continent, uniformity is not to be desired, nor, without hardship, to be secured. Rigid insistence upon certificates of age and physical fitness are likely to lead to hardship to individuals, if not to abuse. The conversion of the factories into schools is not likely to prove acceptable to those chiefly interested. Interference with women and children is likely to prejudice, without materially assisting, those whom it is intended to advantage. Insistence upon regular hours at which work is to commence and to cease, is bound to produce inequality, not uniformity, in view of the different conditions to which it is sought to apply this rigid rule, summer and winter, in hot, cold, and rainy weather. There are parts of India in which the inhabitants do not and cannot come out at 5.30 A.M. without catching colds, chills, and catarrh.

Indeed, the mill hands of Bombay have already held a meeting in order to protest against the limitation of the hours of labour, on the ground that they would lose the chance of earning overtime wages, and so adding to their incomes.

Up till now little interference has been attempted with mines in India, greatly to the profit of the industries concerned. For instance, the Mysore goldfields have produced £20,000,000 sterling of the precious metal, and are still enjoying great prosperity. They are one of the chief features of the economic prosperity of the Mysore state, and are due to the enterprise of British capitalists, of whom the late Sir Charles Tennant was the chief. It would be difficult to find in any country a more pleasing spectacle than is afforded here of long streets of admirable cottages, clubs, churches, hospitals, bungalows, well-kept roads, electrically lighted streets and gardens. The water supply, too, is excellent, and the high standards maintained in the field make it a model labour settlement of great value as a pattern and exemplar, over and above the large pecuniary profit which from this industry accrues to the people of the Mysore state, and of neighbouring British districts.

The miners are satisfied with the wages they receive, which are, of course, far higher than those earned in agriculture, which is the other chief occupation of the plateau, and the wages of which have, perhaps, hardly doubled in the last generation, as they have no doubt in other parts of India.

Of the Indian agricultural labourers it may be said that, under existing circumstances, they do not suffer from want unless crops fail and prices rise, when they would probably perish in large numbers but for the system of relief and famine prevention which now approaches nearer to perfection than is given to most human institutions. Indian agriculture has rightly been described as a perfect picture of careful cultivation combined with hard labour, knowledge, and fertility of resource. Dubois, early in last century, calculated that the agricultural labourer got 12s. a year and his keep. I estimated in 1890 that such an one in South India made £3, 10s. a year in all, without of course counting the family gains, and the estimate lately made by the Government of India gives a family £8 a year, for the wife and children are also breadwinners. To suppose that Government can raise the condition of the depressed classes was, in the opinion of Abbé Dubois, an idle dream, and Mr Crooke at the end of the last century came to much the same conclusion. Mr Justice Ranade pointed out to his fellow-countrymen the encouraging increase in the exports of manufactured goods in recent years, than which the rise in the export of raw produce had been relatively less, and he attributed the change to the influx of British capital and enterprise, and saw a hopeful sign in the already altered relations between Indian exports and imports of raw and manufactured goods. He was a wise man and a real patriot, and there is indeed hardly any limit to the development which might occur in this respect in a country in which vast stores of raw material exist alongside the cheapest and by no means the least efficient labour in the world.

Mr Crooke, writing in 1888, said that a hired labourer in upper India got 3 rupees (4s.) a month, part of which was paid in kind at village rates, and that the wages of blacksmiths and carpenters had doubled within the last generation. There is little doubt that the conditions of artisan life in India are more pleasant and more healthy than those of a mechanic in an English town, for the workers' houses are more airy and there is less confinement, less grinding hard work. They do not produce so much because the division of labour, universal in Europe, is well-nigh impossible in the industral organisation which obtains in India. If the labour of the artisan was aggregated, its volume would make the use of power possible and remunerative, but this is not the case, nor, until communication and distributing agencies become more assimilated to those obtaining in Europe, is such development likely to be experienced.

It is difficult for the English student to realise that the majority of the Indian labouring classes are not dependent upon the rate of wages, because they work upon their own account. In comparing wages, moreover, in India and England that of the English farm-labourer is always over-stated, and the fact that he has, and the Indian farm-labourer has not, to pay rent is suppressed. Generally speaking, too, the Indian average income *per head* is treated as if it was the income *per family*, to obtain which it must be multiplied by five. A coolie on an Indian railway, for example, will get probably 3d. a day himself, while his wife and family will earn 2d., and a penny a day is more than enough to maintain each individual member of the average family of five persons. The coolie pays nothing for rent and fuel, very little for boots and clothes, and his penny for the food he wants goes at least as far as 1s. a day for the British workman's tea, bacon, meat, bread, etc.

Mr Morison, the distinguished educationalist, who was Principal of the Mahomedan Anglo - Oriental College at Aligarh and is now a member of the Secretary of State's Council, has pointed out how different is the type of industrial organisation in India from that assumed to be the normal type in Western Europe and the United States. In India the labourer usually works on his own account, and in addition to supplying the labour necessary for the production of wealth undertakes the risks of production, while in Europe he is usually a hired man working for an employer.

Mr Morison in his Industrial Organisation of an Indian province has also shown that though in Indian towns there are some labourers who occupy the same position as wage-earners in Europe, the urban population is only a small fraction, and the great bulk of the labouring classes are men who work on their own account, and not for an employer. The output of wealth cannot therefore compare with that of countries in which industry is directed by technical skill, commercial knowledge, administrative ability and ample capital, in addition to which the organisation of Indian society does not admit of the all-important division of labour. Authentic statistics, however, show that the indebtedness of Indian peasants is certainly not greater, and is probably smaller, than that of Europeans in the same position, and that both borrow not according to their need, but according to their capacity.

Except under the most intolerable pressure, writes a Congress journal, *United India*, no indigent weaver or mason or petty hawker will resort to another occupation, but will stick to his own till actual starvation drives him to the labour market.

As Mr Morison says, this difference invalidates the application to India of most of the current economic doctrines about the working classes. In the normal Indian province more than half the population are small farmers, whose crops are needed first of all to feed the family, and afterwards to provide from the proceeds of the sale of the remainder, the funds needed for rent and other purposes, such as interest on debt, which, unfortunately, forms a very frequent feature in the budget of the petty farmer in most countries.

Exaction of high interest by moneylenders, and hopeless indebtedness on the part of the borrowing agriculturist, are by no means features peculiar to India. They are, indeed, common to agricultural life in every country. Credit, as Sir F. Nicholson says, is an essential factor of agriculture, and neither the condition of the country nor anything else affects the one great fact that agriculturists must borrow.

The immobility of labour is another factor in the case. In other countries it migrates to places where employment offers, but in India only where special inducements are given, as, for example, in Assam, Mysore, or in Ceylon, or other colonies. Rules and regulations too often impede such disposition as there is to move, and coolies are often protected to their own disadvantage. This is conspicuously the case in Bengal, emigration from which to Assam is so beneficial to both provinces.

It is therefore clear that, with their industrial organisation, the people of India can never compare in wealth with nations in which wage-earners work under the direction of employers, and receive in addition their share of profit, instead of taking the risks of production on their own unaided individual shoulders. In India that system is universal which in other countries only obtains in respect of agriculture, and where land is owned or rented in small holdings, whereas in India the carpenter, potter, and blacksmith, and other village artisans, are all small capitalists without capital, if the expression be allowed, whose labour is, to a great extent, wasted for want of organisation.

To compare the conditions of life, the income and needs of the Indian peasantry with those of similar classes in Eastern and Western Europe, is a useless and, indeed, an impossible task. Upon the whole, the Indian peasant, in ordinary years, is not in a much inferior position—when his wants and his means of supplying them are taken into consideration—to the peasant of Europe. The contrast is in wants. The peasant in Eastern Europe has fewer wants than the peasant of Western Europe, but considerably more than the Indian peasant; in fact, proximity to the tropics determines not a lower standard of comfort, but a simpler standard of wants. The Indian peasant can feed and keep himself in good health, with grain and a few condiments, for a penny a day; he usually has free quarters, or accommodation at an almost nominal rental, and his expenses for clothes are but small. The British working man, on the other hand, has to pay from 25 per cent. to 40 per cent. of his earnings in rent, and his expenses for food and clothing are, of course, very considerable.

It is extremely difficult to teach the Indian peasant thrift. Under former rulers he had avowedly been allowed but enough for bare subsistence, and any margin our lower land-tax leaves him serves but to enhance his credit with the moneylenders, and so contribute to his indebtedness. When the peasant grasps the idea of putting a penny by for a rainless day a great advance will have been made; but the habit of centuries has not as yet been weakened. The question as to the improvement of the peasant's condition is one that can hardly be decided by statistics. Doubtless his nominal income has increased, but owing to payments in cash—instead of in grain, as formerly—and higher prices, he is probably not so very much better off than before, except where he has profited by the local expenditure of British capital, and the establishment of some new, or the development of some old, industry.

In considering Indian economic questions it must, moreover, never be forgotten that tranquillity and comfort rather than the accumulation of wealth, or the acquisition of higher wages, are the objects of the Indian, and that agriculturists will not be attracted wholesale to factories by the offer of higher wages; which indeed are perhaps not higher when the addition of house rent and the greater cost of living in towns are taken into account.

Nor must the fact be overlooked that it is by helping cottage industries that industrial development can be best effected, and its range most widely extended, for the village artisans are as the sands of the sea compared with the numbers provided with employment. That remarkably able and radically minded ruler, the Gaekwar of Baroda, dwelt upon this fact at the East Indian Industrial Conference.

But if the economic development of India depends, as it does, upon the provision of the necessary capital, what are the prospects in this behalf? British capital is still shy, and the agitators, by increasing the indisposition of Europeans to invest in India, have done her the worst turn within their power. South America, with its somewhat unstable republics, is still a far more attractive field. Probably as other countries require less capital more will come to India, but it is difficult to overestimate the set-back occasioned by the present unrest. Commercial confidence is a plant of exceptionally slow growth, and no sooner are we rid of the unstable rupee, and assured of a fixed gold standard, than we are threatened with instability of another character. Though firm and wise treatment has averted the threatened crisis, the effects of it will not so quickly pass away. The creation of the department of commerce and industry should serve to define and develop the economic policy of the Government of India, but the great need is to coax Indian capital, of which it has been estimated that there are no less than £500,000,000 sterling, into Indian industries. If the Congress agitators, instead of complaining about the drain of interest on borrowed capital, would bring indigenous hoards to light, and induce their owners to invest them in the country, they would do some service in their day and generation. As it is, they actually lament that British capital has come into India to develop the country, to create her trade, to cover her with a network of railways and communications, and to endow her with great works of irrigation. It is difficult to briefly define the economic policy of the Government of India, but Lord Minto has clearly stated that the development of home industries in preference to importation from without, of anything that can be produced within, the limits of the empire, is one of its cardinal features, and the Government of India has insisted during the preferential tariffs controversy that there shall not be imposed upon it any system unfavourable to the interests of India, and repugnant to the decision at which it then arrived, the details of which are contained in a blue book on Preferential Tariffs, published in 1904. Of Indian exports foreign countries take more than 60, while the British Empire takes under 40, per cent., so that in the event of a tariff war foreign countries might refuse to take India's exports, while she would be unable to act as her interests might in that case require, owing to the fiscal policy of England. Of her imports on the other hand foreign countries supply 25, and the British Empire 75, per cent. India, therefore, has little by way of preference to offer, and has very little profit to make from an Imperial interpreferential policy. There are, of course, those who hold different views, and the question is not one to be discussed in these pages, but it seems of little practical value to conjecture what would be the wisest course for India to pursue were her circumstances different from what they actually are.

There is little proof to be found in any direction of willingness to sacrifice Indian to British interests. The tea industry has been protected by the Tea Cess Act and indigo by a special grant; efforts at least have been made to improve the somewhat inadequate banking system; the customs service has not long since been reformed; cable rates have been reduced, and, as has been stated above, a department of Commerce and Industry has been created. In no direction is any sign forthcoming of selfish exploitation, in all quarters is evidence seen of increasing prosperity. *The Hindu Patriot* lately admitted that the day labourer who used to get one, now gets two, pence a day, and wages generally have increased by 50 per cent. upon the figures of last generation, while the standards of living among the poor have improved to an extent visible to all whose eyes are not blinded by prejudice and hostility. Since the new currency policy was brought into play in 1893, up to 1905 the expenditure on railways and irrigation has increased by 56, and the capital invested by joint-stock companies by 23, per cent; savings bank deposits have risen by 43, and private deposits in joint-stock banks by 130, per cent.; deposits in exchange banks by 95 per cent.; the income assessable to income-tax has risen by 29, the rupee circulation by 27, and the note circulation by 68, per cent., and imports have gone up 35 and exports 48 per cent.—figures which show that the economic policy of the Government may, in some respects, be satisfactorily defined by its actual results.

Nor, when pessimistic descriptions are manufactured and circulated wholesale, is it unworthy of note that *United India*, a Congress organ, in a series of articles on the Indian agricultural labourer, reveals the unwillingness of the landowner to raise his labourer's wages in due proportion to the rise in the prices of produce, because the average rate of profit on money invested in land is only 6 per cent.

"For a person who invests his money in land in this country, the average rate of profit is only about 6 per cent. It is not therefore equitable to expect him to raise the rate of wages of his labourers."

How fortunate would the English landholder think himself in the same case and how willingly would he raise the wages he pays.

It may be roundly stated that the Government of India pursues a *Svadeshi* policy—that is to say, a policy of encouraging local industries and manufactures, and as far back as 1883 local governments were instructed to supply their wants in the local market of articles of *bona fide* local manufacture. The Government of India expressed its desire to give the utmost encouragement to every effort to substitute for articles now obtained from Europe, articles of indigenous origin, and, except where a material difference in price and quality existed, to give the preference to Indian manufactures. It went further and reminded all its officers that many articles which may not be immediately obtainable in the local markets can be made in the event of Government encouraging their manufacture. Lord Minto has accepted and emphasised this principle, and during his term of office, and while Bengali agitators have set on foot a sham *Svadeshi* movement, intended to further their own objects, and to injure their adversaries, he has in several directions developed and extended the true *Svadeshi* policy.

It is not contended that British rule is perfect, and there are, of course, directions in which improvements are required. One such relates to railway rates, with which the export trade is, of course, intimately connected, and during the last two years strenuous efforts have been made to bring them into fair relations with commercial interests, to increase the rolling stock, and to give greater play to technical and trading, rather than to official, considerations. Mr Morley has also appointed a Special Committee to inquire into railway finance, to report whether larger sums should be spent, and to suggest improvements in the administration. The Indian Government, which owns the whole or part of almost all the lines, occupies a very strong position, and if such a step were deemed advisable could follow the example of the German Government and control sea freights, and influence the course of trade to an extent which would probably be found incompatible with the accepted English policy in regard to such questions. An era of greater activity and better management has set in, and there is no room for the complaint, formerly made, that railway direction was a close official preserve.

Another much-needed reform, but one hardly within the power of Government to effect, is the substitution of coal for other kinds of fuel. The chief domestic fuel of the people is dried cowdung, the use of which for this purpose robs the fields of their natural manure. As land comes under cultivation, which previously was scrub or forest—one of the chief reasons of course for the increase in the land revenue, which malevolence ascribes to the greed of the Government,—fuel gets more and more rare, and cowdung is more and more in request. The provision of cheap coal, therefore, is one of the greatest wants of India, and the matter concerns the agricultural, as much as the industrial, worker. There is plenty of coal in Bengal and in other parts of the continent of India, and cheap carriage by rail is the problem to be solved, and Mr Morley's Commission will no doubt go as near to solving it as is possible in existing circumstances. Meanwhile it has been calculated that Indian rates are relatively from 40 to 60 per cent. higher than those obtaining in the United Kingdom. Diversity of occupation and removal of as many of the people as possible from the practice of an often starveling agriculture, being one of the chief objects in view, the provision of cheap railway carriage is one of the chief ends to be secured. *The Times* has suggested that if the railways cannot afford sufficient reduction the Government should compensate them for loss, but that nothing should retard the introduction of this vital reform, and as so many of the lines belong wholly or in part to the Government, it should be possible to satisfactorily deal with the question.

The problem is how to apply the vast amount of labour available in a manner which will give a decent livelihood to those living by it, and will develop the extensive resources of the country; how to train the millions; how best to employ them; how to establish the larger industries involving an extensive use of machinery, for on such must the industrial future of

India depend, and how to subsidise the not less important cottage manufactures. There are about 200,000,000 to treat, and if the whole country was fed by Indian mills only 1,000,000 of the 11,000,000 of the weaving class could find employment. Railways, jute and cotton mills, tea gardens, and coal and gold mines now employ about 1½ millions. The Indians are at heart agriculturists, new employments can only divert a fraction from their traditional occupation, and Indian industries to succeed on a sufficient scale must still be chiefly rural, a fact which makes the provision of industrial and technical education an even more difficult problem in India than in other countries. If the Government can stimulate the small industries in the hands of guilds constituted on a caste basis, it will go a long way towards solving a large problem, and only in some such direction can light be seen.

The abstention of Government from any unwelcome interference with the labour system, which must develop on lines familiar to, and consonant with, the traditions, feelings, and even prejudices of the people, are of paramount importance. The admirable organisation which exists for dealing with famine is based, as far as the management of the camps is concerned on the family system. But legislation in regard to mining regulates, and interferes with, the employment of the men and of women and children in coal mines. The men cannot leave their fields and cut coal unless their women can bring their dinners, and the women cannot bring the dinners unless they may also bring the children. Nor does the slightest danger result, nor have accidents been frequent when they have been allowed to manage matters in their own fashion. Moreover, Indian coal and gold do not compete with British industries. Recent legislation regarding Assam labour too, was regarded, and in my opinion not without reason, as needlessly harassing to the planter, for, if the coolie can be trusted to know when he is well off, he is so in Assam, in which backward little province he settles wholesale, to its great benefit, as soon as his contract term is over.

Those who, like myself, knew India upwards of thirty years ago, have seen with their own eyes in the present century a higher standard of comfort prevailing, better clothes, better houses, brass instead of earthen pots, and such-like indications of higher incomes and improved circumstances. There is no need of royal commissions for such, as have read what records exist of past times, and can, from personal observation and from actual first-hand communication with the peasants, compare with that evidence the actual conditions of the present day.

CHAPTER XIV

CONCLUSION

Conclusions—Past Anarchy—Present Peace and Progress—Abstract of Former Chapters—Suggestions for Better Government of British Territory—Of Native States—Paramount Importance of Knowledge of Vernacular Languages — Oriental Languages Committee—Political Talent of Bengalis—Future of India—Conclusion

TO sum up the conclusions of this little volume, the early history of India exhibits a vast sub-continent devastated by continual warfare. In the sixteenth century it is reduced, for the most part, to something like order by the Great Moguls, whose rule, for the purpose of depreciating that of Britain, is now in retrospect represented by malcontents as the Golden Age. Elphinstone, however, who was an admirer, almost an apologist, of these princes, wrote that, during the reign of Shah Jehan, when their empire reached its zenith, "the condition of the people must have been worse than in the most badly governed state in modern Europe," while Manucci, the best contemporary witness, testified to the fact "that in the time of the Aurangzeb, in no part of the empire was there any justice; no one thought of anything but how to plunder, the revenue was collected by violence, and no remissions were allowed for loss of crops." During the break up of the Mogul Empire the genius of Clive and Hastings maintained some semblance of order and of government, and their successors destroyed the purely predatory dominion of the Mahrattas, who are also held up to admiration by the critics of the British, regardless of the fact that their rule meant nothing but taxation of the masses for the benefit of the classes, represented by Brahmin Peshwas, who had ousted from their places the founders of dynasty.

An adopted son of the last Peshwa was our enemy, Nana Sahib, whose affix Sahib, which was not at that time, and as a title is not now, peculiar to Mahomedans, obscures the fact that he was a Mahratta Brahmin. Little space is given to the history of India under our viceroys, till the day of Lord Curzon, in whose time the educational yeast fermented. For this reason, and because of its length, extending to nearly twice that of his predecessors, his Viceroyalty calls for particular notice. During its currency, important administrative changes were introduced, alike upon the north-western and north-eastern frontiers, and considerable reforms were effected in the internal civil and military administration. In a controversy with Lord Kitchener he failed to obtain the support of the Home Government and resigned, having acquired great unpopularity among the educated English classes of Bengal in consequence of his determined efforts to introduce into the educational system those reforms of which it stood, and still stands, in such urgent need. In a chapter on land assessments it is shown how little the critics understand, or how greatly they misrepresent, a system, which we inherited from our predecessors in title, and have only altered in so far as we have enormously reduced the share due by immemorial custom to the State. The claim made by critics that the permanent settlement of Bengal is more advantageous to the cultivator is easily refuted, and the reason is explained why this landlords' article of faith is adopted in the creed of the Congress.

A suggestion is, however, made that the Government should effect a permanent settlement with the actual cultivators, who thus would be little inclined to listen to the itinerant agitators, who now do, and in future will, perambulate the land. The demonstrably false and foolish position that the British invented and multiplied famines is easily carried, and next some account is given of the manner in which India is governed, by means of thirteen local administrations. The fact that these are, to an overwhelming extent, staffed by native agency disposes of the assertion that justice is denied to Indians by European judges, magistrates, and administrators, and the danger is shown of further impairing and reducing the authority of the European district officers by depriving them of those magisterial powers, which they now seldom use, but should always retain. The indifferent success of local self-government leads to the observation that the principle of representation has as yet taken no hold of the people of India, to whom, indeed, it is wholly foreign in character. Under the head of finance the suggestions are made that the pension list is capable of some reduction; that the expression Famine Relief should be abandoned in favour of Famine Prevention; that existing banking facilities should be increased, and that the Presidency banks should be allowed access to the London market. In the brief chapter devoted to the native states, for which I have a great affection, founded upon knowledge, the interference in internal affairs, so often practised by British Residents, is condemned as unjustifiable, and altogether contrary to the declared policy of the Government of India, and the fact is noted that such interference is immensely increased in respect of states in political relations with local governments, which directly, or indirectly through their Residents, practically deprive the ruling chiefs of their right to choose their own ministers.

The resulting loss of the precious individuality of ancient Hindoo states is demonstrated and deplored, and it is suggested that such states had better be transferred to the Government of India than further exposed to such irreparable damage at the hands of local administrations. In a chapter entitled Russia in the East I have shown how the Russian political programme, which led up to the war with Japan, was revealed nearly twenty years ago by Prince Esper Ukhtomsky; how easily the Russians, with their present railway facilities, can transport to, and maintain on, the Afghan frontier a numerous and powerful army, how little likely they are to adopt this line of most resistance, and how it has come to pass that the storm centre is the Middle East, the Persian frontier, and the Persian Gulf. This leads by a natural transition to the frontier policy of Lord Curzon's Government, and to the Anglo-Russian Convention, which agreement I cannot but approve as a whole, while regretting that it did not include the Gulf itself, and did not adopt a dividing line in Persia confirming to Britain that sphere of influence she has hitherto retained, and the trade routes leading to the Gulf. It is idle to deny that the arrangement made regarding Afghanistan is satisfactory, or that the fruits of the Tibet Expedition had been by a previous administration already thrown away. It is very easy for party purposes to dwell on the obvious defects of the Convention, but the instrument is one which both parties will equally approve and implement. The lowest depths of political ignorance and ineptitude are reached when a good understanding with Russia is deprecated as an obstacle to the progress in that empire of the cause of democracy and representative government. The Baghdad railway question, which I have several times brought before the House of Commons, is believed to have reached that stage so common, if not universal, in the history of railways at which more capital is needed for the continuance of construction. It is of vital importance either that the whole line from the Taurus to the end should be internationalised, or that the last section from Baghdad to the Gulf should be financed and constructed by Great Britain. The opportunity, which once offered, of participating in the concession granted to the Germans was lost, but it may yet be open to us to join in providing capital, and in that case it may be hoped that we shall not again refuse. Other nations have soldiers, we have money, and it should be used for the furtherance of political advantage, as well as for the promotion of trade, if indeed the two ends can here, or ever, be separated. The already predominating position of Germany in the Turkish Empire will be enormously strengthened whenever a railway which she controls runs from the Bosphorus to the Persian Gulf.

As our troubles on the frontier are, for the present at anyrate, over, troubles in the internal administration of India begin. It is indeed easier to give the causes of the unrest which, unhappily, prevails than to suggest remedies. The causes are given in Chapters VIII. and IX., and, of all those enumerated, our own system of education is beyond all others responsible for the evil results.

Purely secular instruction is given in our schools, and experience shows that this is not supplemented by moral instruction at home, so that not only the British in India, but all the natives, except those who are themselves the product of our system, unite in condemning the results. The Indian graduates are too often youths without any sense of religion or duty to their parents or to the State, and almost all of them have forsaken the religion of their forefathers. Indeed the atmosphere in which they are brought up is an inevitable solvent of their own religious, social, and economic system, which is destroyed while nothing replaces it. But though religious feeling dies away, caste conventions increase and militant Hindooism is ever on the upward grade, while increasing bitterness is developing between the Mahomedans and Hindoos. In no country can belief in the divine right of kings and of obligations to parents be more highly developed than in India, and no country has any class more wanting in a sense of these duties than the Babu class which has been created by our education.

Their great idol is Herbert Spencer, and it would astonish the average educated Englishman to find what a stupendous reputation this writer has in India. It is evident that religious education should have been preserved until some ideal had been evolved to take its place—such as exists, for instance, in the Bushido of Japan. That any such will ever be developed we have no proof, nor is such an event probable, though among the Rajputs a not altogether dissimilar standard of knightliness has flourished in the past, and even exists at the present day.

No little responsibility, however, rests with those who have encouraged, and are encouraging, disaffection by misrepresenting in Britain the character of our rule in India. I thank a taste for native languages, no less than a disposition to stand by my deserving fellow-countrymen, for never having fallen into the net spread in sight of those who love an atmosphere of adulation. How easy the descent, is apparent from a speech lately delivered by an ex-Indian Civil servant to a public meeting in London, in which he said that the attitude of the English towards the Indians was harsh, and justice between man and man in India was far from being fairly administered. His audience, of course, was ignorant of the fact that justice between native and native is, with rare exceptions, dispensed by native. A great deal of cant is current about sympathy, which lends itself with fatal facility to prostitution as a party pawn, or foul play as an agitators' counter. Yet the aggressive manifestation of uninformed sympathy has its compensation, in that it attracts to the side of the seditious and sentimental, recruits whose advocacy is fatal to the cause they espouse.

But a governing Imperial people must practise an Imperial impartiality. Otherwise, with which people, caste, or class in India is it to sympathise? Can its sympathies be given to one, without being withdrawn from another, unit? Should it favour the colonist against the Indian, or the Indian against the colonist? Should it, like the Congress, adopt the cause of the classes, or should it adopt the attitude, now familiar at home, of preferring the masses? It may indeed say to all its many subject peoples, and to all their innumerable subdivisions:

"οὔτοι συνέχθειν, ἀλλὰ συμφιλεῖν ἔφυν";

but it must never forget that sympathy with one, connotes antipathy against another, unit. The least harmful sympathy is that which is extended towards its own people, for this is expected, and those who do not sympathise with their own are everywhere despised. The governing class in India might recognise this truth by giving more encouragement to planters, who can teach them a great deal, are most useful auxiliaries of the administrator, and see and learn more of the masses than most of the civil servants ever do, or can.

At the risk of appearing to overvalue a personal qualification, I will add that the Government of India makes an error of the greatest magnitude in omitting to recognise competent and exceptional knowledge of the Indian vernaculars as conferring a special claim to honour and promotion on the part of those who possess it. Many, nay most, of its highly placed officials, able and valuable men, lack this knowledge, and that personal acquaintance with the real India, and the real Indian, which through its agency alone can be acquired.

The present British Government has appointed a Treasury Committee to consider the organisation of the study of Oriental languages, for which it deserves the greatest credit, none of its predecessors having taken any action in this behalf. It seems therefore almost ungracious to observe that upon this committee there is no member possessing a wide acquaintance with Oriental languages, and experience as an examiner and interpreter.

European district officers, possessing good knowledge of the vernacular languages, with no axes to grind, with unimpaired authority, well supported from above—in the multiplication of such as these will be found the best antidote against unrest. But without the firmness and patience which Mr Morley has preached and practised, nothing will avail. The licentious and disloyal press of Bengal must be restrained or suppressed. Even more than the sedition preached, does the spectacle of an administration pelted with mud, without retaliation, damage the hold of the British upon the Indian peoples.

The loyal Mahomedans, ay, and others who are loyal, should not see, as they have too long seen, that "loyalty does not pay." I fear sometimes that it may become the besetting sin of British Government in India, as it often is in England, that they are too ready to alienate their friends in the vain endeavour to conciliate their enemies.

I have told the whole story of the division of the Bengal province into two lieutenant-governorships. As the classes prejudiced were those who control the local press the clamour against this measure has reached high heaven. But I own I would have let Bengal alone. The previously existing administration was good enough, and there was no difficulty in getting a lieutenant-governor for the old undivided province.

The Indian princes, the old-fashioned natives of the classes, and the multitudinous masses, either support the Government, or are unaware that it is attacked. Nevertheless the Babus have shown themselves such skilful agitators that it is unsafe to assume that they will not go to the hamlets in still greater numbers, and one bad Bengali Babu is capable of corrupting a whole good village, in or out of Bengal. I do not say that all Bengali Babus are bad—on the contrary, I do not say this of the majority—and I know that the Bengali peasant possesses his full share of the great virtues of the ordinary native of India. I do not for a moment say, with Sir Syed Ahmed, that a Bengali faints at the sight of a carving knife, or adopt the unflattering portrait drawn, of the only Indians he knew, by Macaulay, most fascinating and inaccurate of men and historians, but it is fair to say that the Bengali Babus are regarded by the other more martial races, and by the more robust classes, as talkers, not workers, writers not fighters, men of faction not of action.

Sedition should be severely punished when detected. To hold that it, is sufficient to ignore it, is dangerous doctrine among subject Oriental races. It should be distinctly understood that there is no moderate party in the Congress, unless any party can be so designated which desires to put down the British from the seats of the mighty. The same astute electioneering talent which has induced the British socialists and democrats to join hands with the representatives of landlord, class, and caste, is already persuading England that, because there is one party in Congress which is extremer than another, there is one which is moderate. It is clever, but it is not true. Both parties oppose the admirable programme of reforms drawn up by Lord Minto's Government and approved by Mr Morley. Neither party has even a word of thanks for the most conspicuous recognition of Indian aspirations afforded by the appointment of two Indian gentlemen to the Council at the office

> "Where the rulers of India dwell,
> Whose orders flash from the far land, who girdle the earth with a spell."

Both parties prefer to disparage the eminent and superlatively representative men selected rather than to rejoice in seeing their fellow-countrymen in positions in which they can exercise supreme influence. The only suggestion I have here to make is that more native lawyers might be appointed District and High Court Judges. No one does, or can, dispute their fitness, and, if European judicial standards be higher, what matter if the governed are content with the standard in this behalf of their own kith and kin.

The real feeling of the people, however, like truth in an affidavit, will come out, and in Ludhiana recently they protested against the wholly Hindoo administration to which they were subjected and prayed for an European District Officer, who would observe strict impartiality and not favour one community at the expense of another. The dislike of the people was intensified in this instance because the chief official was not only an Indian, but of a caste they were not prepared to tolerate in high places, a difficulty which must occur under any system of competitive examination or representative government.

The people of Kurnool, in like manner, after having a succession of native district judges, lately asked, "why Government was not pleased to bless them with an European judge as a relief for some years at least." Still, native judges are good judges, and I would increase their number, and I would more and more increase the independent powers of local governments, and of all their agents, down to an assistant-collector.

In the field of social reform, there is no particular reason why the foreigner should continue, when the native has ceased, to labour. I am driven to the use of the word native, because the word "Indian" no more particularises than the word "European," and I know no word common to the many peoples, castes, creeds, and classes of the continent. The word "native" should convey no offence, and certainly none is intended. India has experienced a Hindoo revival, and the reformer has had to reconsider his attitude since the days when Ramtanu Lahiri's friends threw beef about the streets of Calcutta, and regarded drinking as a proof of civilisation. He now very properly respects the gods, and is bound

> "Retrorsum
> Vela dare, atque iterare cursus
> Relictos."

His present attitude may be pose, but is preferable to his earlier cyclonic fury of reform. As soon as we ourselves join hands with the social reformer, we offend a thousand, to please one, of our subjects. The Age of Consent Act, undertaken at the instance of a Parsee journalist, is a conspicuous case in point, and the evils of Indian social customs are the subject of habitual and monumental exaggeration, and their merits are invariably suppressed. I believe we are, by Queen Victoria's proclamation, pledged not to interfere in such a case as this, and that we do not interpret that pledge as strictly as we should. At any rate, Hindoo domestic life needs little or no apology, and I have given some account of it in Chapter XII. Few have the opportunities given to those who have served on the Malabar coast of being received upon friendly terms into the houses of Hindoos, of whom it may be said that, the more they are known the better they are liked and appreciated, A "Hindoo Home" such as I described in *The Nineteenth Century* for May, 1901, possesses a unique and extraordinary charm, which is in no way lessened by the fact that in no part of the world with which I am acquainted are the women more beautiful, or more dainty in their dress and appointments.

In Chapter XIII. I have endeavoured to deal with a subject which would exhaust an encyclopædia, and found no space for setting forth the results of comparisons between the economic condition of natives of India and those of other Eastern countries, and of Eastern Europe. This subject, which always appeared to me to possess an especial interest, I have treated, in 1902, in *The Fortnightly Review* and in *The Nineteenth Century.* It is positively painful to anyone possessing the most elementary knowledge of the issues to hear the inhabitants of India comprehensively classed as poor, and compared with the people of England and France, the richest countries in the world, whose inhabitants are therefore courageously and comprehensively described as rich. The condition of the Hindoos does not greatly differ from that of the inhabitants of other Eastern countries, and is indeed, I think, not inferior to that of the peasant of Russia, and of Eastern Europe. But cosmic, climatic, ethnic, and economic conditions are of no account to the class of critic who sees a beggar in an Indian because he does not wear trousers. In order to improve industrial conditions, which have been so admirably analysed quite lately by Mr Theodore Morison, the policy to be adopted is the true *Svadeshi* policy expounded by Lord Minto, plus the influx of British capital, which the agitators are doing their best to scare away. It would help to a correct understanding of the problem if an authoritative memorandum were published explaining the home charges, and dissipating the accretions, which have collected around "the drain." India is no doubt destined, if she continues to be blessed with good government, to become a great manufacturing country, to which end railway rates must come down, coal must replace wood as fuel, cottage industries must be developed, and the Government must let labour alone.

Finally we must make up our minds that India cannot be governed upon democratic lines. In spite of the agitation of a small, but not influential, party in Parliament, and notwithstanding the aid of sincere members of the Labour Party, who necessarily are without knowledge of the circumstances, the representatives of the British people are not likely, within any limit of time which we can foresee, to be willing to give up India, Indeed as the democracy becomes more and more educated, it will see more and more plainly the absolute necessity of keeping this great possession, from a labour point of view—for no class in England would be more immediately and more adversely affected than the wage-earners by any such disastrous blow to our trade as would follow upon the loss of the only part of our Empire, which is at once an Empire, and a market frequented by one fifth of the inhabitants of this planet.

We must avoid like the plague, than which it is no less disastrous, the introduction into India of our party politics. Any servant of the Crown who committed this offence would be promptly and rightly dismissed from his office, and I own I regret that the same penalty does not attach to the like conduct on the part of a pensioner. Every ex-official turned anti-official possesses, as an agitators' counter a value, perhaps wholly disproportionate to that at which he would otherwise be rated.

I do not underrate the importance of the movement inaugurated in Bengal, adopted by the Congress, and fanned from a flicker into a flame by its English branch, and I do not deny the ability of the Babu. I realise that he has captured the vernacular press, and that his propaganda proceeds apace. All that is happening has been, or might have been, foreseen. But I do deny that Britain will ever let the Babu govern India on his own lines, under the protection of an army maintained by the British taxpayer, and I know that without such protection the warlike races and the other classes will not allow the Babu to govern for a single day.

Sir Alfred Lyall, in the second edition of "Asiatic Studies," while manifesting no sympathy with the sentimentalists, who are friends of every country but their own, or with the separatists, who would regard our hold upon India as temporary and provisional, yet sees that prosperity, education, and acquaintance with European methods lead to the development within a dependency of political rights, which have to be reconciled with the preservation of political supremacy. He does not see, nor at present do I, any likelihood that the existing ferment will lead to the sweeping away of British rule, under which the natural conditions that develop strong native rulers and powerful dynasties have disappeared. There is a world of difference between Babu S. N. Bannerji, or even Babu B. C. Pal, and Sivajee and Hyder Ali. "But the very increase of riches, population, and intelligence in India is producing an upward pressure upon the superstructure of foreign rule, so that alterations and modifications from time to time become necessary." Such are the wise reforms under consideration at the present time.

And, since "the words of the wise are as goads," Sir Alfred's warning that we, as possessors of India, are still interested to the last degree in the maintenance of the Empire of China should never be forgotten.

We must make up our minds upon the great education problem, and should, I think, follow Lord Curzon's courageous lead in refusing to subsidise the manufacture of half-baked Bachelors of Arts and full-fledged agitators. It is too late, I suppose, to go back upon the decision in favour of the Anglicists, but is there any particular reason why Herbert Spencer, for instance, should be given in the Indian system so prominent a place? Is there any need to fill Indian students with philosophy, the study of which, even in Oxford, induces a regrettable tendency towards vain speculative dreams and socialistic sophistries? Cannot our educationalists remember that even Jowett, who loved Plato, wrote: "The Socratic pang of philosophy—that is to say, the fascination of abstract ideas—may easily interfere with the growth of the mind in youth or in early manhood. Poetry, language, physical science, mathematics, the works of great writers—Greek, Latin, or English—are a much better basis of education than metaphysical philosophy."

Jowett, no doubt, read Plato, as we all should, for the beauty of his language, not for the value of his ideas. Indeed Plato persuades us to deplore the condemnation and execution of Socrates, which, as John Inglesant's friend the Cardinal said, appears to have been considered necessary by men of good judgment in that day, to preserve the framework of ordinary everyday society from falling to pieces. Rightly understood, the death of Socrates is an object lesson of great value in practical politics, and should be an example for all time to those who go about making the worser appear the better cause. The Indian youth wants Lord Kelvin, not Herbert Spencer; and philosophy, which does little good at Oxford, works positive mischief at Calcutta, Madras, and Bombay.

We must clear our minds of cant, practise Imperial impartiality not only between the different peoples of India, but between India and our Colonial possessions, and ignore, as the Government wisely did in respect of the Transvaal Indians, with satisfactory results, pressure from either side. We must refrain from encouraging idle dreams called "autonomy under the British ægis," which means India for the classes, whilst peace is maintained amongst the masses, at the expense of the British taxpayer.

Among the Indian newspapers received as this book goes to press is the *The Amrita Bazaar Patrika* of Calcutta, which writes: "How can the Congress be called 'national' when it consists almost exclusively of English educated middle-class men? Unless other important sections of the community join, it cannot claim to be national, or to represent all interests in the country." In like manner Mr Welinkar, the Superintendent of Municipal Schools in Bombay, himself an Indian gentleman, when lecturing before the East India Association said: "The Indian graduate does not command much influence among the masses of his countrymen, and does not represent them."

Another late arrival is *The Wednesday Review* of Trichinopoly, in an editorial article in which it is stated that "the great masses are in happy ignorance of all that is said in their behalf, and in their name. *Svaraj*, without any quibbling, means complete independence of British rule, else *Svaraj* would be a misnomer."

Now if a lunatic in the plains of India wore the Canadian fur coat, of which Mr Morley lately spoke, he would inevitably melt away, and so, in the like case, would dissolve our Indian Empire, the possession of which is the greatest factor in the place of pride, power, and pre-eminence, which Great Britain fills within the world.

INDEX

L

M

N

THE REAL INDIA